D1083615

How sweet the sound. We hear the big bird before we see it: a pleasing annunciation. More than 3,000 heads are turned skywards, hoping for a first glimpse of the helicopter of our blue and white dreams, the one which is bearing the Holy Grail. The whirring of the chopper blades gets louder and louder, and suddenly the yearned-for, prayed-for, to-die-for flying machine is sighted, glinting in the sunlight. Amid loud cheers it circles the battered, worn-out, Fife amphitheatre which has staged some glorious and some truly dreadful events over the past century or so, but is now touchingly ennobled by breeze-blown saltires, and Brazilian and Finnish national flags. Central Park, the crater which lies at the heart of the once-vibrant mining town which goes by the name of Cowdenbeath, feels like an international stadium. Well, sort of. That is what euphoria does to you. After all, we have waited 67 years for this. That is why we are cheering, and dancing. Some of us are crying. It matters to us.

But why does it matter quite so much? That's what this book is about.

Dan (2) and Olly (4) Ferguson

Helicopter Dreams

The Quest for the Holy Grail

RON FERGUSON

Dedicated to all those lower league fans who follow their team
in good times and bad, especially the supporters of the
mighty Blue Brazil, past, present and future;
and to my grandchildren Olly and Dan Ferguson *(opposite),*
the latest of Granny Pollock's Bairns

Northern Books
from Famedram

CONTENTS

PREFACE: THE ZEN OF CENTRAL PARK

How many books about Cowdenbeath Football Club can a grateful nation absorb? That was the question in my brain when *Cowden123* (David Welch from Ipswich) suggested on the excellent Scottish football website Pie and Bovril that I write a sequel to *Black Diamonds and the Blue Brazil*.

When it was first published 13 years ago, BDBB was regarded as a rather eccentric book, an oddity. (Bookshops at first didn't know whether to site it in the jewellery or travel sections.) After it was well reviewed by the leading Scottish poet and novelist, George Mackay Brown, it got mentions in the heavyweight Sunday papers, and there was heady talk about "new genre" and all that. I didn't know what they were talking about, but it did the book no harm. The *Daily Telegraph*, no less, despatched their fine football writer Robert Philip in a plane to Kirkwall to write a full-page feature on *Black Diamonds*. By this time it was being described as a "cult book"!

Thirteen years on it still sells, especially in England. Cowdenbeath FC's chairman, Gordon McDougall, tells me that readers south of the border have made pilgrimages to Central Park, simply to stare – inexplicably - at the unprepossessing old ground in awed silence for several minutes. The Zen of Central Park. Something is going on here.

Anyway, I quickly declined David's invitation, mainly due to other writing commitments. Then I thought about it. The last time Cowdenbeath won a Championship was 67 years ago, before I was born. And *Black Diamonds* was – not intentionally – about a truly appalling season in the history of Cowdenbeath Football Club. Wouldn't it be good to record one of the finest seasons in Cowdenbeath's history? Not only that, Cowden's Championship victories in the 20th century had been followed very quickly by world wars. There could be an even bigger history in the making.

I decided to float the idea of a sequel on the Third division forum of Pie and Bovril. The response was overwhelmingly positive – though I did like one hesitant contribution from an Arbroath supporter who posts under the name of farflunglichtie: "*Black Diamonds and the Blue Brazil* is a great book, must've read it twice. However that may be as much as I ever want to know about Cowden in this world or the next. (I know the line between the two is blurred in West Fife.) But I'm always looking out to read about the lower league fans' experience in general. So if you kept the Cowden details down to palatable levels, it may be digestible - which is more than you say for any fare sold at Central Park."

The man's got style. Anyway, I got in touch with Bill Williams, proprietor of Famedram, the Scottish publishing house which took a gamble on *Black Diamonds and the Blue Brazil* after it was turned down – with incredulous laughter - by my regular publisher, HarperCollins. The crazed man, who had just returned from holiday in Spain and was in upbeat mode, said yes, go for it. *Helicopter Dreams* is the response - written indoors, slaving over a hot computer, during one of the most glorious summers Scotland has seen. That's what supporting this wretched football team does to you.

One early decision I had to make was about how much of the ground covered in *Black Diamonds* should be traversed again. I obviously couldn't make the assumption that everyone reading this tome would have read BDBB; on the other hand I didn't want to bore readers who had read the first book. I believe strongly that a football club can't be understood without a bit of background about the club's history and traditions and the story of the community in which it operates. Consequently, some of the historical territory covered by *Black Diamonds* is here, but I have handled it differently. Not only that, new information has come to light in the last 13 years.

A major difference in the football world since 1993 has been the explosive growth of internet websites. In the "good old days", football fans had to rely on local weekly newspapers for information about their team. Now news of signings – and rumours of signings - is posted on websites immediately. Football is all about opinions – often passionate opinions – and internet football forums are the perfect vehicle for information, misinformation and debates. The opinions can be partisan, insane, informed, spectacularly inaccurate, witty or defamatory, but they are the lifeblood of the game. So a major development in this new volume is the inclusion of posts from supporters of all of the clubs in the basement division of the Scottish Football League. I am grateful to Dave McDonald (webmaster of Pie and Bovril), Neil Ferguson (webmaster of Cowdenbeath's official site) and Brian Fraser (webmaster of Cowdenbeath's unofficial site) for permission to quote freely from their sites.

I'm grateful to all who have co-operated in making it possible to produce this book so quickly. My debt to them will be obvious throughout the course of the text. Particular thanks are due to the immensely helpful Hilary Patrick, Supervisor of Cowdenbeath Library, for permission to publish the photograph of the Cowdenbeath Ladies Football Team of 1921, Jonathan Cape for permission to quote a few lines from *A Lie About My Father,* Windfall Books and Jim Douglas

for permission to use material from *dugs doos & dancing* (which can be obtained
from Windfall Books, 2 Railway Cottages, Westcroft Way, Kelty KY40AT).
Thanks also to Ally and Sarah Ferguson for image work, and to DC Thomson, Paul
Browne, Steven Ferguson, John Cameron, Alan Rhodes (Queen's Park website)
and Colin Whyte for permission to use photographs of the last games of the season.
(Any who wish copies of Paul Browne's professional pictures will find contact
details on www.cowdenbeathfc.com.) Football quotations came from a variety of
sources: The Umbro Book of Football Quotations (Ebury) and Scottish Football
Quotations (Mainstream) were particularly helpful. Thanks also to Fiona Ferguson
and Neil Ferguson for advice on the text and to Sandy Ferguson for interviews. My
thanks to our MP and Chancellor of the Exchequer Gordon Brown and Cowden
legend Craig Levein for kindly contributing Forewords, and thanks once again
to Bill McArthur, who regularly wins the Scottish Cartoonist of the Year Award,
for his cover illustration and image of Magaret Pollock. David Allan's help with
history has, as ever, been superb, but he need take no responsibility for the uses I
have made of his researches. Finally, I'm once more indebted to Bill Williams of
Famedram, who is committed to publishing "off centre" books and puts his money
where his mouth is. *Helicopter Dreams* is a labour of love and madness, and all
author's royalties will go to the Blue Brazil Youth Development Fund.

This book is about football, but it's about more than football. No, I'm not
going to prattle on pretentiously about football as a metaphor for life and all that,
but there's stuff here about dreams, tragedies, excitements, loyalties, coalmining,
religion, economics and politics. That's because the "beautiful game"- and the
sometimes not-so-beautiful game - doesn't exist in a vacuum.
You'll see that I have dedicated *Helicopter Dreams* to the fans of lower league
clubs. Soccer hype surrounds the big clubs, of course, but following teams in the
lower divisions requires commitment, loyalty, doggedness, humour, and a strong
digestive system. Keep the faith, strange people. May the sound of the helicopter
blades be yours at least once in your lifetime. (When I posted a similar sentiment
on the Pie and Bovril website, an Arbroath fan, *Ray of Licht*, responded: "Heard
that plenty of times......Sadly it was the Condor Marines returning from Norway.")

There is a subtext running through this book: that football in Scotland is
more than the story of the dominant Old Firm of Rangers and Celtic, or even of the
Scottish Premier League. Many of those at the upper levels of the Scottish football
food chain have made it clear over the years that they would like to get rid of the
small clubs – yet many of these big clubs have recklessly wasted their substance
on inflated fees and wages for foreign mercenaries instead of paying close attention
to the grass roots of the Scottish game. An expensive foreign pudding is still a
pudding, and there have been some spectacularly bad ones. There is a certain black
humour about clubs – run by normally prudent businessmen - going to the brink
of bankruptcy in order to support the lifestyles of less than enthusiastic European

nomads wearing gloves and tights on raw November nights in Fife.

If football is to flourish again in a healthy Scotland, it has to be developed from the bottom up, rather than from the profligate and arrogant top down. Clubs like Cowdenbeath, which provide excellent, qualified coaching for six youth teams, need encouragement rather than abuse.

Want to know more? Read on, MacDuff.

FOREWORDS

1. Rt. Hon. Gordon Brown, MP, Chancellor of the Exchequer

My family came from Brighills around Lochgelly and my father used to tell me of being at the match that decided Cowdenbeath's promotion in 1923-24 season. He must have been only nine and for him it would have been a special privilege to have been allowed to go with his father to the match.

And he told me of the crowds that flocked to see Cowdenbeath win on that day. So I was delighted to continue the family tradition - being at the historic match this year when Cowdenbeath not only won another promotion but took the Championship trophy. The whole Cowdenbeath club from team on the field to backroom support deserve praise for securing promotion.

It is so important because Cowdenbeath Football Club have always been at the centre of Cowdenbeath - literally and in every aspect of community life including today's successful youth policy. For all of us Cowdenbeath is a community which has had to triumph over depression, adversity and even pit disasters - and yet - has emerged stronger as a community. Cowdenbeath is a community where men and women can travel thousands of miles to the ends of the earth - and still think of Cowdenbeath as home.

All the local stories that Ron Ferguson brought together in *Black Diamonds and the Blue Brazil* are themselves part of the richness of the decades of community life we celebrate. And I am delighted to contribute to this new book which will also show just how important Cowdenbeath Football Club is to local community life. Cowdenbeath Football Club has been at the very centre of Cowdenbeath since the town we know today first grew as the coal mines grew. I'm proud that it was miners from the Little Raith colliery, and particularly the Pollock family, that started Cowdenbeath in June 1880, first as Cowdenbeath Rangers.

It's interesting that Raith Rovers was formed in Cowdenbeath in 1881. And it is when Cowdenbeath Rangers and Raith Rovers merged that Cowdenbeath FC joined the newly formed Fifeshire Football Association, winning the Fifeshire cup for the first time in 1885 then joining the Scottish Football league in 1905, and then securing the Second Division Championship in both 1914 and 1915 - and it takes us through to that match in 1923-24 season my father attended when 'the Miners' team at last won promotion to the top division, coming fifth in 1924-5.

Just like the pits, Cowdenbeath's fortunes went up and down - so it was after a period when success faded and they were relegated that Cowdenbeath saw a Championship return in 1938-39, a return to the top flight that was stillborn because of the war and it took years to get back to that position. I recall the career of Andy Matthew and it was his side that took Cowdenbeath back up - but just for a short time. And it was a great centre half, Craig Levein - brought up locally - who became Cowdenbeath manager and reinvigorated the club. Promotion from Division 3 was earned in 2001. Only new boss Mixu Paatelainen has managed a similar feat this year for which he and his team deserve to be congratulated.

This summer I saw a great Cowdenbeath performance and was part of a great crowd as the team clinched promotion, beating Elgin - and then that helicopter dash to get the trophy I had the privilege of handing to the Cowdenbeath team. So our family feels privileged that, starting with my father 82 years ago, it's now been my good fortune to present the Championship trophy this season. We've seen some great historic matches and witnessed, as we will again this season, one or two Raith Rovers derbies too.

What I know is that in recent years, through thick and thin, Gordon McDougall has been a wonderful chairman. Backed up by his board and with a youth policy that is a credit to the club, to win a League Championship - the first since 1939 - has been a remarkable success for the whole club. And it is really fitting that promotion was won in the year Cowdenbeath celebrated its 125th anniversary and 100 years as part of the Scottish League. And the experts tell me that during our promotion-winning season we recorded the 5,000th goal scored by the club in the Scottish League. In football, fortunes rise and fall - but it is when you have the strength of the community behind you that you can withstand the hard times and share the good times.

Gordon Brown

2. Craig Levein, Cowdenbeath player, manager and legend.

Some things just make you smile!

Thinking back on my time with Cowdenbeath both as a player, and more recently, a manager does if for me every time.

Meeting many new interesting people, leading to friendships formed and since strengthened. Being educated in the art of playing football and, more recently, managing football players. For these things I am eternally grateful to Cowdenbeath Football Club.

Cowdenbeath, like many clubs of a similar stature, has a vital role to play in Scottish football and in their local communities. Bringing through young players to go on to greater things and giving the town moments of great pride and a sense of togetherness.

Cowdenbeath's last Championship was delivered in 1939. Between then and now there have been sporadic successes. Promotions under John Brownlie and Gary Kirk in recent times spring to mind.

Not for the Blue Brazil supporters the heady heights of yearly cup finals, European exploits in famous stadia or the League Flag unfurled every second season. No, the wait between trophies can be measured in decades rather than years, but don't tell the supporters of the "big teams" that at Central Park the sweet smell of success lingers in the nostrils that little bit longer.

Congratulations to Gordon McDougall, Mixu Paatelainen and the players, staff and supporters of the Blue Brazil on a truly remarkable achievement.

Cowdenbeath Football Club, 3rd Division Champions 2005/2006

Like I said, some things just make you smile.........

Craig Levein

HELICOPTER DREAMS

PART ONE

The Story and the Season

1. MAD COWDENBEATH DISEASE

They fuck you up, your mum and dad.
They may not mean to, but they do.
They fill you with the faults they had
And add some extra, just for you.
- Philip Larkin, This Be The Verse

If a man watches three football games in a row, he should be declared
legally brain dead. - Erma Bombeck

My name is Ron, and I'm an addict. I suffer from a rare disorder called Mad Cowdenbeath Disease. There is no known antidote to the condition. Once it attacks the brain, the cells responsible for rational thinking shut down for good.

Mad Cowdenbeath Disease manifests itself in peculiar ways. For instance, I find myself strangely compelled to travel from my home in Orkney – pitching across the boiling Pentland Firth, then travelling forever in a bus designed for anorexic dwarfs, as the will to live slowly ebbs away – in order to stand on a litter-strewn terracing in a Kafka-esque stadium in Cowdenbeath, participate in a West Fife Tourette's Syndrome convention, and watch a brand of Scottish Third Division football which can sometimes feel like a rehearsal for purgatory. Fellow sufferers will also pay hard-earned money to travel by bus or train to other dilapidated grounds in various parts of Scotland to watch similar fare, fuelled by scalding Bovril and lumpen pies which make a formidable assault upon the human digestive system. Neither brain surgery, nor analysis, nor cognitive therapy – not even electric shock treatment – can cure this rare compulsive disorder. What I do know now is that my father and grandfather also suffered from Mad Cowdenbeath Disease. The records show that when my father and mother went on honeymoon to the Ochil foothills in

14

1934, they were strangely drawn to watch Alloa versus Cowdenbeath. At least my father was: and my mother, who was strangely drawn to Joseph Ferguson and had foolishly promised to obey him during the wedding ceremony, went along as well. Mind you, Recreation Park, Alloa: what bride could resist its allure?

My brother, two sons and daughter have also succumbed to MCD, and I have two small grandchildren who are already exhibiting signs of the condition. Tests to establish whether the disorder is transmitted through the Central Park pies have so far proved inconclusive. The search for the Cowdenbeath Gene has produced very little hard evidence, and because of the rarity of the disease, funding bodies are not prepared to pour money into the necessary research. Thus the nature-nurture argument goes on in obscure medical journals.

What we know from the nurture side of the debate is that stories are formative. They lay down neural pathways in the brain. They shape human identity. They provide the mental and spiritual lenses through which we see life. I have no earthly idea what it would have been like to have been born a Hindu girl in a village near Calcutta in the 18th century, but I do know what it is to be a white Christian Scottish male, born in the 20th century and still manifesting a pulse in the 21st. I also know what it is to be raised in a mining community in West Fife, and to support a football team with the coolest nickname in the world. These experiences have both limited me and allowed me to flourish. I am regional and partial and partisan; at the same time I am a citizen of the world. Even as I communicate with that world from a "remote" island and earn a living as a writer - thanks to the opening up of a technological cornucopia undreamed of in the coal-dusted Cowdenbeath of my youth - I also live in the Kingdom of Blue Brazil, a territory characterised by fierce and formative tribal loyalties and a defiant hope unmodified by experience.

I was brought up in the faith - indoctrinated, some would say. When I was a child, my father told me stories about the great Cowdenbeath footballers of his day. Of course, I didn't know at that time that he was crazed, but while my childhood peers were being entranced by Peter Pan and Captain Hook, I thrilled to tales about Hooky Leonard, Willie Devlin, and Alex Venters. When other children struggled to memorise the two times table, I could recite the Cowdenbeath Championship-winning side of 1939.

I loved the stories about Tewfik Abdullah, Cowdenbeath's legendary Egyptian inside forward in the 1922/3 season, who came to Cowdenbeath via Derby. In one game for Derby County, he ran on to the sandy pitch shouting "Where's me camel?" At least, that's what the laughing players thought he said. Apparently, what he had been shouting was "Where's Mick Hammill?" (Hammill was an Irishman making his debut for Manchester City, and "Toothpick", as he was known, was supposed to mark him.) Abdullah, who was dubbed "Abe" at Central Park, had clever ball skills, but was a little on the slow side. It was presumably with a touch of pre-postmodern irony that a Cowdenbeath miner named his greyhound after him.

And then there was Willie Curle, who scored six goals in one game and was rewarded with six pounds of sausages by the local butcher. John Falconer, the legendary Cowdenbeath goalie who went on to play for the Scottish League, saved three penalties in a match against Hibs in March 1926. All three penalties were for handball offences, each one committed by embarrassed Cowden fullback Davie Hopewell. I have a photograph of Hopewell with his arms folded, and no hands are visible. Presumably they were forcibly amputated. I heard lots of stories about Cowdenbeath Football Club's Golden Era in Scotland's top league from 1924 to 1934. The decade produced Scottish internationalists and great characters in an adventurous free-scoring Cowden team, at a time when the mining industry was booming and big crowds came to watch Cowden play the elite names of Scottish football. In their first season in the First Division, Cowdenbeath finished near the top, only two points behind Celtic. Cowdenbeath's highly successful manager, Scott Duncan, moved from Central Park to Old Trafford, the first and last Cowden boss to become manager of Manchester United.

Sitting beside my grandfather and father in the front of the Cowdenbeath stand, I absorbed tales of record crowds, famous victories over Rangers and Celtic, and robbery by biased and short-sighted referees. My father also told me about my relatives who founded Cowdenbeath Football Club and narrated stories which had been passed on to him by his father and grandfather. (I in turn have fulfilled my paternal obligations by transmitting the Cowdenbeath canon to my children. They, of course, didn't know that I was crazed as well, but they loved the tales. Now they themselves watch the games and eat the pies.)

I was also reared on stories of the rise and fall of the mining industry in west Fife. I heard tales of pit disasters and heroic rescues, of strikes by the miners for better pay and safer working conditions, and of lock-outs by the mine-owners. I heard about rabble-rousing orators who were blacklisted by the coal companies and never allowed to work in the west Fife coalfields again. I heard too about another Cowdenbeath relative of mine, Jennie Lee, who became the youngest MP in the House of Commons at the age of 24.

In my boyhood and youth in the 1940s and 1950s, the whole West Fife economy still revolved around coal. In the town itself, the signs and scars of mining were everywhere. Then the coal boom ended. As a teenager I saw the pits close, one by one. The fortunes of the football club fell with the town's economic decline.

The dream of every boy in the town was to play for Cowdenbeath. I certainly fantasised about such an event. At primary school I played football, of course, but because of my frailty thanks to a life-threatening illness (are you crying yet?) my mother tried to restrict me by warning me not to head the muddy ball. My protestations that I had complied with her rules were undermined by the mud-smear and the mark of the lace on my forehead. (Remember these two-ton sodden cannonballs with the leather lace that lacerated the skin?) By secondary school, my devastating left foot had come into its own, but the Number 11 jersey at Beath High School inexplicably went to a lad who was even skinnier than me, one Jim Baxter by name. I reckon it was favouritism.

The opportunity to live the dream came two years ago, when the Blue Brazil visited Orkney on a pre-season tour. When the chance arose to come on as a sub and raise money for charity, I jumped at it. I almost didn't make it. While I was training in Stromness a few days previously, a group of local lads started a kick-about. It was too good an opportunity to miss. The young men were used to wee boys asking them for a game, but a request from an auld geezer in a Cowdenbeath strip freaked them out. It was great fun until I over-zealously stretched for the ball, and felt my thigh go. When I got home, I could only get up the stairs of my hoose with difficulty. A torn muscle was diagnosed. Having publicly committed myself to play, and having got sponsorship for two local disability charities – would I be a visual aid? – this was not good news. However, ultrasound physiotherapy on my wounded leg – one nurse suggested brain surgery might be more appropriate – got me back into shape. In truth, a leg-break wouldn't have kept me off the park.

In the half-time tactics talk, the Cowden manager, former Hibs and Scotland striker Keith Wright, told the lads that he wanted to use my blistering pace to unsettle the tiring Orkney defence. When I did come on 12 minutes from the end, it was a fantastic thrill to play for the club I've loved since childhood. I had dyed my hair blue for the occasion - it's payback time when you can embarrass your kids – and the rain threatened to turn my face into a parody of Braveheart. The bigger worry was that I would be scythed by a gorilla from Stromness, some huge Orcadian farmer used to carrying a bull under each oxter. If I'd retaliated, I could have become a new religious icon – Saint Off. The *Daily Record* reported that I had scored six goals in the game. That's how facts become legends, how true tales become tall tales. Mind you, I did lead Cowden to a 9-1 victory (actually it was 8-1 when I came on).

This Mad Cowdenbeath Disease can bring its own challenges. In 1970, I was thrilled when Cowdenbeath won promotion to the old Scottish First Division. As a student at Edinburgh University, I had followed the free-scoring team to many of the games that season. By the time the team had started playing in Scotland's top league against the likes of Rangers and Celtic, I was in the USA, doing postgraduate study at Duke University. It was bad enough not getting to the games, but how would I know the all-important scores? Nowadays, with the internet and text messages, it would not have been a problem, but finding the Scottish football results in North Carolina in 1970 was a little tricky. After the first game of the season I searched frantically through every paper in the university library and, finally, there they were - the Blue Brazil - in the sports pages of the *Jerusalem Post*, which I devoured avidly ever Monday thereafter.

Mad Cowdenbeath Disease, then, may have its origin in pies, genes, or stories. The tales I heard about Cowdenbeath were characterised by a mix of truthfulness,

17

spindoctoring, and wishful thinking. So to write a history of Cowdenbeath Football Club which is more accurate than my father's partisan version, I needed to consult a real historian, someone with at least one foot firmly on terra firma. Only one person could do the business for me: David Allan, who knows more about football in Fife than any sane man ought to know.

David began his working life at the Lochgelly branch of the Trustee Savings Bank, one of the great financial centres of the western world. Now a banker in Edinburgh, he walks normally and talks normally, but his secret obsession is not known outwith the Blue Brazilian cult. You see, Mr Allan also suffers from Mad Cowdenbeath Disease. It is traceable back to his birth in Cowdenbeath on Saturday 29th December 1956. He made his first appearance on earth just as the football results were coming through. Cowden, who were in second place in the old Division 2 and going all out for promotion, unfortunately lost 5-1 at Coatbridge, so his dad wasn't too upset at missing the game.

The authentic story of how Cowdenbeath Football Club was founded will follow soon. But before we go there, it's time to tell how the rollercoaster of the historic 2005/6 season – Cowdenbeath Football Club's 125th season and the centenary of the club's membership of the Scottish League - began.

2. PIE AND BOVRIL

What I need are people who want to play for me at Cowdenbeath on a chilly Wednesday night. Prima donnas won't do a thing for us where we're going.
– Jimmy Bone.

Pies are probably the most sacrosanct thing in Scottish football. - Aberdeen commercial executive, David Johnson, 1990.

Before looking at the new season, an update for readers of *Black Diamonds and the Blue Brazil* might be useful. The summary will confirm that following Cowdenbeath Football Club does not consist of an endless series of celebrations of glorious highlights.

At the end of BDBB, we took our leave of Cowdenbeath Football Club after truly appalling 1992/93 season which ended in early relegation. Would the next season bring some joy to the disconsolate Blue Brazil punters? After a run of five games without a win, hapless manager Andy Harrow was replaced by former Dundee United striker John Reilly as player-manager. Under the new man's guidance, Cowdenbeath still could not shake off the hoodoo hanging over league games at Central Park. At last, on April 2, 1994, *having established a world senior record of 38 games without a home league win in almost two years,* Cowdenbeath finally beat Arbroath at Central Park, thanks to a single goal by local hero Willie Callaghan. The final six league games produced just one point, and downwardly mobile Cowden dropped through the trapdoor to the new Third Division. Exit John Reilly, enter youth coach Paddy Dolan as manager.

The next few seasons ranged from the terrible to the disastrous. Paddy Dolan gave way to Tom Steven, who gave way to Sammy Conn. There was a big row in December 1996 when East Fife fans appeared on a BBC football programme and sang the following ditty to the tune of the Addams Family:

They come fae near Lochgelly
They hivnae goat a telly
They're dirty and their smelly
The Cowden Family.

Coming from Methil, of which the Duke of Edinburgh had famously remarked, with marvellous succinctness, "What a dump!" - and which had a public drainage problem dubbed "The Methil Ming"- this song caused a stooshie which thankfully distracted fans from the dreadful football. The Methil fanzine editor who wrote the offending song was bombarded with bars of soap, and Cowden spent the next decade routinely humiliating East Fife on the field of play.

Sammy Conn eventually went the way of all Cowdenbeath managerial flesh. Cowden fans wondered when the torture would stop, and were looking for a messiah rather than a manager. In the five years since John Brownlie had been sacked by Cowdenbeath after he had just achieved promotion to the First Division, the Blue Brazil had plummeted to the depths of the Scottish League. Five more managers had come and gone. Of these ex-managers one was now driving a taxi, one was in prison on drugs and firearm charges (a sawn-off shotgun was found under his bed), and another was much further down the social scale - a tabloid sports journalist. Ach well.

In a rather patchy career as a manager-spotter, Gordon McDougall made one of the most inspired decisions of his life when he appointed Cowdenbeath hero and former Scotland captain Craig Levein as the new team boss. His first 18 months at the helm were far from great. In a memorable match against Ross County, ex- Juventus and Hearts player Pasquale Bruno made a cameo appearance for 60 minutes when he was back in Scotland on holiday. The Italian looked a class act until he gifted a goal to County whilst lapping up some terracing banter. It could only happen at Central Park. Season 1999/2000 saw a change of fortune, as Craig Levein re-shaped the team and got the players playing the way he wanted. It seemed a good omen when in one match at Boghead, the Dumbarton goalkeeper managed to head the ball into his own net. What fun!

The following season was the biggie. Levein perhaps had some sympathy with Alan Hansen's adage "you don't win anything with kids", and he knew that he needed more experience in the ranks. Thus Cowden fans saw their youth policy augmented by a number of old codgers. (John Martin, who was almost 42, was a great character. The fans would sing "Johnny, Johnny swing on the bar" and the toothless custodian would oblige with a big grin. You don't get nearly so much fun at SPL matches.) As the season progressed, Hamilton, Brechin City and Cowdenbeath broke away from the pack. With the Blue Brazil playing really well and top of the league, the inevitable happened. Hearts came knocking on the Central Park door and made their former captain Craig Levein an offer he couldn't refuse. Gordon

McDougall announced that Craig's replacement would be Peter Cormack, who had been manager of Partick Thistle and national coach of Botswana. Cormack's style didn't go down well with the senior players, and there was a threat of a player revolt. Gordon McDougall acted decisively and Cormack was asked to meet with him at the McDonald's Restaurant beside the Forth Bridge. It was there that Cormack was given the proverbial 'Big Mac'. *The new manager hadn't been in charge for a single game.*

Craig Levein's assistant, Gary Kirk, stepped up to become manager. Come the last day of the campaign, Cowden were in second place with 73 points, just behind Hamilton on goal difference. Brechin, who were the visitors on the last day of the season, were one point further behind. I well remember the excitement of that last game. The kick-off was long delayed as around 3,500 fans crammed into Central Park for a day of exquisite drama. With the score locked at 1-1, Murray McDowell's injury-time cross was headed high into the net by Cowden skipper Craig Winter. Seconds later it was all over. Hamilton meantime had won their last game to take the Championship on goal difference, despite never winning a match against Cowden.

Towards the end of Cowden's season in the Second Division – made special by loan-signing Craig Gordon from Hearts for four months - Cowden looked destined for relegation, and Gary Kirk was replaced by Keith Wright, who led the club to safety. One of Cowden' stars was young Graeme Brown, who was one of the four players nominated for Division 2 Player of the Year. The following season, enlivened by Derek Riordan's loan spell from Hibs (he scored a hat-trick in Cowden's 7-5 crazy victory at Brechin) ended in relegation. Back in the Third Division, Keith Wright lost some of his best players to bigger clubs. At the end of the season, the Blue Brazil were well adrift of the league leaders. The 2004/5 season got off to a bad start, and Chairman Gordon McDougall decided relieve Wright of the manager's job. Keith had been one of the club's better managers, bringing in some decent players.

The new man appointed was David Baikie, a manager with a proven track record of success. He had transformed Tayport Juniors into a championship-winning side, gaining several trophies, and he had also guided Arbroath to promotion from bottom of the Third to the Second Division. Here was a man who knew about winning promotion. His reign didn't get off to the best of starts, though. The first weekend after his appointment, Baikie was arrested after a fracas in Dundee City centre. He pleaded not guilty, and his trial was fixed for early August. It was hoped that the charges would be dropped in the course of time.

One of his first games in charge was a bit of a disaster. The all-conquering Gretna came to town, and hammered Cowdenbeath 8-0. I knew when the score got to 7-0 that we weren't going to turn this one around. When the Cowden players turned up for training the following Tuesday, they wondered how their gaffer would react. Team captain Innes Ritchie told me what happened.

"When we arrived, the gaffer gave each player a small packet. When we opened them, we found inside an After Eight mint. We all fell about laughing. Dave Baikie was laughing as well. Then he said that we'd got to move on from that defeat. That was all that was said about it. It was great man-management."

Under Baikie's direction results improved, and a late surge saw Cowdenbeath secure third place.

So the fans looked forward with anticipation to a season which would celebrate the 125th anniversary of the founding of Cowdenbeath Football Club and the centenary of the club's election to membership of the Scottish Football League. And what better way to celebrate these significant milestones than by winning promotion to the Second Division?

The historic script was just waiting to be written. Dave Baikie had made it clear that promotion was his aim, and if he could do the business with Arbroath, he can surely do it in this historic season with Cowden?

*****

The new season doesn't begin with the first kick of the ball, but with the final kick of the ball of the last season. Football fans always live for the next season. Supporters of most teams harbour the fantasy that this will be the special year.

By the middle of May, the fans are restless. And when 21st century football supporters are bored, they take to their computer keyboards. The Pie and Bovril website gets its name from the traditional fare at Scottish football matches. P&B was founded in January 2003 by lifelong St. Mirren supporter David MacDonald, a 34-year-old IT professional hailing from deepest, darkest Paisley. The site was the spawn of the successful "soapdodgers" website that had a small cult following back in 2000 but eventually bit the dust.

Although take-up on Pie and Bovril was initially slow, the forums eventually reached the all-important critical mass, and three years on, one million posts have been made on the site by just over 5000 members. The site also runs an annual five-a-side tournament, and it's fair to say that many friendships have been formed on a forum that is famous for its cutting edge humour and no-nonsense style.

It's reported that there will be a new play-off system at the end of the season. The team that wins the Championship will be automatically promoted to the Second Division, but the teams finishing second and third will face one another in a play-off semi-final. The fourth-placed team will face the side finishing second bottom in the Second Division in the other semi before a grand final. This is a complete change from the normal arrangement whereby the two top teams are promoted automatically.

The bookies make Arbroath, who were relegated last season, favourites to win the Championship, with Montrose second favourites, at 4/1. Stenhousemuir, who have signed the experienced former Hearts striker Colin Cramb, seem to have the strongest squad. On Pie and Bovril, most fans of Berwick Rangers are confident that they will win the title.

Martin Prince: Basically, we are going to pish all over this league. I have put £350 on Berwick at 8/1. They might as well pay out right now.

Black & Gold: I borrowed another grand to do the same bet. It's in the bank and will ease my debts come May.

Berwick Mad : We are all looking forward to the season and have a far better chance of winning the league than the pathetic team playing in your shit-stinkin' midden. Crawl back to your slums, Cowden smellies, and just wait for the season.

But Cowden supporters don't take it lying down.

Blue Brazil Forever: I do hope it will be the Blue Brazil's year. I have total faith in the board and in Dave Baikie who has a great track record. But as always at this level, hope triumphs over expectation. I really should know better by now.

The posts exhibit the usual summer mixture of boastfulness, insults, and unrealistic optimism, sometimes covering up an underlying fear that things are going to be as bad as ever. The fans simply want the action to start, praying for a good beginning to the season. As we move into July, the Cowden fans are hopeful that Dave Baikie's men will do the business, and at least win a play-off place.

The pre-season friendlies go reasonably well, and Cowden fans have a spring in their step as they contemplate the first action of the new season – a first-round Bell's Challenge Cup tie away to First Division Partick Thistle.

The Berwick fans are excited by the signing of a new striker, the exotically-named Bruno da Silva. Under the heading: "The New Thierry Henry?" they express their confidence.

Black&Gold (Berwick): I feel the lad will set the league on fire with his ability to not only score goals but create them.

Ally (Queen's Park): More likely he will be the equivalent of Terry Henry who plays up front for the Red Lion pub team near to Highbury.

Let the chattering stop and the action begin. Can Cowdenbeath create a shock by going to Glasgow and beating a team two leagues above them?

July 30, 2005
Partick Thistle 2, Cowdenbeath 0
Cowden are out of the Bell's Challenge Cup. Partick win the game fairly easily. Still, the fans are optimistic. Dave Baikie will get things sorted out, and will get Cowden off to a winning start.

August 1, 2005
Cowden fans wake up to shocking headlines. TEAM MANAGER ADMITS ATTACK. The news story makes sorry reading. Dave Baikie has pleaded guilty to assaulting a man to his severe injury. The victim of the serious attack was the father of one of Baikie's former players at Tayport. The sheriff has deferred sentence until August 29.

This is a disaster for the man assaulted, a disaster for Dave Baikie, and a disaster for the club. The consensus is that Baikie will go to prison.

On Pie and Bovril, *Gordon EF* (an East Fife fan) changes his atavar (the image accompanying his posts) to that of Baikie behind bars. Fans are divided over what should happen.

Cowdenbeath: The club should give him the boot. Now he has been found guilty, reading what happened to the poor guy who got beaten up was disgusting and anyone who can stoop to that level shouldn't be managing a senior football club. He has brought shame on our club.

*Ronaldincoo (*Cowden supporter): Whilst appreciating the gravity and sheer stupidity of what Baikie did, I hope the chairman waits and is willing to give the man a chance to make amends. He has a well-proven track record in football management, a commodity which the likes of Cowden rarely manages to get its hands on, and a despite a moment of drunken idiocy I would want us to bite the bullet and hang in there. Football has never, ever, been a cathedral of good behaviour either by players, management or sometimes the fans.

Hampden Diehard (Queen's Park): Cowden should do the right thing and horse him out the door. To keep him raises questions about what sort of image they want for the club. To keep him because he might be a good manager is ridiculous, but then this is almost acceptable in today's game.

August 3, 2005
The headline says it all again.
BAIKIE RESIGNS!
Following his court appearance, Dave Baikie has lengthy discussions at Central Park with chairman Gordon McDougall on Tuesday and tenders his resignation on Wednesday. McDougall, making the announcement, describes the situation as "extremely regrettable". He adds: "I won't be making any further comment other than to say Dave Baikie was an excellent manager for Cowdenbeath FC."

Vince Sinclair (Cowden fan): Sad news, only a few days before our opener at Shire and we've no manager. The man is a winner and many at Cowden were hoping to challenge for promotion/play offs.

*Auld Pete (*Cowden fan): Yes, Dave was a good manager for Cowden and he will be sorely missed. Still you can't condone what he has done.

Blueminer (Cowden fan): If DB serves his time, if/when he's sentenced then I don't see why he can't come back. Everyone deserves a second chance if they have been punished for the crime they have committed and they have shown remorse for what they have done.

Central Parker: Grievous Bodily Harm on his CV will guarantee him a job in the Juniors.

So Cowdenbeath's promising 125th anniversary season, with all its high hopes, is in tatters before it has even begun. On Pie and Bovril, *Ronaldincoo* sums up the feeling of the fans: "Oh dear God.......someone please tell me this is just a bad dream. How to go from a glory-promising season to a likely season of struggle in one fell swoop....Is it too much to ask that once, just once, someone up there give us a chance? How deeply, deeply depressing."

3. IN THE BEGINNING WAS THE BA'

*You see, all these people here who look down at us as peasants know
nothing of history. If you have a history, you have a pride* - Chanu, a
Bangladeshi immigrant in Monica Ali's novel, Brick Road

The past is not dead and gone, it isn't even past. – William Faulkner

It all began with a football. It was bought for the then princely sum of 13 shillings
by a determined woman who went through from Cowdenbeath to Glasgow to buy a
new leather ball for her sons. That is how football started in the burgeoning mining
village of Cowdenbeath, in the year of Our Lord 1880.

We'll talk about my great grand aunt Margaret Pollock, the formidable founding
mother, in a minute, and also about how Cowdenbeath Football Club has had its
founding date wrong on its official literature for years. But first, for the sake of
clarity, we need to spend just a little time considering history and myth. Stay with
me, if you will.

The word "myth" gets a bad press these days. In modern usage, "myth" is
usually contrasted with "truth". But myth is a much richer concept than that. A myth
is a powerful story which seeks to give meaning to a series of events. These events
may or may not have happened in the way they have been described; what matters
is that some truth is conveyed through the telling of the story. In the words of Pablo
Picasso: "Art is a lie that makes us realize the truth".

"In the beginning was the Word", the opening of St John's gospel, is a stunning
piece of theological artistry. Another myth which still has powerful (and even
lucrative) contemporary resonances is that of the Holy Grail. The term originally
referred to the chalice or dish used by Christ in the Last Supper, and it was reputed
to have miraculous powers.

Down through history, the Holy Grail story has been told in a variety of forms,
most recently in the Da Vinci Code. The powerful appeal of the ancient story,
even into the 21st century, is shown by the fact that Dan Brown's novel has sold a
staggering 50 million copies world wide. It is a page-turning detective yarn, but is

26

largely fanciful tosh. (It says that Jesus and Mary Magdalene actually got married, and have descendants in France. Jacques Chirac, perhaps? Did Jesus and Mary have a white wedding? Was the Apostle Paul best man, with a black gay lover?) Yet in the midst of all this risible guff, the story contains a legitimate powerful warning about how authorities – religious, political or royal – can distort history for their own purposes.

Such a tale could only still be relevant if it spoke to modern yearnings – and it does. The quest for the Holy Grail translated into modern parlance signifies the human longing to find some object or quality which will transform your life. So, your personal symbolic "Holy Grail" might be anything from a winning lottery ticket to personal peace. For a football club, it's likely to something you can grip with both hands, like an elusive Championship trophy.

Big institutions, be they religious, political or sporting all have their own founding myth - a narrative which explains how it all began. In the telling, the myth is usually populated by larger-than-life characters who make important decisions and act in ways which have significance for the future.

So after that quick but necessary run around the philosophical block, let's get back to the fitba. Even wee football clubs like Cowdenbeath have their founding myths. The chatter in this chapter will be about football heroes, and about one particularly significant heroine (to use a non-PC but helpfully descriptive word). Accurate history enhances and refines good mythology, and this is where David Allan comes in. The club's resident historian has unearthed more details about the origins of Cowdenbeath Football Club than were available to us when *Black Diamonds and the Blue Brazil* was being researched and written more than 13 years ago. What follows is current state-of-the-art history filtered through my own interpretive lenses.

To understand the significance of Mrs Pollock's football, we need first pay a visit to the killing fields of Ayrshire junior football, or at least the coalfields of Cumnock. That's where the Pollock dynasty originated. Given the proud radical political traditions of Cowdenbeath, it's also fitting that Cumnock was the home of Keir Hardie, founder of the Labour party.

James Pollock, the father of what was to become a large clan, was born in Airdrie in 1835. His trade as an ironstone miner took him to Old Cumnock. There he was enchanted by one Margaret Miller, a comely local seamstress, and they were married in the town's Free Church on 23rd November 1855. They settled in the Blue Tower district of Cumnock. From the Blue Tower to the Blue Brazil is quite a stretch. James and Margaret Pollock had nine children before moving to Glasgow, then Newcraighall near Edinburgh, then Townhill in Fife. By then they had 12 children, two of whom would become founders of Cowdenbeath's fitba club.

Let the founding family drop out of view for a moment, while we switch the focus to another Fife district, Cowdenbeath. Up until the 1850s, Cowdenbeath had been a small, impoverished and declining agricultural area, with some crofts and small farms. The population only began to grow when iron ore was discovered; when shafts were sunk, accessible coal seems were found. When the value of Fife's iron ore dropped after large quantities were found in Sweden, the industrial focus shifted to coal mining. The Cowdenbeath Coal Company was formed in 1870 to exploit the potentially rich coal reserves.

The demand for west Fife's "black diamonds" - as coal was known – led to an exodus of experienced miners from the overworked Ayrshire iron and coalfields to the promised land of Cowdenbeath. My great grandfather, Joseph Ferguson, was among them. They were joined from Townhill in late 1879 by the Pollock family.

As the population of the area grew, it was felt desirable to fix on a name for the whole district. A public meeting was held to decide on a name, and it was narrowed down to a choice between two of the existing areas, Cowdenbeath and White Threshes. Cowdenbeath won the day.

Football, which had been played for centuries in a variety of wild forms – such as the Orkney Ba' game - had become more popular in the second half of the 19th century. The first senior club in Scotland was Queen's Park, formed in 1867, and the Scottish Football Association was established in 1872, the year in which Glasgow Rangers was formed. In Edinburgh, Heart of Midlothian Football Club was established in 1874, and a year later a new club was formed by Irish-born football enthusiasts and given the name 'Hibernian'.

For years it has been universally quoted that Cowdenbeath's football club was formed in 1881. The club itself has long put forward 1881 as its date of foundation on stationery headings and in programmes, and indeed still does so. *Helicopter Dreams* can reveal that this is the wrong date. David Allan's researches establish that there is absolutely no doubt the club came into existence in 1880. Indeed, the club's formation can be more or less pinpointed to a specific date in June 1880.

The local library archives have a copy of correspondence sent by a man called Eck Hunter to Alex Westwater, who for so long was the proprietor of the *Cowdenbeath Advertiser* and the *Lochgelly Times*. One of Eck's letters tells how he was a neighbour of the Pollock family when they moved to Cowdenbeath.

"The Pollock family came to Cowdenbeath in 1879 just before the Tay Bridge disaster," Eck wrote. "The oldest son Andrew was a house painter and his brothers James, John, William, Sandy and Davie all started work at the Raith Colliery. Their sister Jenny was married to Thomas Greig – she was the grandmother of Jennie Lee (Mrs Nye Bevan).

"They then moved to the Oakley Raws….. and Mrs. Pollock who had a second hand shop purchased a football for her sons in Glasgow. On the Saturday before the Miners' Gala Day in June 1880, Cowdenbeath Albert cricket club and Kinross played a cricket match. After the game, the football was put down and kicked all over the park. When the ball was picked up it was decided to form a club."

(In the *People's Friend* in 1952, the then 84-year-old Davie Pollock recounted:

"Mither decided that we'd got tae hae a ba' so she went tae Glesgae and brocht ane back. That ba' was really the start o' footba' here.")

Helicopter Dreams can reveal that the famous founding ba' (pronounced baw) was purchased at Matthew Brown's in the Saltmarket, Glasgow, in June 1880. I'm sure that David Allan will have the receipt. This was the first time a leather sphere had been sighted in Cowdenbeath.

Freeze-frame the narrative at this point. I want to keep the spotlight on Margaret Pollock, the unsung heroine of the Cowdenbeath FC story. What was it, I wonder, that made her so determined to make the journey through to Glasgow to buy a new leather football for her sons? Why not a set of encyclopaedias, or a Bible? Short of finding a hidden diary, we'll never know the answers to these questions, but it does seem an unusual thing for a woman to do at that time.

Thirteen shillings was a lot of money to spend on a football, at a time when a miner's weekly wage was around 22 shillings and six pence. In 1880, you could buy a man's suit for 26 shillings, and you could get 62 pints of Guinness for what Ma Pollock paid for the football! Thirteen shillings in 1880 is equivalent to £52 today. The money came from the proceeds from the sale of second-hand furniture and bric a brac. She had established an antiques shop in Cowdenbeath's High Street, opposite the entrance to what is now Central Park.

To return to the main story: the two men who picked up the famous ball in June 1880 and founded the club now known as the Blue Brazil were John and James Pollock, two of the lads born at the Blue Tower in Cumnock. The team was initially known as Cowdenbeath Rangers and played in red, white and blue striped jerseys.

I must declare a personal interest at this stage of the holy narrative. My great grandfather, Joseph Ferguson, was married to Agnes Miller, sister of Margaret Pollock. That makes the Blessed Margaret of the Holy Ba' my great grand aunt, and the two founders of the club, John and James Pollock, my first cousins twice removed. Joseph and Agnes Ferguson's son, Alex, established a painter and decorator's business in Cowdenbeath. The business was then taken over by his son, my father, Joe Ferguson. As I was completely handless, I became a reporter with the *Cowdenbeath Advertiser and Kelty News* at the age of 16. Alex Westwater, to whom Eck Hunter wrote, was my first employer. I'm also related to Jack Dougary, editor of the other Westwater paper, the *Lochgelly and District Times* and later of the *Central Fife Times,* and son of one of Cowdenbeath FC's greatest managers.

My God, this feels like an apostolic succession right back to the foundation of the club, in the way that the Roman Catholic Church traces its lineage back through time to the apostle Peter in Rome. Were there contagious traces of Mad Cowdenbeath Disease in that famous football? My similarly-afflicted brother Sandy is vice-chairman of the Cowdenbeath Supporters Club and my son Neil runs the Cowdenbeath FC official website. My daughter Fiona is a staunch supporter who comes to most games, and my younger son Ally, when asked what he wanted for his 10th birthday, unhesitatingly replied that his greatest wish was to be a mascot at Central Park. (Cowden lost 2-0 to Brechin.) My two grandchildren, Olly and Dan are already kitted out in the Blue Brazil regalia. There is something ancestral about this obsessive-compulsive disorder.

Meanwhile, back at the foundation of the fledgling fitba club. After some practice, a match was arranged with Dunfermline United in October 1880 in Cowdenbeath. It ended in a 1-1 draw. John and James Pollock were in the team. As founders, they not only got to pick the team, they got to play. Eat your heart out, Vladimir Romanov.

It's reputed that soon after the formation of the Rangers another team was set up under the banner of Cowdenbeath Thistle. The evidence suggests that the team played on a pitch near that of Cowdenbeath Rangers and merged with the Rangers in April 1881. The club retained the name Cowdenbeath Rangers and played its first post-merger game against Fife's premier club Dunfermline (founded 1874), on 23rd April 1881.

By now, football clubs were springing up all over Fife and it was no surprise when a group of miners at the Raith Colliery decided to set up another club in Cowdenbeath. They named their new club Raith Rovers. The Cowdenbeath version of Raith Rovers was founded around October 1881 and thus predated the Kirkcaldy club of the same name by two years. A year later, the Fifeshire Football Association was formed and 10 clubs joined the new Association, including both of the Cowdenbeath-based clubs. However, it appears that Cowdenbeath Rangers and Raith Rovers got together and decided to amalgamate so that one club could represent Cowdenbeath in the new Fife Cup competition. The merged club adopted the name of Cowdenbeath Football Club – the name that the club proudly carries to this day.

The newly united Cowdenbeath FC played at a field at the north end of the village. It was to be Cowdenbeath FC's home ground until 1917, and remains in use as a football venue to this day. Indeed, I've played on it several times myself.

With the development of the railways as a cheap mode of travel, football became more attractive to spectators, who flocked to watch the newly-arranged cup and league fixtures. Celtic Football Club was formed as a charity by Brother Walfrid eight years after the founding of Cowdenbeath FC. As football became Scotland's most popular spectator sport, people saw the commercial possibilities of football; Celtic, like most other clubs, became much more of a professional business venture. The day of the football gentleman amateur, symbolised by Queen's Park, was over.

What happened to Cowdenbeath's football founding fathers, John and James Pollock? John set up his own drapers business in Cardiff. While in Wales, he concentrated on a different pastime, joining Cardiff Bowling Club in 1900. In 1907 he became World Bowling Champion at Crystal Palace - a victory greeted with much joy at Cowdenbeath Bowling Club where John was also a member. Every year it was his custom to visit Cowdenbeath for a holiday to catch the start of the football season and play some bowls at the Cowdenbeath green. Perhaps his proudest day was in 1924, when he watched the wee club he had founded 44 years earlier take their bow in the First Division of the Scottish League in a match against Hearts before an 18,000 crowd at Central Park. I find it rather touching that one of the club's founders lived to see Cowdenbeath greats like Hooky Leonard and Willie Devlin. He must have been a very proud man. John's brother James was not so fortunate. He died in Australia in 1913. John died in Cardiff at the age of 74.

Margaret Pollock died aged 79 in Cowdenbeath in 1914, a year after her son James's death, just before Cowdenbeath Football Club won their first Championship. In one of the local papers it was reported *"Granny* (Margaret) *Pollock died on Friday 3rd April. She was regarded as an authority on antiques."* Her husband James Pollock, had died in Cowdenbeath in 1882.

A little more dynastic history and the early story of the club and the town is done. Margaret Pollock's sister, called by the unusual name of Gibson Miller, married John, a member of the Dougary clan. Their son, John Dougary, played alongside his cousins John and James Pollock for Cowdenbeath. John Dougary's son John went on to become a legendary Cowden manager in two spells at the helm both before and after the Second World War.

So the crucial years from 1870 to the turn of the century saw the founding of Cowdenbeath's coal industry, football club and town (which received burgh status in 1890). As the demand for coal soared and Cowdenbeath Coal Company merged into the Fife Coal Company, the town became a bit more prosperous and the football club began to flourish.

Cowdenbeath FC reflected the toughness and resilience of the mining community of which it was an integral part. It also proudly flew the flag for a town which knew much sorrow, and which always had to struggle for its very existence. The club's Golden Age in the 1920s and 1930s reflected the growing vibrancy and confidence of a proud town with strong communitarian traditions. Through the excellence of its flagship football team, challenging even the Rangers and Celtics, the name of the town would become known throughout Scotland. Darker days would follow, though, as the miners lost political battles and the coal mines would close, one after another. The economic fortunes of the community would be mirrored in the slow decline of its football team, punctuated by defiant hurrahs.

One thing for sure is that those of us who stood on that terracing on April 29th, 2006, straining for the sight of a helicopter in the sky, were looking for more than we knew. And we would not have been there had it not been for a strong woman's journey, from Cowdenbeath to Glasgow, to buy a football for her boys.

Granny Pollock, bearer of the iconic ball, I am glad to salute you.

4. ONLY TWO PAATELAINENS

It would perhaps be dishonest if I went as far as to say that when I was a boy growing up in Finland I had always dreamed of one day being at Central Park! – A smiling Mixu Paatelainen confesses all

Reporter: *This might sound like a daft question, but you'll be happy to get your first win under your belt, won't you?*
Gordon Strachan: *You're right. It is a daft question. I'm not even going to bother answering that one.*

The wires are buzzing. All the talk is of who will succeed Dave Baikie as manager. The main names in the frame are David Hannah, John Connolly, Eddie Wolecki and Campbell Money. We shall see.

August 6, 2005
East Stirling 0 Cowdenbeath 1
Graeme Irons registers a win in his first game as stand-in boss. It's an important victory, given the turmoil at the club. There's a sense of "Let's win this one for Dave" about this performance. The only goal of the game comes from Cowden's towering centre back John Ward, Dave Baikie's most significant signing.

August 9, 2006
Cowdenbeath 2 St Johnstone 3
A late winner for the First Division side knocks Cowdenbeath out of the CIS Insurance Cup. It's a pulsating end-to-end game, with Cowden matching their higher-placed opponents. Cowden twice come from behind to level. John Ward equalises the first St Johnstone goal. The second equaliser, a stunning 40-yard strike from Darren Gribben is a candidate for goal of the season.

August 10, 2005

The waiting is over. Every single rumour has been wrong. Cowden chairman Gordon McDougall has pulled off a surprise by appointing former Finnish internationalist Mixu Paatelainen as new manager. The 38-year-old striker, capped 70 times by Finland, has no managerial experience, but has been coaching St Mirren's Under-19 side. During a distinguished career he has played for Haka, Dundee United, Aberdeen, Bolton, Wolves, Strasbourg, Hibs and St Johnstone, as well as earning 70 international caps with Finland. Mixu says at the press conference: "I jumped at the chance of joining this club as I had nothing but good reports about it. It is a great opportunity for me to start my managerial career."

Over at Pie and Bovril, the comments pour in. The appointment has taken people by surprise, and there are reservations about Mixu's lack of managerial experience.

Nelly (Cowden fan): I think he could in time turn out to be a good manager at Cowden and he will have a lot of contacts in the game to get in loan players etc.

Not Really John McVeigh: Apart from allegedly taking the Under-19s for training now and again, what managerial experience does Mixed-up Pantieliner have? Football management should be left to those with professional football experience, not amateurs. Some chairmen don't have the sense they are born with.

MarreZ (St Mirren): Mixu will do a grand job for Cowdenbeath - he's done brilliantly as reserve and Under-19 coach, and will be missed at St Mirren.

Referring to the notorious girth of former Cowden player Mark Yardley, *Hampden Diehard* (Queen's Park) writes: If Cowden sign old boy Mark Yardley and play him up front with Mixu, you'd see an eclipse over Central Park.

DonnieDarko (East Fife): I wish him well. I have lots of friends in Finland, and have been over there many times. I speak a bit of the lingo, and will be able to give him dug's abuse in his own native tongue!

Djn (Berwick): Mixu can speak English well, but can the Cowden fans?

This is a real challenge for Paatelainen. It can't be easy to take over a team of somebody else's players, succeeding a popular manager who has left in such difficult circumstances. The challenge for the new manager is to find out very quickly how many of the summer signings are really up to it and inspire the others to beat the best in the division. Apart from that, it's dead easy.

August 11, 2006
The official Blue Brazil website (www.cowdenbeathfc.com) is re-launched to celebrate the club's 125th year. The site, which has been run manfully by journalist and club director Ian Fraser for some years, has been completely revamped under the direction of webmaster Neil Ferguson and web design company Okta. There are sections covering the club's history, player profiles, fans' view, youth system, facilities, etc, and there is also an on-line shop selling club merchandise. The new

site complements the long-running unofficial site (www.cowdenbeath.net) run by Ian Fraser's son, Brian. As well as giving club news, Brian's site provides a forum for Cowden fans. To have these two excellent sites dedicated to Cowdenbeath Football Club is a bonus for the fans in his special year.

After the Baikie drama, there is a new spring in the step of Blue Brazil supporters, despite the question marks over about the new boss's lack of managerial experience. Everyone is looking forward to Saturday's home game against Queen's Park.

August 13, 2005
Cowdenbeath 0 Queen's Park 2
Ouch! Reality check. The game effectively ends for Cowden just after the hour mark when young defender Darren McGregor concedes a penalty and is sent off two minutes later for a reckless lunge which earns him a second yellow card.

Hampden Diehard: We ran out quite comfortable winners, but poor Mixu must have wondered what he's come to when Cowden's discipline just went out the window later on. PS a good pie and Bovril at Central Park for £1.20 - quality!

Vince Sinclair (Cowden fan): We were very poor today and got what we deserved – nothing.

Oh dear, is it all going pear-shaped already? Now we face a hard away trip to Elgin.

August 20, 2005
Elgin City 0, Cowdenbeath 3.
That's more like it. Mixu enlists the help of his 22-year-old brother Markus to record his first success as a manager. Markus, who is a Finnish Under-21 internationalist, is fielded as a trialist and has an impressive 90 minutes. Iain Machlen scores with a penalty, young Liam Buchanan scores his 21st goal for Cowden, and 18-year-old striker Ryan McCallum also gets a goal. The Cowden fans feel better.

Asked on the official website about his early impressions of the squad, Mixu replies: "The squad is very fit and the players have an excellent attitude. I am looking for changes, though, and I want to help them improve their game. They need to take more care in their passing. I am looking for more hunger and determination."

The Cowden fans are looking forward to Saturday's game against their local rivals East Fife at Methil. Remarkably, East Fife haven't managed to beat Cowdenbeath in the last 11 years. The Blue Brazil fans are confident that that record will still be intact after Saturday.

Many of the East Fife fans are in a stand-up dispute with their club's chairman, Derrick Brown, and have taken to demonstrating against him from a mound outside the ground. The fans, many of whom are members of the East Fife Supporters Trust, feel that the chairman is taking the club in the wrong direction. The debate hots up on Pie and Bovril.

Faither (East Fife fan): In a truly amazing display of contempt for fans - even by Scottish football standards - East Fife FC Chairman Derrick Brown has just rejected an offer by the EF Supporters' Trust to invest £10,000 in the club. The absolute priority is getting this creature away from our club - and preferably out of Scottish football altogether.

Igor (East Fife): Supporters should be running clubs because we have no hidden agenda, we have the club's interests purely at heart. Many football clubs are run by supporters and this has proven to be extremely successful, from AFC Wimbledon to FC Barcelona.

The debate goes back about two years, when about 100 East Fife fans met to set up the Trust. *Faither* (Eugene Clarke) told *Helicopter Dreams*: "The entire problem came about because of a lack of trust on the part of the club chairman who saw us as some sort of threat to his own position."

Eugene Clarke is confident that the Trust will eventually win the argument. "This confidence comes from the increasing political support for community involvement in clubs; it comes from the fact that we have received so much support from our local community; it comes also the support we have received from the fans of other clubs –even our arch rivals Cowdenbeath!"

It is destructive when supporters of a small club are seen as the enemy. Surely commonsense can prevail, and a deal can be worked out whereby the East Fife FC Board and the Supporters' Trust can work in harmony for the best interests of the club?

August 27, 2005
East Fife 1 Cowdenbeath 0.
Another reality check. With the same successful line-up as last week, Cowden are terrible. The back three are very uncomfortable, and the midfielders seem hardly able to pass the ball. The pony-tailed Markus Paatelainen looks off the pace. "Mixu, get your sister off," shouts a frustrated fan. Is Cowden's great white hope going to be another foreign flop?

The reality is that the club's proud 11-year record is broken. The fans are despondent. Stuart Juner sums it up in the Fans' View section of the official website: "When you've played your local rivals and have gone undefeated for the past several hundred years, the law of averages will ride into town and place his steel toe-cap in your backside to give you a reminder that nothing should be taken for granted. East Fife had made several changes in their playing staff and style – they had marginally improved, going from really poor to selling the Big Issue. In short, they scored and won, we never turned up."

With the transfer window about to close, Second Division side Forfar Athletic sign Cowden striker Darren Gribben for £3000. Mixu signs 17-year-old striker Andy Jackson on-loan until January and right-sided player Mark Baxter from Mixu's old club St. Johnstone. Markus Paatelainen, currently a free agent, completes a trio of signings, having already appeared twice in his big brother's team as a trialist.

August 29, 2005

Dave Baikie comes up for sentencing. The sheriff says he was mindful to send Baikie to prison, but in view of the fact that he has no previous convictions for violent behaviour, he would sentence him to complete 300 hours of community service. Baikie is also ordered to pay £3000 compensation to the victim of the assault.

The official Cowden website introduces a new sponsorship scheme. Fans or companies can sponsor a player or member of the backroom staff for £30 for the 2005/6 season. Supporters immediately start to sign up.

With the changes Mixu has made to the squad, the fans are upbeat again. Maybe the season isn't over after all. A huge game is coming up: against league leaders Berwick Rangers at Central Park. Mixu Paatelainen is beginning to make his presence felt, and the fans and players like him. The supporters sing: "There's only two Paatelainens!"

The tide will surely turn. Bring on Berwick!

September 10, 2005

Cowdenbeath 0 Berwick Rangers 1

Special guests at the game are a group of Blue Brazil fans called "Cowdenbrummies". Who are they? Their leader, Simon Pearson, tells me the story: "Basically I took up an interest in the Blue Brazil during the 38-game run without a home win. For some bizarre reason it appealed to me. In early 1994 a friend and I made our first trip north of the border to see the away cup tie at Greenock. We got talking to some members of the supporters club as we looked at bit out of place wearing claret and blue shirts! During the second half we got on so well that we were told not to catch the train as we planned but join them on the coach back to Central Park, dropping us off on the way. With friendly people like that how could we not come back? Come back we did, and have done at least once a season since then with a hardcore of six of us, but up to ten people. The other five of the hardcore group are Andy, Loz, Boydie, Reg and Cliff. There are also another five people who've made at least one pilgrimage."

Kevin Haynes scores for the visitors after only five minutes. The Blue Brazil have more of the play but in a scrappy and hard fought game they can't find the cutting edge. The best opportunities for the home team fall to Markus Paatelainen, but he's out of luck. This means that Cowden have lost their second home league match in succession. Is the dreaded home hoodoo going to strike again? If so, we can forget about the play-offs.

There's some trouble in the ground between young Cowden and Berwick fans. Some of the visiting fans have turned up wearing masks and giving out soap in order to wind up the locals, and there is a small group of young local "hard men" who are always ready for a scuffle. The police are called. A debate rages on Pie and Bovril.

*Oliver Tobias (*Berwick): People at the club know who these idiots are who spoil the good name of the club and usually tarnish the good reputation of the people that matter, decent supporters who go to the match and watch a game. Name and shame them. I'm not saying all our fans are angels. Let's nip it in the bud.

Hampden Diehard: If you turn up at a game, particularly somewhere like Cowdenbeath, full of drink, fling soap and tennis balls about and wind up the (admittedly excitable) locals to the point where they want to give you a doing, then you should really be looking a bit closer to home when it comes to sharing out the blame.

On the club website, chairman Gordon McDougall responds: "Sadly we have it at the stock cars as well. It seems to be a problem involving society and the community at present. Football matches and other events where crowds congregate give some elements the chance to carry out their nonsense and hide. I would ask our core supporters to help in identifying the troublemakers."

On the football side, Berwick and Stenhousemuir look to be running away with the league. We'll have to be much more consistent if we are to stay close enough to the leaders to win play-off place come April.

5. THE BLUE BRAZIL HALL OF FAME

The match against Brazil was football at its best. Both sides had opportunities to win the game – Michel Platini

When I signed Jim Holton from Shrewsbury for £100,000, Harry Gregg said, "You've got a player who doesn't know the meaning of the word defeat." A week later I phoned Harry and said, "Aye, and defeat's not the only word he doesn't know the meaning of. There's pass, control, dribble...."
– Tommy Docherty

Brazil! The very sound of the name conjures up exciting football. The most thrilling soccer team in the world, the exemplars of Pele's "beautiful game", have been the standard-bearers for "total football" excellence.

Despite what seems an almost genetic predisposition to skilful soccer, football came quite late to Brazil. In fact, Cowdenbeath Football Club had been playing for at least a decade before Charles Miller landed in Brazil, carrying a football. (Did he buy it at Margaret Pollock's emporium at Cowdenbeath? I like to think that it might have been the original thirteen-shilling Ba' - hopefully sold on for twenty shillings – that sparked off the great world football revolution. Should the Brazilian national team really be known as the Yellow Cowdenbeath?) What we do know is that the Englishman hoped to create interest in the sport that was becoming popular in Britain.

He was successful beyond his dreams. Football immediately took on in Brazil, and by the 1930s the country had begun to make its mark in South American football. In 1950 Brazil hosted the World Cup and built the largest stadium in the world, the famed Maracanã. Brazil's defeat by Uruguay in the final triggered heart attacks, brawls and even attempted suicides, such were the passions soccer evoked.

In 1958 in Sweden, Brazil won its first World Cup with a team featuring players such as Santos, Garrincha, Vavá and Zagallo - and a precocious 17-year-old by the name of Pele. Brazil went on to win four more world cups, featuring players like Clodoaldo, Gerson, Jairzinho, Rivelino, Tostão, Falcão, Sócrates, Zico, Júnior, and latterly Ronaldo, Ronaldinho, Rivaldo, Cafu and Roberto Carlos. Many of them had developed their footballing skills on the Copabanco beaches, and they played the kind of fluent soccer that football fans love to watch.

With Brazil being an international byword for state-of-the-art soccer, how did Cowdenbeath come to be known as the Blue Brazil? Well, it might have been because Cowden had a good European pedigree. Yes, you have read that sentence correctly. In 1925, after finishing fifth in Scotland's top division, just behind Celtic, the Miners were invited to play in Gibraltar. Most of the players were sick on the journey, and a rumour swept through Cowdenbeath that the team had been wiped out in a road accident after a Sunday afternoon at a bullfight. Apart from that, everything went fine. Far from being deid, Cowden won all three games, with Hooky Leonard and Willie Devlin exciting the crowds with their skills.

Three years later Cowden went to Germany, supposedly to teach the locals how to play fitba'. The trip was a great success - the Fife players enjoyed visits to night clubs in Cologne and a sail down the Rhine – apart from the football. In the first game, the coin had neither a head nor a tail, and when it came down the referee awarded the choice of ends to the Germans. Ve vill make ze decisions. Cowden lost all four games, and in the last match in Dortmund, the same biased ref as the first game was in charge. Same coin. Cowden lost 5-1. Still, the German players gave the Cowden players three cheers at the end, which was nice.

No, it wasn't because of their European tours that Cowden became known as the Blue Brazil. In fact, the nickname didn't actually come into being until the 1980s. In *Black Diamonds and the Blue Brazil,* I reported that a Cowden fan called Big Bob had said that the name came about "because Cowden play in blue and have the same debt as a Third World country."

Thirteen years on, *Helicopter Dreams* can exclusively reveal the true answer to the mystery which has perplexed football fans all over the world. (They still talk of nothing else in Brazil.) We tracked down the main man to his home in Lochgelly, and he gave me the definitive answer in his own words: "It was in the early 1980s, 1982 or so. I'd always loved Brazil and the way they played the game. I was standing on the terracing one day and Cowden were playing well – in fact they were playing like Brazil. So I shouted, 'C'mon the Blue Brazil!' It just seemed to take off."

Who was that man? Step forward Colin "Chalky" Whyte. Unless anyone else comes forward to contest Colin's convincing claim, he is responsible for the sharpest nickname in the football world, one which the Cowdenbeath players are proud to wear on their chests. Cowden chairman Gordon McDougall, grateful for such an instantly recognisable brand name, said to me that whoever coined the nickname was a genius. This means that Lochgelly has produced at least two characters of Einsteinian proportions - Jim Leishman and Chalky Whyte. Chalky, you are indeed a genius and you deserve the accolades.

****

The fact that Cowdenbeath Football Supporters Club has decided to institute a Blue Brazil Hall of Fame has evinced much mirth in the higher echelons of Scottish football. A Third Division Hall of Fame! In Cowdenbeath! Such elevated notions are normally reserved for the Rangers and Celtics of the world, with their bulging trophy cabinets.

Cowdenbeath Football Club have had some great players, a fair number of good ones, and a lot of truly terrible ones. Cruise liners have turned quicker than some of our lumbering central defenders. We've had strikers who could miss an open goal while standing on the goal line. We've had midfielders who should have been charged with mistreating an innocent football. We've had fullbacks who could well have been charged with being drunk in charge of a football. After one particularly excruciating season, the fans voted in the Player of the Year poll for the player who had played fewest games during the season on the grounds that he had inflicted least damage.

Robert Philip of the *Daily Telegraph* writes: "I thought it was a wind-up at first; Cowdenbeath have invited fans to nominate their favourite 25 players for inclusion in a Hall of Fame to celebrate the club's 125th anniversary. It was the first time I had seen the words Cowdenbeath and Hall of Fame in close proximity. Here are a club who have spent the 60 post-war years unnoticed by the rest of world football, playing in front of a few hundred supporters."

Just when it looks as if Robert is going to put the boot in, he goes on: "But why shouldn't the Blue Brazil, as they are affectionately known, indulge in such nostalgia? If Manchester United and Arsenal, Rangers and Celtic followers can drone on about their 'Dream Teams', surely the good folk of Cowdenbeath deserve the same opportunity. Dipping into *Black Diamonds and the Blue Brazil*, I was reminded that the Fifers have a history as rich as any. While the battalions of Rangers and Celtic fans march to the beat of triumphalism, those who follow Cowdenbeath and their lowly ilk wallow in romanticism. If Robbie Burns had been a footballer, he might have played for the Blue Brazil. . . with Laurel and Hardy at wing-half."

Wallow in romanticism? What can the man possibly mean? Let me tell you again about Margaret Pollock, and the historic Cowden victories over Rangers.....

Robert goes on with an invitation to *Daily Telegraph* readers: "And so, inspired by Cowdenbeath's initiative, I invite you to name post-1945 'Dream Teams' of your own favourites. There are two rules: a) the clubs involved must not have won their national championship in the past 60 years; b) any player named must have made at least one first-team appearance."

Soon, fans of lower league clubs are searching the memory traces and club records to produce their dream teams. The boring domination of the nation's press by the tedious Old Firm is mercifully set aside for a time while fans of lowly clubs, often with a proud history, dig out the old photographs again

The Cowden Supporters Club, who are determined not to let this historic season go by unnoticed, are working with the Blue Brazil On-line and the *Central Fife Times* to create the Hall of Fame. Players will be grouped into five eras, each of 25 years duration, with biographies of each player. The five candidates with the highest votes in each era will be admitted to the hall of fame.

*****

In a straw poll on Pie and Bovril about how people think the league will finish, some posters predict Cowdenbeath will finish fifth, sixth or seventh. The line of thinking is that Mixu has inherited someone else's players, and it will be next season before he can mount a really serious promotion challenge. Speaking about the upcoming game against Montrose, Mixu says: "We will continue to work away in training to improve the way we play as a team and as individuals. But it is difficult as, with part-time players, you don't have a lot of time to spend with the players on the training ground and that has been the biggest difference for me having been used to full-time football."

September 17, 2005
Cowdenbeath 2 Montrose 0
The Blue Brazil dominate from the start, although Montrose cause a scare by hitting the crossbar early on. Few chances are created in the first half as the team settle into Mixu's latest attacking 4-3-3 formation. Cowden answer the manager's half-time call to be more ruthless in front of goal as the three young front men revel in the new formation. Teenager Ryan McCallum opens the scoring in 53 minutes, then Graham Guy scores with a free kick. At the final whistle there's relief all around that Cowden have recorded their first home win of the season. Innes Ritchie's jubilant reaction in the tunnel at the end shows this is more than just a run-of-the mill victory. Could this be the confidence-boosting result that will kick-start the season?

BROWN BRAZIL! Cowden's new web sponsorship initiative reaches the national papers with the *Daily Record* and the *Sun* running stories on the Rt. Hon. Gordon Brown sponsoring Blue Brazil prospect Mark McEwen. Chairman Gordon McDougall says, "We are delighted to have Gordon Brown on board and thank him for his support. We are not sure whether to bank the cheque or frame it!"

There is a slight embarrassment when it is revealed that the player the Chancellor has sponsored has actually been farmed out to a junior club. Oops!

September 21, 2005

The Cowdenbeath Supporters Club hosts a 'Meet the Manager' event with Mixu Paatelainen at Central Park. There is a good turnout of fans, with Mixu's honesty, charisma and charm making a big impression. The supporters are cheered by the manager's commitment to attacking football. Mixu highlights the tremendous backing given by the fans. "A bit of encouragement even when things go wrong is invaluable and helps stop players losing confidence," he says. "Football is 80 per cent confidence, it's mainly played in the head."

September 24, 2005

Arbroath 0 Cowdenbeath 3

Cowden are playing attractive attacking football, with their three young attackers, Liam Buchanan (20), Andy Jackson (17) and Ryan McCallum (18) causing all sorts of problems. Buchanan scores after 28 minutes, Innes Ritchie scores with a header, and Ryan McCallum adds the third ten minutes from time. After the game, Arbroath's manager, Harry Cairney, resigns.

Mixu is gradually getting his young side playing the attacking football he wants, and the 4-3-3 formation is resulting is some great football. The result takes Cowden into third place and sets the team up for the clash with high-flying Stenhousemuir in seven days time. The Warriors are unbeaten in the opening seven games of the season but will travel to Central Park to face a Cowden side in good form. Markus Paatelainen, who has emerged as the team's playmaker, is voted as Fan's Player of the Month on the club's website. On Pie and Bovril, Berwick fans have started a thread wondering if the triumphant Berwick side, with a clear lead at the top of the league, will go through the whole season without losing a game. But it's the Cowdenbeath versus second-top Stenhousemuir game which grabs most of the attention.

6Boothy6 (Stenhousemuir fan): Cowden fans need to calm down with their "Bring on Stenny" posts. Cramb is back next week and will be amongst the goals in a 4-0 win.

Francesc Fabregas (Stenny): "People who think that Cowdenbeath will beat Stenhousemuir are either gay, a woman, or mental." He adds: "I've never heard of John Ward, or have any idea about his ability or prowess, but Colin Cramb will kill him."

Filling Francesc in on John Ward, Cowden fan *Blue Brazil Forever* says: "Scottish Junior internationalist, captain of Tayport and winner of two Scottish Junior Cup medals, 6' 4" tall, psycho totally committed to the Blue Brazil. Plays alongside Innes Ritchie in a defence that is now tighter than a mouse's vagina."

Tighter than a mouse's vagina? Unusual analogy, that.

******

In the vote for the best five players of the 1880-1905 era, the following win a place in the Hall of Fame:

Bob Law *(Wing half, 1881-95)* - One of the founders of Raith Rovers in Cowdenbeath. After the merger with Cowdenbeath Rangers, Bob was appointed captain of Cowdenbeath FC and led the team on the field for many years. He was capped several times by Fifeshire. He also played for the Albert Cricket Club in Cowdenbeath.

Willie Mercer *(Outside left, 1894-1909)* – Local miner Willie Mercer joined Cowdenbeath in 1894. He was to prove one of Cowden's best ever investments and gave the club almost 15 years of faithful service. In 1905, Willie had the honour of scoring Cowdenbeath's first ever goal in the Scottish League. He spent three years as trainer of Cowdenbeath FC and was a referee.

John Pollock - *(Outside right, 1880-85)* – One of the founders of Cowdenbeath FC and was a star player in the team. He was capped by both the Fifeshire and Edinburgh FAs. His Cowdenbeath career culminated with the winning of the Fife Cup in 1885 when Cowdenbeath beat the holders Dunfermline 2-0 in the final. John Pollock's brilliant solo counter was the highlight of the game.

James Pollock (Outside left, 1880-88) – The other official founder of Cowdenbeath FC. James played on the opposite flank from his brother and again represented Fifeshire on many occasions. James was a clever footballer and gave Cowden many years of stalwart service.

George 'Doddy' Wilson *(Outside left, 1902-03)* - Doddy Wilson was perhaps the best winger ever to don a Cowdenbeath jersey. The chunky Wilson was extremely skilful and exceptionally fast. After only one season he was sold to Hearts, and in 1904 he won his first of his six caps for Scotland. Then, in April 1906, he scored the only goal of the final to take the Scottish Cup to Tynecastle.

6. THE TRUE PRICE OF BLACK DIAMONDS

No man is an island, entire of itself...any man's death diminishes me, because I am involved in mankind; and therefore never send to know for whom the bell tolls; it tolls for thee – John Donne, 16th century poet and clergyman

Erith isn't twinned with anywhere, but it does have a suicide pact with Dagenham. – Linda Smith, broadcaster, who comes from Erith.

If coal hadn't been found in the farmlands of Cowdenbeath, there would have been no town of that name, and no senior football club. Without the "black diamonds", there would have been no Blue Brazil. The fact that the football club is still in existence four decades after the black diamonds ran out is a tribute to the resilience of those who run the club and the fans who support it.

In the early days of coal mining at the turn of the 20th century, labour was cheap, and so was life itself. Digging for coal in the bowels of the earth was hazardous. Many were maimed; far too many lost their lives.

The Moss Morran disaster at Donibristle colliery in 1901 was the biggest mining catastrophe since coal mining began in Cowdenbeath. A number of men had been working in a section of the mine when they broke through into a bed of moss and peat. They were trapped by the thousands of tons of the liquid moss and peat which surged in upon them. Two rescue parties were ensnared, then yet another rescue party was formed, and although some were found alive eight men lost their lives.

Going to the rescue of doomed colleagues was a badge of honour in the coalfields. A miner's safety depended on the vigilance of colleagues, and he needed to know that if he got into difficulties he could count on his fellow miners to try to rescue him. Cowdenbeath Football Club's captain Bob Law was lowered on a rope into the yawning chasm of Moss Morran where he rescued three men who had been entombed. He was honoured for his heroism with £100 from Andrew Carnegie and a gold watch from the Daily Telegraph. The very name Moss Morran hung like a cloud of dread over the area for a long time, and is part of the West Fife mining community's keening litany of grief.

Miners' pay was poor, and there was no provision for illness or the premature ageing which so often afflicted miners. People had to care for each other. This interdependence created the strong sense of brotherhood so characteristic of mining communities. There was a strong sense of sisterhood as well. In the early days of the coal rush, some women worked underground. Miners' wives at home with the children would get up early to make their men's "pieces" before they left for work at five am to work a 12-hour day. When the men emerged blinking in the sunlight after a long shift in the darkness, they went back to overcrowded houses in miners' "raws" to wash off the coal dust in tin baths in front of the living room fire.

The damp conditions and the swirling coal dust left many miners suffering from serious lung diseases. When I was a boy, I would often pass miners sitting on their "hunkers" at street corners gasping for breath, smoking, and hawking up coal-dusted phlegm and blood.

Kelty-born Jim Douglas is an extraordinary sportsman, poet and artist. The mining industry in which he grew up has been a major theme of his art and poetry. The illustration and these verses from his poem "Workin Doon the Pit", part of his excellent collection *dugs doos and dancing,* vividly capture aspects of the life of the miner:

Workin doon the pit, workin doon the pit.
Wi a cough and spit, workin doon the pit.
Dinnae get much pey, that's aye been the wey.
Like ma Dad and Dai, workin doon the pit.

Burry like a mole, burry like a mole,
Searchin for the coal, workin doon the pit.
Water tae yir waist, coal dust tae yir taste,
No for man nor baist, workin doon the pit.

Hear the timbers creak, hear the timbers creak.
Fairly maks yeh seek, workin doon the pit.
Is this day yir last or the day yir gassed.
The danger's never past, workin doon the pit.

Where are departed mates, where are departed mates?
Beyond the pearly gates, no workin doon the pit.
Or are they below, near tae where we go?
Hell's no far awoh, workin doon the pit.

There came a time when miners didn't want their sons to go down the pit, and sons worried about their prematurely-ageing fathers. This is captured well in a verse from another poem by Jim Douglas, called *The Miner's Son:*

It's awfy dark doon there, Dad,
Yir day must be like nicht.
Ye said yir bones wir sair, Dad,
Are ye share ye'll be a'richt?
Dae ye hiv tae work in water?
Why are the roofs sae low?
Ah widnae send a dug doon there,
Why should ma Faither go.

With ever-increasing demand for coal by the burgeoning railways, Cowdenbeath continued to expand. The population of the town jumped from 3,000 to 14,000 in less than 20 years. In the early part of the century, Cowdenbeath had something of a "wild west" feel. Unlikely to be twinned with Aix-En-Provence, it could never be mistaken for a tourist resort.

46

The Fife Coal Company, which owned nine collieries in the Cowdenbeath area, soon became the largest coalmining enterprise in Britain. While the company's profits grew, the men who dug out the coal continued to be paid poorly and safety was not as high a priority as it should have been. The black diamonds were mined at a cost, which was paid in red blood.

In 1912 there was a strike throughout the Fife coalfields, and this led to the passing of the Minimum Wage Act. After the Great War, the Miners' Federation demanded a 30 per cent wage increase and a six-hour day; the Fife Coal Company responded by announcing that miners wages would be cut. To avert a damaging strike, the government set up a commission on the mines, whose recommendations it promised to abide by. When the commission recommended a six-hour day and joint control of the mines, the government went back on its word. The stage was set for a national strike.

****

If this was what was happening in pits and politics, what else were the miners up to? They were playing football. When the Scottish First Division reached 16 clubs in 1905, Cowdenbeath Football Club, which had turned professional in 1897, made the step up from regional football to the Scottish League's new Second Division. In 1907, the club changed its colours from maroon to the familiar royal blue. (The Maroon Brazil doesn't quite work, does it?) 'The Miners', as the team were known throughout Scotland, did well on the park, but financially the club struggled at first in its more demanding new environment. With debts of £600 in 1909, it was proposed that the club be closed down, but the move was defeated.

An additional source of income was required, and it came from another traditional sport of the miners - greyhound racing. When I was a boy, the sight of a miner walking along the road with his "whippet" was a very familiar one. They greyhound promoters leased Cowdenbeath's North End park, and the annual rent of £104 helped keep the football club alive. The new financial security emboldened the club's directors to aim for the Scottish League's top bracket – the First Division. At the end of season 1913-14, Cowdenbeath beat Dundee Hibs 7-0 to win the Second Division Championship for the first time. There was no automatic promotion in these days, and the west of Scotland mafia combined to keep Cowden out of the top league. The following season Cowdenbeath won the Second Division Championship again, but this time the Great War put paid to their hopes. After the war, it was decided to have only one league. When Cowdenbeath, who by this time had moved to Central Park, applied for a place in the First Division, they found themselves tied with Albion Rovers. The chairman of another west of Scotland club gave his casting vote for the club from the west. No surprises there, then.

In 1921 the Scottish League officials at last dealt with the scandal of cronyism and decided that promotion and relegation should be automatic. In 1924, a year after opening their brand new 3,500-seater stand, Cowden won promotion to the First Division, one point behind champions St Johnstone.

The winning of promotion began a decade of unprecedented success in Scotland's top football league. It was the Golden Era of Cowdenbeath Football Club. As well as the players mentioned below, full back Bill Murray was transferred to Sunderland for £8000 – a huge transfer fee for those days - and goalkeeper Bob Middleton became the first Cowdenbeath player to be capped for Scotland. In their first season in the elite league, the "Miners" finished just behind Celtic. Not bad for a club from what not so long ago had been an agricultural settlement which hardly figured on the map.

Voting for the Hall of Fame for the 1905-30 era was particularly difficult, because there were so many outstanding players to choose from. Here are the ones who made it into the pantheon.

Willie Devlin (*Centre forward, 1922-26, 1929-30*) – In Cowden's great season in 1924/25, Devlin scored 33 League goals to end up as the First Division's leading marksman - one goal ahead of Hughie Gallagher. He was at his peak in 1925/26 and was transferred to Huddersfield for £4,200. He had scored 38 League goals in 30 games and ended the season as the leading scorer in Division 1, ahead of Jimmy McGrory of Celtic. In two spells at Central Park, Devlin scored a club record 120 League goals in 155 appearances, a wonderful record which is likely to stand the test of time.

John Falconer (*Goalkeeper, 1921-30*) – Falconer was a regular for two seasons but when asked to re-sign in 1923 he demanded an exorbitant signing-on fee. Cowdenbeath soon learned that he had been tapped by Celtic and refused to allow him to leave. Falconer was idle throughout the next season but when Cowdenbeath clinched promotion, the club and player agreed to bury the hatchet. He was a virtual ever present throughout the next seven seasons. In 1928 he was capped by the Scottish League v the English League at Ibrox.

Jim 'Hooky' Leonard (*Inside forward, 1923-26, 1927-28, 1930*) - In 1924/25, Hooky was in and out of the side and was suspended for missing training sessions due to a fondness for the bottle. In season 1925/26 he was third top goalscorer in Division 1. In December 1926, Hooky walked out on Cowden to join Indiana Flooring in the thriving American Soccer League. He came back to Cowdenbeath for season 1927/28, then spent a further two years in the States before returning to West Fife to sign for Cowdenbeath for a third time. He was selected to represent the Scottish League against the Irish League and then was signed by Sunderland for a £3,000 fee.

Duncan Lindsay (*Centre forward, 1926-30*) - A bustling, powerful centre forward with great pace, Duncan scored 31 league goals in season 1927/28. He also scored six goals in a Scottish Cup tie v Johnstone. Duncan signed for Newcastle for £2,700 in 1930. Unfortunately, he was expected to fill the boots of Tyneside legend, Hughie Gallagher. Duncan Lindsay scored 82 goals in 126 Scottish First Division appearances for Cowdenbeath. No one has bettered this tally for Cowden in the top flight.

Willie Paterson (*Centre Forward, 1914-25*) - Willie Paterson from Hill of Beath was the son of Sandy Paterson, the Cowdenbeath manager. His father signed him for Cowdenbeath and he played a small part in Cowdenbeath's 1915 Second Division championship success. In the following season, Willie became established as the first choice centre forward. After service in the Great War, he was transferred to Derby County for £3,500. He returned to Central Park in the close season of 1923/24. In 1933 after his father died, Willie had a short spell as caretaker boss at Central Park.

Fast forward to October 1, 2005, the day when the Blue Brazil play Stenhousemuir. The Stenny fans will be out in force, confident that they will increase the gap between them and Cowden. A group of the Stenny fans form what is known as the "Akabusi Loyal", named after Kriss Akabusi, the British medal-winning athlete, television presenter, prominent business motivational speaker and part-time preacher. I like these Akabusi guys. They are loyal fans of their club, and on P & B their badinage is witty and largely generous, even when they're taking the mickey out of you and your team. Before the match I meet up with *Francesc Fabregas, 6Boothy6,* and *Fudge* at Wee Jimmie's Bar in Cowdenbeath. After all, *Francesc* had posted: "I'm actually looking forward to meeting some Cowden fans and sitting down and having a nice long chat with them, and talk about the arts, literature, science and the cosmos." As one does at Wee Jimmie's.

They are pretty confident that they will stuff us, and that they'll be able to shout their triumphant cry AWOOGA! We carry on the conversation with the Stenny fans in the social club at Central Park. The Cowdenbeath Supporters Club plays host to visiting fans before every match at Central Park, with free sandwiches on the menu. In the Raith Rovers v Dumbarton match programme of 3rd December, 2005, writer and Dumbarton fan Harry Glass is asked what his favourite and least favourite grounds in Scotland are. He replies: "The ground I most enjoyed attending in recent times was Cowdenbeath where the hospitality and conviviality of the local fans was exemplary."

The game starts with home keeper Davie Hay making a couple of brilliant blocks to keep Stenny at bay. Then Cowden take command. The match catches fire in 27 minutes when Stenny keeper Willie McCulloch somehow manages to parry a crashing free kick from Graham Guy, but Buchanan is first to react and he steers the rebound into the corner of the net. Buchanan, who is proving a handful, is fouled. From the resultant free kick, John Ward, who has dominated Colin Cramb, scores with a looping header. Top scorer Ryan McCallum wraps up the points before half-time with an overhead kick from six yards.

With Markus Paatelainen controlling the play, Cowden drop the tempo and play possession football. Then comes the goal of the game. Young striker Andy Jackson picks the ball up in midfield, steps forward and cracks a 30-yard screamer past McCulloch. Frankie Carroll nets a late consolation for a dejected Stenny side who have been totally outplayed in what is their first league defeat.

"This was our best display since I took charge and it was very pleasing to watch," says a delighted Mixu. "The commitment and team spirit were first class."

Frances Fabregas: I am eating humble pie, and the taste is bitter.

Hey, this season may not be a disappointment after all. AWOOGA!

****

Before the end of each game at Central Park, the familiar sound of roaring car exhausts is heard. No, it's not fans leaving because they can't stand the football, it's the sound of stock cars revving up, ready for the races which will start at Central Park not long after the final whistle. Without that throaty sound in the late-afternoon air, there would be no senior football in Cowdenbeath.

After the Second World War, the club faced a series of financial crises which threatened to bring senior football in the town to an end. it was clear that another source of income had to be found if the club's future were to be secured. Chairman Andrew Gronbach negotiated a deal with stock car promoter Roy Cecil. One man who drove there was champion stock car racing driver Gordon McDougall. He first raced at Cowdenbeath in August 1965. In 1981 started his own stock car enterprise in Newtongrange. He returned to Central Park in 1989, renting the stadium for an annual sum of £30,000. With Cowdenbeath FC a quarter of a million pounds in debt, McDougall was concerned about the financial stability of the club, and how it would impact on his own business. He embarked on a take-over venture, which was successful after a bitter battle with chairman Tom Currie. This was followed by Cowdenbeath's winning promotion in 1992, and the exit of manager John Brownlie over disputes about budgets.

When Gordon McDougall took over, there were fears among supporters that football would lose out to stock car racing. The situation worsened following a disastrous season in the First Division, which was chronicled in *Black Diamonds and the Blue Brazil*. The fact is that McDougall wanted Cowdenbeath Football Club to be rid of its debts and the heavy interest payments, and to live within its means. This necessitated a period of financial stringency, low wages, and consequently the inability to attract better quality players. He also wanted to invest in a new youth policy, which he saw as the way forward for the club.

His judgment has been vindicated in that several big-spending Scottish clubs got into severe financial difficulties through living beyond their means. Twenty five years on, Cowdenbeath Football Club lives to fight another day. Gordon McDougall has presided over three promotions, and the development of a youth policy which is the envy of many clubs. The Central Park Racewall has hosted many championships, including the World Stockcar Championship. The throaty sound of the revving of these car engines on Saturday afternoons is music to the supporters of the Blue Brazil.

7. YOU'VE GOT TO MAKE MAGIC

*As for you, I tell you what the epitaph on you Scottish dissenters will be –
pure, but impotent. Yes, you will be pure all right. But remember, at the price
of impotency. You will not influence the course of British politics by as much
as a hair's breadth. Why don't you get into a nunnery and be done with it?*
– Aneurin Bevan to Jennie Lee, 1931.

*Life is theatre, you've got to make magic, that's what you've got to do,
create magic* – Jennie Lee.

You can choose your friends, but not your relatives. We all know that. But there are
some relatives you would choose to have as friends. For me, that would certainly
be the case with my third cousin, Jennie Lee, the firebrand politician who is one of
Cowdenbeath's finest daughters.

At the time of her marriage in 1931, Jennie Lee was a national figure, much
better known than her groom, Aneurin Bevan. The fiery Welsh orator, though, rose
to prominence as Minister of Health in the post-war Labour government. He had
overall responsibility for the setting up of the National Health Service – arguably the
finest legislative achievement of any British government. It meant that for the first
time ever, poor people could have access to first class health treatment. After that,
Jennie lived somewhat in Nye's shadow, though she herself became a minister in
Harold Wilson's government and was responsible for another fine national project,
the founding of the Open University.

To understand Jennie Lee, we have to go back to where so much begins - the
Pollock dynasty. Margaret Pollock, the founding mother of Cowdenbeath Football
Club, was Jennie's great grandmother. As Cowdenbeath expanded quickly during
the coal rush, Margaret Pollock's son John, one of the two brothers who founded the
club, built the Grand Theatre and Temperance Hotel in Cowdenbeath's High Street.
John's sister, Janet Greig, ran the hotel for him. Janet Greig's dark-haired daughter
Euphemia helped her with the cooking, even after she married miner James Lee,
son of the well-known Fife miners' leader, Mick Lee. The hotel was built over a

shopping arcade – the one in which Margaret Pollock had her antiques shop.

Six contractors had been engaged in building the Grand Theatre, which could accommodate 1200 people. Its painting and decoration was undertaken by my grandfather, Alex Ferguson. Margaret Pollock and my grandfather and grandmother were official guests at the grand opening in 1904. I love the image of Margaret Pollock and my grandfather, who was a rabid Cowdenbeath supporter, conversing during that surreal gala evening in Cowdenbeath. Did they talk about Cowden's planned application to join the Scottish League? Did Margaret flush with pride and say that she never realised what that journey to Glasgow to buy the football would lead to? Did they talk about how one-year-old Joe (my father) was doing? Or about the pregnancy of Euphemia Lee, who probably cooked the gala meal that evening? (Romanticism? What calumny!) Euphemia's daughter, Jennie, was born on November 3, 1904

When Janet Greig died in 1908, Euphemia and husband James reluctantly continued to run the hotel and theatre. For the next few years it was home to Euphemia and Jim and their family, Jennie and son Tommy, aged two. Jennie was to write: "The new hotel was ramshackle and gloomy, a fire trap and damp. The noise was relentless. Pit engines shunted outside the bedroom windows while miners tramped past to the pithead cages." Jennie loved the arcade with its toy and sweet shops and old Margaret Pollock's Aladdin's cave of a furniture shop. She also loved the theatre and all the eccentric characters, such as actors, conjurors and ventriloquists, who came about the place.

Jennie's father was miserable in the rat-infested hotel which did not give them much of a living, and in 1912 he went back to the pits. The family moved to a cottage with its own indoor lavatory in Foulford Street, Cowdenbeath. Time in the "magical place" was over. There was, though, the magic of the imagination. Jennie Lee loved books. Garvie's Bookshop in Cowdenbeath became a regular haunt. Mr Garvie was blind, and Jennie used to read to him from his favourite book, *A History of the Working Classes Throughout the Ages*.

Jennie's father was chairman of the local branch of the Independent Labour Party, which had been formed under the leadership of Cumnock's Keir Hardie in 1893. Some of the best known ILP platform orators were Scots such as James Maxton and David Kirkwood. They came to speak at the Cowdenbeath branch of the ILP, and young Jennie Lee was entranced by the visitors, who stayed overnight in the Lee household.

This was an extraordinary political education for a precocious girl. The 14-year-old was also a clever pupil, coming top of her class at Beath High School. With only two mouths to feed and living in a reasonably comfortable home which was furnished with items from the hotel, the Lees, by mining community standards, were not poor. The house in Foulford Street was full of books, and Jennie had piano and violin lessons. Unlike most teenage girls who had other siblings to look after, Jennie was encouraged to read rather than to do domestic chores, and she was allowed to stay on at school beyond the normal leaving age of 14.

Neighbours thought that Jennie was a bit spoiled and "difficult", and this verdict accords with the tales I heard of her in the family story cycle. That kind of judgment depends on one's perspective. My guess is that Jennie Lee, growing up in a political environment in which she was tutored by her radical father and grandfather and stimulated by some of the greats of the burgeoning socialist movement in Scotland, was a confident, good-looking, unconventional and independent-minded woman who was disinclined to defer to men and was determined to make her mark on the world.

Thanks to a grant from the Carnegie Trust, Jennie was able to become a student at Edinburgh University at the age of 17. The Cowdenbeath girl flourished in this new environment. She preached her evangelical and passionate brand of socialism at the Mound, learning to deal with aggressive hecklers who disputed her claims that women should have votes on the same terms as men.

When the general strike was called off by the TUC, the miners decided to hold out. By this time the Lee family had moved to nearby Lochgelly, and Jennie returned home to give support to the miners. As the coal owners attempted to starve the miners back to work, extra police were brought in to quell the resultant violence. (In a previous strike in 1921, many of the local bobbies were personally sympathetic to the striking miners; indeed the local police played a football match against the Cowdenbeath Ladies Football Team to raise money to support the starving miners' families.)

The 1926 strike was especially bitter, and the miners were eventually starved into submission. A year later, at national conference of the Independent Labour Party she caught the eye with a passionate speech. Here is how veteran Labour activist Fenner Brockway remembered it: "A young dark girl took the rostrum, a puckish figure with a mop of thick black hair thrown impatiently aside, brown eyes flashing, body and arms moving in rapid gestures, words pouring from her mouth in Scottish accent and vigorous phrases, sometimes with sarcasm which equalled Shinwell's. It was Jennie Lee making her first speech at an ILP conference. And what a speech it was."

The speech propelled Jennie to prominence in the Scottish Labour movement, and she was invited to become the ILP candidate for North Lanark by-election. She turned a 2,028 Conservative majority into a Labour majority of 6,578. Jennie Lee was only 24 years old. She was not even old enough to vote. Her maiden speech was an attack on Winston Churchill. Here is how she recalled it: "Winston Churchill was at that time Chancellor of the Exchequer and I directed my attack mainly against his budget proposals. Later in the day, in the Smoking Room, he came over to me and congratulated me on my speech. He assured me that we both wanted the same thing, only we had different notions of how to get it."

Jennie's youthful appearance and forthright views began to attract much attention. One MP she became very friendly with was Aneurin Bevan. Her commitment to the ILP, which renounced the official Labour Party, prompted Bevan to issue his famous rebuke, reproduced at the top of this chapter. The difference of opinion, however, did not stop her marrying the miner M.P. for Ebbw Vale in 1934.

Jennie Lee, latterly Baroness Lee of Asheridge died in 1988. She represented a radical West Fife political tradition which was forged by the experience of the miners' struggle for a living wage and better working conditions. For several years, the make up of Cowdenbeath Town Council was eight Labour members and four Communist. Each May Day, the red flag flew from Cowdenbeath Town House. The real political battles – sometimes bitter – were between Labour and Communist, with democratic socialism pitched against revolutionary socialism. Jennie Lee had many battles with the Communists, resenting what she saw as their simplistic condemnations of anyone who did not follow a revolutionary Leninist line.

The politics of the area was largely communitarian rather than Marxist. The Co-operative movement was very strong, and the local Co-op store, producing its eagerly-awaited quarterly dividend, dominated the town's shopping options. Outside of the pitched ideological battles, the general ethos, born of struggles in times of adversity, was one of interdependence and solidarity. The black dust of this tradition has left traces in my own bloodstream and, in spite the fact that it flirted from time to time with totalitarian themes coming from Russia, I am glad to own it. And I'm proud of my feisty, independent, argumentative and passionate relative, Jennie Lee.

****

When the Blue Brazil's 17-year-old striker Andy Jackson hit the back of the Stenhousemuir net with a 30-yard rocket, it marked the 4,999th time Cowden had scored in Scottish Football League matches. Now the race is on to hit the magic 5000 mark at Cliftonhill, and whoever scores first for the Blue Brazil will go into the Central Park history books.

Following on the success of their first-team individual sponsorship scheme, which is now fully subscribed, Cowden have now extended the scheme to their youth squad. As part of the celebrations to mark their 125th year and the 100th anniversary of joining the Scottish League, Cowdenbeath FC and the Cowdenbeath Supporters Club have launched an initiative to recruit Honorary Supporters with Cowdenbeath connections. Acceptances have already been received from the Chancellor of the Exchequer, the Rt Hon Gordon Brown, and from MSPs Dennis Canavan, Helen Eadie and Tricia Marwick. Scotland's finest defence advocate Donald Findlay QC, best-selling crime novelist Ian Rankin, Cowden legend Craig Levein, former Cowden player Roy Erskine and his grandsons, Scotland tennis star Andrew Murray and his brother Jaimie, have all signed up.

October 15, 2005
Albion Rovers 0 Cowdenbeath 3

Striker Robert Downs, awarded a starting jersey in place of the injured Liam Buchanan, takes only six minutes to earn himself a permanent place in the Cowdenbeath FC history books. Robert's sublime chip into the far corner of the net is the club's 5000th goal in the Scottish League. It is Robert's first goal for the club. Markus Paatelainen, who is winning many admires with his virtuosity in midfield, also scores his first goal for the Blue Brazil, with 18-year-old Ryan McCallum finding the target for the fourth game in a row. There is one amusing incident during the game. Let *BlooCoo* on Pie and Bovril tell it like it was: "The Albino Raver centre forward receives a pass and turns quicker than a thing that turns really quick - and runs straight into Innes Ritchie. It takes the poor guy several minutes of treatment to realise where he is (bloody smelling salts - they could've let him dream on a little longer). Cue the shout from the terracing – 'You've been flat-packed.'" (Cowden captain Innes Ritchie works for Ikea.)

Club chairman Gordon McDougall receives a letter from Albion Rovers general manager John Reynolds praising the Cowden fans for observing Saturday's minute's silence at Cliftonhill impeccably. The message board on the Albion Rovers website is also full of praise for the conduct and humour of the Cowden faithful. In addition, Peter McClurg, the Tam Cowan lookalike tannoy announcer, emails to say "The fans were a true credit to the club and colours. They will be most welcome back at Cliftonhill. Keep believing and you will go up."

October 22, 2005
Cowdenbeath 5 East Stirling 1.

The Blue Brazil continue their impressive form by demolishing East Stirling. The victory not only extends the unbeaten run to five games but also made it five consecutive wins - scoring 17 goals and only conceding two in the process. Robert Downs scores an early double, Stephen Dymock scores for the Rovers, and John Ward and Markus Paatelainen add a further two goals before half time. Andy Jackson scores his second goal for the club in the second half.

October 26, 2005
Queen's Park 0 Cowdenbeath 2

Cowden dominate the opening spell at a wet Hampden and open the scoring after 17 minutes through Andy Jackson. Queen's play better in the second half, before a deserved victory is sealed with a Markus Paatelainen header 10 minutes from time.

It's starting to get tighter at the top, with Berwick stuttering and Stenny wining with late goals even when they're playing badly – the sign of Champions. With their bigger, more experienced, squad and Colin Cramb, the league's top scorer, scoring goals for fun, Stenny are looking strong. Mind you, the free-flowing Cowden, led by the outstanding Markus Paatelainen, are starting to look like serious title contenders – at least in the eyes of one neutral observer.

Attendant (Queen's Park fan): Berwick, Stenny and Cowden are well worth their places, and on what I saw the other night I wouldn't bet against Cowden continuing their run all the way to first place and the Championship.

Cowden and Berwick fans are building up for the big game at Berwick on Saturday. Berwick are well ahead at the top of the league with Stenhousemuir in second place, but an increasingly confident Cowdenbeath side are looking forward to inflicting some damage on the league leaders. They will be backed by a vocal travelling support.

When Cowdenbeath are playing away from home, two travelling factions are involved. You might reasonably think that the Cowdenbeath travelling support would be too small to have two factions, but you would be wrong. We are entering the realms of esoteric knowledge here. We're not talking about the Cowdenbeath People's Liberation Front clashing with the People's Front for the Liberation of Cowdenbeath, a la *Life of Brian,* but about the ETB and the Tea and Sconers. Remember you read it first in *Helicopter Dreams.*

Let's complicate this a little further. The ETB is an organisation that doesn't really exist or have any members. The initials stand for the Early Train Brigade, whose origin lies in the frustration of arriving at away games on the supporters' bus with too little time to, er, socialise before the game. In other words, there are those fans who like to set off from Cowdenbeath late enough to arrive fairly close to kick-off time, and others who prefer to leave much earlier so that they can enjoy a small beverage before the match. Or even ten small beverages.

When Cowden were in the Second Division, enough fans wanted to travel to away games to run two buses. (Old Firm supporters, who are used to travelling to games in several Panzer divisions, will be on the floor with laughter at this stage. Two whole buses!) The different needs of the Blue Brazilian punters were met by laying on an early bus and a later bus. Back in the basement division, there were only enough volunteers to fill one bus, and the majority felt they had better things to do with their Saturday than hang around dingy hostelries in places like darkest Berwick-Upon-Tweed. That was when the option of travelling by train was seriously looked at. Fan Derek Neilson took responsibility for finding out train times and circulating the information to those interested.

The first game when this plan came into operation was Gretna versus Cowdenbeath in the 2003/4 season. The itinerary for travelling to Gretna involved leaving from Lochgelly and Cowdenbeath stations, changing at Inverkeithing to get the train to Carlisle before boarding the train from there to Gretna! On the train to Carlisle a few beers were consumed, a card game enjoyed and some Cowden songs sung. So they were in good fettle when they arrived in Gretna only to find out, when they arrived at the ground, that the game had been called off because high winds were threatening to whip the roof off the old stand!

"Tea and Sconers" is the name applied by the ETB to those fans who travel on the bus to away games when the ETB are on one of their special away days. But it's not always simple. Sometimes ETB people travel on the supporters' bus, and the odd Tea and Sconer has been known to travel by train. Some even travel by car, motor bike, cycle, or rickshaw. Quite a few Tea and Sconers like a drink, and there are ETB people who are quite partial to a nice cup of tea and a wee scone. They are totally united in their support for the Blue Brazil. The ETB folk believe that they sing more vociferously – which may be largely due to the amount of alcohol consumed. No ETB person presents this case too loudly though, for fear of being concussed by a large flying scone.

October 29, 2005
Berwick Rangers 1 Cowdenbeath 0
Disappointment for the large travelling support as the league leaders run out winners in an evenly contested game in front of a healthy attendance of 715. The game is decided by a controversial decision in Berwick's favour. Goalkeeper David Hay picks the ball up just inside his area and bowls the ball out to Kevin McBride. The linesman rules that Hay has carried the ball outside the box and Chris McGroarty fires in the resulting free kick into the top corner.

Nelly (Cowden): The game was poor, pure and simple. Didn't think Berwick were top quality but they have beaten us twice 1-0 so they are doing something right. Berwick will win the league pure and simple, but Cowden will definitely get a play- off place. The best thing about the game was the two burgers I had, they were fantastic!

Mixu Paatelainen wins the October Bell's Third Division Manager of the Month award, thanks to Cowden winning four out of five games in October and scoring an impressive 14 goals with only three conceded. For the second successive month, Cowden fans have voted for Markus Paatelainen as the Supporters Web Player of the Month. Markus is Making Magic.

November 05, 2005
Cowdenbeath 3 East Fife 1
Cowden return to winning ways in the Fife derby. Craig Smart scores for East Fife against the run of play after 28 minutes but the Blue Brazil storm back in the second half with goals from Innes Ritchie, Ryan McCallum and the aptly named Graham Guy.

November 12, 2005
Montrose 0 Cowdenbeath 1

Cowden continue their impressive run, recording their eighth win from the last nine fixtures. Markus Paatelainen opens the scoring after only three minutes. Cowden play flowing football, with Markus running the show in midfield, but despite creating many chances the score remains the same. Montrose never threaten the Cowden goal.

Berwick, who are now faltering, lose 3-2 at Arbroath. The Blue Brazil are only six points behind the league leaders with a game in hand. Things are getting really tasty at the top. Cowden fans on P & B are in good form.

Blue Brazil Forever: I do sincerely believe that the Blue Brazil under Mixu are on the verge of true greatness. Present team spirit is fantastic and the side are playing a brand of football which is a revelation.

Cowden Cowboy (Blue Brazil fan): First half Cowden were so on top it was like an exhibition game. At one point after about half an hour a Montrose player actually managed to get the ball from Markus Paatelainen. This provoked a shout of "Jesus Christ - make him Montrose Player of the Year now!"

A Brechin fan asks how David Hay, the Cowden goalie who was freed by Brechin City, is doing. The facts speak for themselves: So far in the league, Cowden have conceded 8 goals in 14 games. Hay has had seven shut-outs.

Ivo den Bieman: (Montrose): The fact that Hay could have taken to the pitch in a string vest and carpet slippers, and got pissed in his goalmouth because he had so little to do, will make this his cheapest clean sheet of the season, I fancy. We were shite. Again.

Morale at Central Park is high. The player and backroom team sponsorship scheme has continued to attract backers with a total of 46 players and backroom staff now sponsored. Meanwhile, Dave Baikie has been appointment manager of Junior club Bo'ness.

8. GET YOUR PITS OUT FOR THE LADY

Half a league, half a league,
Half a league onward,
All in the valley of Death
Rode the six hundred.
'Forward, the Light Brigade!
Charge for the guns!' he said:
Into the valley of Death
Rode the six hundred.
-Alfred, Lord Tennyson, The Charge of the Light Brigade

There is something undeniably sexy about a woman in power. We may not agree with President Mitterand's assertion that Margaret Thatcher had "the eyes of Caligula and the mouth of Marilyn Monroe" but some of her cabinet were certainly in thrall to her. – Helen Frith Powell

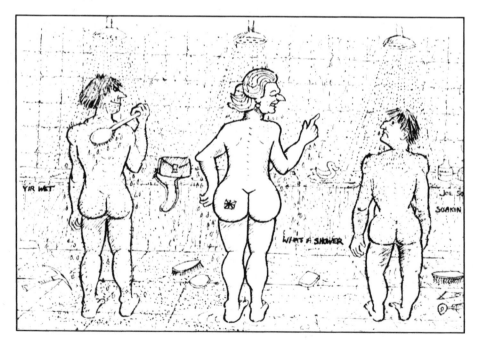

Well, did the Iron Lady ride into town and put the miners to the sword? Did the Right Honourable Margaret Thatcher MP, prime minister of the United Kingdom, visit Fife and go down a coal mine? Mibbees aye, mibbees naw, as Kenny Dalglish might say. She certainly came to a township in the mind of Kelty's mining Poet Laureate and artist Jim Douglas, who has mythologised a visit by Mrs Thatcher to his own internal West Fife. Jim's poem and illustration from *dugs doos & dancing* certainly capture the arrogance, disdain, and even eroticism of the Iron Lady. She seems to get her kicks from either putting down or being adored by men. As neither a psychologist nor the son of a psychologist I couldn't possibly comment. These verses from Jim's poem "The Visit" and his illustration cover the territory well. Over to Mr Douglas.

Good morning. Sir, yes it's me.
I'm Margaret Thatcher, the M.P
Now what is all this fuss about,
I'm here to sort the Miners out.
They want more money I am told,
Do they think I'm made of gold?
They should thank their lucky stars
I haven't clapped them behind bars.

Would I like to see below?
Of course, where any man can go.
I can too, I'm willing, ready.
I'm after all the Iron Lady.
Must I step into this cage?
Come now men and act your age.
Because I know you'll all agree

A cage is just the place for me.
Sir, take me to the top again.
I've seen enough of working men.
I must say they're a bit uncouth,
And I've developed quite a drouth.
I feel just like a wilted flower
And what I'd give for a good shower.
Oh, I can join the men you say,
Is that a dare? Show me the way.

I'm in the shower, oh what bliss,
To think the working men get this.

I feel my spirits start to soar,
Haven't you seen a girl before?
The men are modest though, I hope,
Won't hide behind their bars of soap.
I must say they seem thrilled to bits.
 They don't know yet, I'll close their pits!

The miners certainly hated Margaret Thatcher. To understand why, we need to wind the reel back to her hero, Winston Churchill, who was hated by the miners as well. When riots occurred in the Welsh town of Tonypandy in 1910, Churchill put troops on reserve. During the general strike the troops were brought in, and the strike collapsed after 12 days. As we have seen, the miners stayed out, but at tremendous cost. The government was determined to break the miners, and the sight of warrant sales in the streets of Cowdenbeath was a familiar one. There were many arrests and imprisonments. That is why the miners of Cowdenbeath hated Winston Spencer Churchill.

The only good news to come out of Cowdenbeath at this time was that its football team was (now and again) beating the Rangers and Celtics of Scotland's top football league. It began to feel like acts of defiance on the part of a mining town under siege.

When Labour came to power after the Second World War, it nationalized the mines. Miners' wages and conditions improved, and safety in the pits was a priority. And the five-day working week – the miners' Holy Grail – was at last achieved. There was a real sense abroad of having won a hugely significant victory. More disposable income meant more choices for miners' families, and the 1950s and especially the 1960s provided more options in terms of leisure and travel. With Cowdenbeath back down in the Second Division, young miners with free Saturdays headed towards Glasgow in increasing numbers, dressed in blue or green. The old communal bonds, forged in times of hardship, began to be loosened. Even the old political loyalties were strained as ordinary people became more affluent.

There are two tragedies in life, said George Bernard Shaw. One is not to get your heart's desire. The other is to get it. In the nationalised mining industry, what also developed was the growth of bureaucracy and a "jobs for the boys" mentality. NCB directors failed to read the signs of the times. Many of the existing seams in the Cowdenbeath coalfields were unsuitable for the new methods of coal extraction, and coal from other mechanized pits was cheaper to produce. Not only that, the coal industry was facing increased pressure from oil. Towards the end of the 1950s, the National Coal Board was making thousands of miners redundant. This was not the new dawn the miners had expected. In 1960, the No 7 pit, the last working pit in Cowdenbeath, closed. There was something poignant about this particular closure because the No 7 pit stood in the heart of the town, right beside Central Park, symbolizing the close link between coal and football in the town's history. The "Number Seeven" was part of the folklore of Cowdenbeath Football Club.

Let me give one illustration. On September 21, 1949, I was part of Cowdenbeath's biggest-ever crowd of 25,586, lifted high by my dad, to watch Cowden play Rangers in the second leg of the quarter final of the Scottish League Cup. In the first leg at Ibrox, Cowdenbeath had faced one of the greatest-ever Rangers sides, which included Bobby Brown, Willie Woodburn, George Young, Tiger Shaw, Sammy Cox, Ian McCall, Torry Gillick and Johnny Rutherford. Sports writers protested that such a mismatch should even be allowed. Rangers must have wished it hadn't been allowed, because Cowden humped the Huns by three goals to two, becoming the first Second Division club to go to Fortress Ibrox and beat the mighty Rangers. Not only that, they did it with style.

At the end of the Ibrox match, Alex Menzies, Cowden's heroic and fearless captain, had danced a Highland Fling in front of the baying Rangers punters. A boyhood hero of mine, "Big Ming" would be prepared to die for the cause. He resolutely refused to acknowledge defeat even when it stared him in the face – and as a Cowdenbeath defender it stared him in the face often. My old mentor, Cowdenbeath's firemaster Tommy Deas, now in his 96th year, used to say of Ming, "After Ming got a kick on the heid he played better!"

Alex Menzies was actually born and brought up in Lochgelly. One child who revered him, when Ming played for Lochgelly Violet – great name for a team of macho miners! - was Ron Hunter, fellow pupil of mine at Beath High School, and a former wing half with Raith Rovers. "When you grinned shyly at him at nine years old and he said 'Aye min' to you," Ron told me, "you knew that you had been spoken to by a superstar and you carried on along to the Store baker's in a state of unmitigated euphoria." Star quality, in Lochgelly.

Everyone in Cowdenbeath knew Big Ming and admired him. (Fans – including his wife – used to shout affectionate abuse at him from the stand.) Ming belonged to the Desperate Dan school of Scottish footballing manhood, with his diet of pies, fish suppers and beer. Nowadays, of course, elite footballers eat lettuce, drive free BMWs, flaunt jewellery, and wear Italian designer suits. Most of today's foreign players speak English better than Alex Menzies ever did. Big Ming, with an earring, strutting his stuff in Cowdenbeath High Street dressed in a Versace suit? I try to picture it, but there are some images which stubbornly refuse to form.

But I digress. With most people expecting a thrashing from the wounded Glasgow giants, upstarts Cowden had the audacity to take the lead in six minutes. The scorer? Big Ming, of course. Rangers pulled one back, making it 4-3. With only 13 seconds left, Cowden forward Frank Armstrong wins the ball in the Rangers penalty area. Alex Menzies shouts in a voice that can be heard throughout the ground, "Don't try anything clever, Frank, just kick it down number Seeven pit!" Instead, Frank tries to torment big Geordie Young of Rangers one more time, but fails. Young lumps it into the Cowden penalty area and Johnny Rutherford scores. 4-4. Rangers win in extra time, 5-4. As a child, I cried. So did the men around me. So did Ron Hunter.

"I was there when Rangers scored the winning goal in the gloaming. I was at the back of the goal at the Beath High end, high up on the terracing and just a wee bit too heavy by then to be on my faither's shoothers. And of course I wept with the grown men. I can see it as clearly as if it were five minutes ago. 'See yon Airmstrong…' they would say. 'He wid rin as long as there wis gress. If ye opened the gates at the bottom end he wid rin richt an' nivver stoap till he goat tae Brighills! If only he'd run oot the park at haulf-time an' nivver come back.' Poor Mr Armstrong. What commitment. Such inordinate and consummate skills. What utter bloody stupidity – taking on big Corky at the eleventh hour!"

Some of the West Fife pits were closing not because the seams had been exhausted, but because coal was becoming too expensive to extract, given the competition. The great days of coalmining in Scotland were over. Some of the NUM leaders, like many of the other big union bosses, strutted on the political stage. A few, like Arthur Scargill, aligned themselves with totalitarian East European political leaders. The union bosses misread the times, which was a dangerous thing for even big beasts in the jungle to do when one Margaret Thatcher was on the prowl. The somewhat chauvinistic union barons were dismissive of this upstart woman, who had become Britain's first ever female prime minister in 1979. Winning the 1983 election with a landslide victory following the Falklands war, Margaret Thatcher had the trade unions in her sights.

Whatever one thinks of the Iron Lady, she was a fearless and driven radical who was determined to re-shape what she saw as a stagnant Britain. Breaking the power of the miners was a kind of political virility test for this fragrant but dangerous woman with a much-mocked swinging handbag. She decided to ambush the NUM leadership. In March 1984, the trap was set. With coal stocks high, Ian McGregor, chairman of the NCB announced that several high-cost pits would cease production. The NUM leadership, without even balloting their members, called a national strike. The trap snapped tight. Gotcha!

Scargill may well have been right that the government had a "hit list" of other pits, but precipitate action was not what was called for. The odds were always going to be against him, but what was required was a strategy, not an undemocratic strident call to arms. There was a good case to be made that Britain had no viable national fuel strategy and that reliance on oil and foreign coal was not in the country's long-term interests, but the grandstanding, hectoring supporter of dodgy East European regimes was not the man to make it. He was a gift to the

Thatcher-supporting tabloids. When the Light Brigade charged, the NCB boss and the prime minister must have thought it was Christmas.

The old familiar soup kitchens were back. Mick McGahey addressed a big rally at Central Park, bringing back memories of the old struggles. But Britain had changed. The six million readers of the right-wing *Sun* newspaper included a high proportion of working-class people who had bought their Council houses under Tory legislation and even had investments. These readers included car-owning and house-owning miners. The Labour old guard might have felt betrayed, but this was the new reality. The strike lasted a year, but the miners were defeated. The feminine/masculine Iron Lady had had her wicked way with them, cheered on by much of the country. The broken miners had to accept redundancy money to pay off their debts. Welcome to the new Britain.

The Iron Lady would go on to become the longest serving UK prime minister for more than 150 years. As she became more and more messianic, her hubris became unbearable. Her entranced cabinet of drooling fellow-believers were in thrall to this British Joan of Arc, who to them was made beautiful and sexy by the aphrodisiac of power. Even old Tory public schoolboys were so turned on by the sense of danger, the whiff of cordite, that they wanted to be spanked by this authoritarian nanny who knew what was good for them. She had woken up a complacent nation, but she also created an industrial desert and called it peace.

No, she didn't come to Fife and go down a pit, in the flesh. But she did so in a hundred thousand nightmares. She opted for cheap oil and cheap foreign coal on the false assumption that Middle East oil and eastern European coal and gas would always be there for Britain at cheap prices.

The once-vibrant mining town of Cowdenbeath, the Chicago of Fife, was now a rather dispirited place characterised by high unemployment. The burden of maintaining pride in the town's name now fell upon its football club. But with the umbilical link between coal and football now severed, could a team which was playing in the lower divisions in front of diminished crowds carry the extra weight which had been thrust upon it?

******

The inductees for the Blue Brazil Hall of Fame for the era 1930-55 are as follows:

Tom Glancy (*Wing half/Inside forward, 1925-34*) – £350 was money well spent by Cowdenbeath to sign Tom Glancy from St Johnstone. Glancy found his niche at Central Park in the right-half berth and went on to give his home town club nine seasons of faithful assistance. He made 264 league appearances for Cowden, all in the top flight. His versatility and consistency made him a real favourite of the local fans.

George Jordan (*Right back, 1938-40*) – A superb full back. Arsenal offered a massive £8,000 fee for him but Jordan wished to play for no one but Cowdenbeath. He marched into manager John Dougary's office and laid it on the line: "Are you not

wanting me to play for Cowdenbeath? If not, I'll no' be playing for anybody else."
George remained at Central Park to share in the 1938/39 promotion success. Private
2759374 George Jordan of the 7th Battalion, the Black Watch was killed on active
service in North West France on 8 July 1944. He was only 27 years of age.

Alex 'Ming' Menzies *(Half back, 1948-55)* See above. Lord Ewing recommended
that the new stand being built at Central Park be named after Alex Menzies and this
suggestion was adopted by the Board of Cowdenbeath FC.

Alex Venters *(Inside Left, 1930-33)* – Played for Cowden when he was 17, and was
soon the club's brightest star. In season 1933/34 he was selected to represent Scotland
v Ireland. Rooted at the foot of the league table and nearly broke, Cowden sold him
to Rangers for £2,000 at the age of 20 after scoring 37 goals in 95 top flight league
games In season 1938/39 he was leading scorer in the First Division with 35 goals.
He won two Scottish caps v England to add to the one gained with Cowdenbeath,
two Scottish Cup winners medals and three league championships with Rangers. Aly
died in 1959 at the age of 45, and was immortalised when the playing field at Park
Street, Cowdenbeath was renamed the Alex Venters Memorial Park.

Rab Walls *(Centre Forward, 1937-45)* - Rab was renowned for his powerful shooting
which several times knocked out opponents unlucky enough to get in the way of a
ball launched from his boot. Sometimes goalkeepers who attempted to save were
carried into the back of the net with the ball in their grasp. After playing for Hearts,
St Bernards, Hibs and Aldershot. Cowden then brought Rab back to Scotland and
he became the idol of the local fans with some extraordinary scoring feats. He had
a club record of 54 league goals in Cowden's runaway Division 2 championship
success in 1938/39. His tally has only been bettered once in Scottish football history.
Rab scored an extraordinary 103 league goals in 79 games for Cowden

****

November 26 2005
Cowdenbeath 0 Morton 3
There's a lot of snow on the pitch, but the referee is happy enough with the
conditions underfoot to allow the Tennent's Scottish Cup first round tie to go ahead
– provided the surface snow can be cleared within two hours. Cowden fan Stuart
Watson *(Blueminer)* goes down to the ground to find Mixu, Gordon McDougall and
some of the ground staff on the pitch, clearing the snow. Stuart contacts some fans
to ask them to come to Central Park, and he goes home for his snow scoop. To get it,
he has to walk along his own snow-covered path, which his wife reminds him he is
never too keen to clear! The pitch is cleared.

Pity about the game, though. Stuart Watson wonders whether clearing the
pitch was such a good idea after all.

December 3, 2005
Cowdenbeath 2 Albion Rovers 1

The Blue Brazil open the scoring after 33 minutes with Markus Paatelainen heading home Kevin McBride's free kick. Rovers equalise through Donnachy courtesy of a defensive mix-up six minutes into the second half. Both teams make further chances in the second half, including a missed penalty from Markus Paatelainen, but it's Cowden who score the winning goal with Liam Buchanan heading in a corner after 67 minutes.

December 06 2005
Cowdenbeath 3 Arbroath 2
Cowden get off to a flyer when Liam Buchanan heads home after only 90 seconds. Arbroath hit back, literally, and they are reduced to ten men when Paul Watson is red-carded after Marc Millar is cynically felled. Cowden should be on easy street, but their once-invulnerable defence is caught playing statues as they stand and watch a powder-puff header from Pat Clarke crawl over the line. Worse is to follow after the interval when Steven Cook puts ten-man Arbroath 2-1 ahead. This goal spurs the Blue Brazil into top gear at last. First, Liam Buchanan controls a Ryan McCallum cross, makes space for himself, then blasts the ball past keeper Mark Peat from ten yards. Loan star Andy Jackson notches the winner when the ball breaks to him following a goalmouth scramble.

This tenth win in 11 games moves Cowdenbeath into second place in the league. On Saturday, Cowden will travel to play Stenhousemuir in what will be the most critical game of the season so far. If Cowden can beat the Warriors, they will move into top position.

December 17, 2005
Stenhousemuir 2 Cowdenbeath 0
Stenny start better as their midfield take control, and they take an early lead through Colin Cramb. Worse is to follow before the interval when indecision in the Cowden defence allows the unmarked Jim Mercer to steer a weak shot into the corner of the net. Cowden come out fired up for second half but they can't get an opening goal to spark a comeback. The result means that Cowden slip five points behind league leaders. The Stenny fans on P & B are quite pleased.

Fudge: Pitalineon looked a good player, the only one in the Cowden team who tried to play football. Ward received a white sphere at his feet, thought 'what the f**k is this', then humped it up the park on every occasion. I think his training schedule is solely to header brick.

Cowden fan *Kierkegaard* composes a biblical greeting for Christmas. He calls it The Stenhousemuir nativity: "And it came to pass in ancient times that three wise men from the East, from the village of Sten-house-manure, followed a star to see where a baby who would lead their people to glory might be born. When they

67

came to a broken-down hovel, Boothy, Francesc and Fudge entered, and knelt down before the one they believed would be their saviour. He was called Coco, of the House of Cramb. Then they handed over their gifts of gold, frankincense and hair gel. But the Lord said to them: 'Your GPS monitor is defective, and you've gone to the wrong hoose. The real star is shining in Finland, where Markus of the House of Paataleinen has been born. In the future, Sten-house-manure will be in the lead for some time, but a team called the Blue Brazil will overtake them at the final hurdle.'"

Stenny fan *Dubya* is dismissive of Kierkegaard's coded prediction: "I'm writing all your tosh down for the end of the season when you will eat a very large maroon-coloured slice of humble pie."

Blue Brazil fan *Nelly* has a problem on his mind. His great friend Garry Moyles, another lifetime Cowden fan, is due to be married in May – on the day of the play-offs. Nelly and his friends start telling Garry gently that they would prefer an evening invitation because they'll be going to the Cowden play-off game. Garry just smiles and says, "Don't worry, Cowden will still win it."

As we look towards the New Year, Stenhousemuir look most likely to reach the finishing post first, with Berwick and Cowden fighting it out for second place. The Stenny fans, though, try to hide their worry that the blue horse from Fife will overtake the maroon mount on the final rail.

Does Cowdenbeath's Kierkegaard know something that Dubya doesn't? And is groom-to-be Garry Moyles right to believe that his friends will be at the wedding on the play-off date, because Cowdenbeath will already have won the Championship?

9. HARRY POTTER AND THE MYSTERY OF THE SMOKIE PENSIONER

When I was a teenager at Dundee and I saw the senior players I used to think, 'Well, if I'm with Arbroath at that age, getting £30 a week and all the kippers I can eat, I'll be doing pretty well for myself. – Gordon Strachan, captaining Leeds United at age 33.

Most football teams are temperamental. That's 90% temper and 10% mental.
 - Doug Plank

Did you know that Aung San Suu Kyi, brave leader of the Burmese opposition party, is a Cowdenbeath supporter? No, this isn't a joke. She has never visited Central Park as far as I am aware, but there is evidence to suggest that news of the fortunes of the Blue Brazil is not entirely absent from her consciousness.

But before I talk about this courageous lady, I need to turn to Professor Sir James Black, one of Cowdenbeath's most gifted sons, who has been enlisted this season as an Honorary Supporter of the Blue Brazil. Born in 1924, James Whyte Black chose not to follow his father into the mines. His father worked his way through the pits until he became a mine manager. As a brilliant maths and science student at Beath High School, Cowdenbeath, Jim became a lecturer at St Andrews and at Glasgow Veterinary School. In 1958 he moved to ICI. There he devised a drug called Inderal, which saved the lives of many people suffering from coronary disease. In 1972, while working for Smith-Kline, he produced Tagamet, a wonder drug which transformed the life of ulcer sufferers. In 1988 Professor Black received international recognition when he was awarded the Nobel Prize for Medicine. Not bad for a miner's son from Cowdenbeath.

Anyway, back to Aung San Suu Kyi. She is an astonishing person, one of the most impressive women in the world. I've been a fan of hers for a long time.

When she married Dr Michael Aris, the couple made a pact that if it were the right thing to do, she would return to Burma. She did so in 1988, with Michael's full support. Ever since her National League for Democracy won a landslide election victory in 1990, Suu Kyi has been either in prison or held under house arrest. She has been courageously critical of the junta's actions, and has repeatedly drawn public attention to their abuse of human rights. She is democracy's most potent symbol in that part of the world, and her presence there is an inspiration to many people whose human rights are repeatedly denied.

But what about this business of supporting Cowdenbeath? Not long after *Black Diamonds and the Blue Brazil* was published, I received a letter from a woman in London. Her father, Dr Duncan Young, had been a GP in Cowdenbeath in the 1930s, and he took his enthusiastic daughter to home games. She also talked about Professor Black, and she told me that her beloved daughter-in-law was also a Nobel Prize winner. Her name? Aung San Suu Kyi. The writer of the letter was Mrs Evelyn Aris, mother of Michael.

Fantasy mode – a common form of consciousness among lower division footie fans - immediately took over. Did my heroine confuse her bewildered interrogators by reciting the Cowdenbeath scores of 1938, as taught by her Blue Brazil-supporting mother-in-law? Is the Myanmar Special Branch currently poring over a confiscated copy *Black Diamonds and the Blue Brazil*, searching for hidden meanings among the tales of glorious defeat and disaster? OK I'm being a little disingenuous in suggesting that this iconic woman is definitely a supporter of the Blue Brazil, but if she's paid attention to her mother-in-law's stories of dramas at Central Park she might well be. And there may be an inspector in the Myanmar Secret Police who is Burma's leading authority on Hooky Leonard.

****

Soon, we will have to make the long trip to Arbroath, the well known East coast fishing centre which is particularly associated with kippers and Abroath Smokies (smoked haddock).

Arbroath is also in the football record books. In 1885, Arbroath Football Club beat Aberdeen side Bon Accord 36-0 in a Scottish cup tie – the highest score in world senior football. Their centre forward John Petrie scored 13 of the goals. Their goalkeeper, Jim Milne senior – also known as "auld Milne" - had so little to do on that rainy day that he borrowed an umbrella from a friend in the crowd to keep dry. The final tally could, however, have been much more had referee Dave Stormont taken a harder line with the Aberdeen team. Many years later he revealed that the Lichties could actually have won 43-0, as he might have been wrong in chalking off seven goals for offside. Did you know that on the same day that Arbroath rattled 36 goals past Bon Accord, less than 20 miles away Dundee Harp were thrashing Aberdeen Rovers 35-0? It was one of my leading researchers, Mr Google – who still comes second to Mr Allan in the esoteric Fife fitba information league table – who

70

revealed this to me. At the end of the game, the referee told Harp's committee that it had been difficult for him to keep count of the goals, but he thought it was 37. The Dundee men admitted, however, that they had recorded 'just' 35 goals. The referee accepted their version and telegraphed the official result through to the SFA as 35-0.

Another thing Arbroath is famous for is the Declaration of Arbroath in 1320 – a ringing statement about Scottish Independence. There is a mystery about this Latin statement; no one is sure who wrote it. But, as Cowdenbeath Football Club are about to find out, Arbroath is a place of many mysteries. We shall have to consider the Mystery of the Smokie Pensioner. But before we make the journey north, there are other domestic matters to attend to.

The terracing song has to be amended to "There's only Three Paatelainens". Mikko Paatelainen (25), brother of boss Mixu and midfield star Markus, joins Cowdenbeath on a two month loan deal from FF Jaro in the Finnish premier league. The Cowden fans are delighted. With Andy Jackson being called back to St Johnstone, Ryan McCallum being farmed out to the juniors, and Robert Downs going back to the juniors, we are seriously short in the striking department. With three Paatelainens now signed up at Central Park, *Farflunglichtie* comments wittily on P & B: "I'd hate to see Cowden - its nickname a byword for cosmoplitan internationalism - turn into an inbred, purely family venture offering merely an assembly line of opportunity for the latest Finnish wonderboy. Incidentally, is cloning more advanced in Finland?"

Mixu also announces the signing of 18-year-old striker Paul McBride from Tower Hearts and defender or midfielder Pat Scullion (19) from Elgin City. The fans are upbeat about the trip to Methil for the New Year's Day derby against East Fife. Honours are even so far with Cowden going down 1-0 at Bayview but avenging this with a 3-1 victory at Central Park.

January 1 006
East Fife 2 Cowdenbeath 1
A group of East Fife fans demonstrate against chairman Derrick Brown on top of the mound (now nicknamed "Mount Killamanforhisgiro"!) Cowdenbeath start the game well, and miss several chances. The Blue Brazil defence looks a bit shaky, and Cowden find themselves two goals down after 18 minutes. Cowden come out for the second half fired up, and John Ward scores in 55 minutes. Despite having several chances, Cowden can't conjure up an equaliser. The fans are despondent at losing to their local rivals again.

Mixu is disappointed as well. "Hopefully this will act as a wake up call to the boys that they can not afford to switch off at any time." The boss returns to his former club St. Mirren to secure the services of promising young forward David

McKenna (19) on loan till the end of the season.

Saturday's match against Berwick, who are lying second in the league with Stenhousemuir in pole position, promises to be a cracker. Our problem at the moment seems to be scoring goals. Berwick have the same problem, while Stenny keep winning matches late in the game and extending their lead at the top of the table. The Cowden and Berwick fans on P & B are up for the match.

The Minertaur: Huge game, one of the biggest of the season. A draw would scupper both teams' chances of automatic promotion. I would take a 1-0 for Cowden just now!

BerwickMad: If we win, it is us who are back in the race. If our new signings show us we can start scoring again, then we are back in the race.

Francesc Fabregas (Stenny)*:* If we don't win the league this season, I will rip off my face and throw it into the burn. But it won't come to that, as we will win the League by April. AWOOGA!

January 14, 2006
Cowdenbeath 1 Berwick Rangers 1
Mixu Paatelainen makes a number of changes, with new signing David McKenna making his debut. Berwick open the scoring after only 10 minutes. Cowden press for the remainder of the half without finding a cutting edge in front of goal. In the second half the Blue Brazil move up a gear and equalise through Markus Paatelainen.

Markus, whose dazzling displays in midfield have impressed opposition fans as well as Blue Brazil supporters, has won the fan's website Player of the Month award for the fourth consecutive month. The problem for the club will be to hold on to their star, who is attracting attention from envious managers.

January 21 2006
Cowdenbeath 2 Montrose 0
New loan signing David McKenna opens the scoring after just four minutes when he shoots home an inch-perfect cross from Markus Paatelainen. Cowden are well on top but suffer a major setback five minutes before the interval when Darren McGregor is sent packing after receiving two yellow cards. The crucial second goal arrives seven minutes from time when Markus Paatelainen chips the ball through to Liam Buchanan who calmly lobs the advancing goalkeeper to seal victory for Cowden.

The Blue Brazil remain in third position and now face a trip to Arbroath before hosting league leaders Stenhousemuir. Mixu is optimistic about the trip north, despite the fact that the previous games against Arbroath have been hard and bad-tempered encounters. "The trip to Gayfield will be a real test for us," says the boss. "Arbroath showed what a physical side they can be on their last visit to Central Park but are also an experienced and skilful team. I am quietly confident though that if we play to our capabilities we can come away with a victory."

January 28, 2006
Arbroath 4 Cowdenbeath 1

Cowden begin in superb form, playing some wonderful football, winning grudging admiration from the home fans. The Blue Brazil put the Arbroath goal under sustained pressure, but can't get the all-important opening goal. Then Arbroath take a shock lead against the run of play in 30 minutes. Gavin Swankie latches onto a through ball from player-manager John McGlashan and lifts the ball over the advancing David Hay. The turning point of the game comes in 69 minutes when an Arbroath supporter throws the ball in Mark Baxter's face as the full back waits to take a throw-in. Baxter loses the plot and hurls the ball back at the fan. The referee immediately sends off the Cowden player. Jay Stein makes it 2-0 for Arbroath. Then, with nine minutes remaining, Iain Mauchlen makes a reckless challenge on John McGlashan and is rightly red-carded. This sees almost all the players on the park congregating to "debate" the matter. McGlashan subs himself off and disappears down the tunnel, where there is an altercation. Paul Watson and Steven Cook score further goals against the nine-man Cowden, and Mikko Paatelainen scores his first goal for the club in injury time.

On Pie and Bovril, a thread headed "Mark Baxter, you are a fucking disgrace", starts a furious debate involving a total of 141 postings.

SimonLichtie : Should be fucking ashamed of himself. A man between the age of 65 and 80 chucked the ball back from the crowd to give it to him, and Baxter seemed to feel he had chucked it so hard, and was aiming for his face. Who knows if he meant to or not? The old man had no incentive to do it, as the game hadn't got out of hand at all by then.

Cowdenbeath: The guy shouldn't have hit Baxter with the ball. I believe that the police are involved in the incident and I hope the Arbroath supporter gets done for it. You can't have supporters assaulting players, the Arbroath players are good enough at that without their fans doing it.

HillStreetBlue (Cowden fan): I know that Arbroath's style of play has prompted complaints by a number of clubs but it's a new dimension to add surprise attacks from all corners of the ground!! Is bin Laden the new Director of Football? It was like a day at the Ayrshire Juniors.

xbassLichtie: I didn't see the incident properly, but I suspect the guy was simply throwing the ball to the guy, as many other people do. But at 80 years old, it's easy to misjudge.

Kierkegaard (Cowden): This innocent Abroath fan, who, according to Simon, was really just trying to help Mark Baxter by gently handing him the ball, is getting older with every post. By noon today he'll be a blind, peace-loving 150-year-old with a wooden leg, who helps old ladies across the Arbroath streets and feeds starving children in Africa.

*Hampden Diehard (*Queen's Park): This is easy to sort out. The two of them to have a square go on the pitch at half time the next time Arbroath visit Cowden; the old guy gets to use his zimmer and the Cowden player has one hand tied behind his back. Get Sky involved and you'd get a bumper crowd.

Djn: Is there any truth in the rumour that Baxter killed Bambi's mum?

*FarflungLichtie (*Arbroath): In the wrong hands, a football can be a lethal weapon. We may be dealing with a serial killer here.

Kierkegaard: Simon's OAP will probably turn out to be a 29-year-old weightlifter whose complexion has aged as a result of curing one haddie too many. It was Simon who told us the culprit was a pensioner. Surely Simon isn't using that as a smokescreen to cover.......himself? Surely not.

xbassLichtie: It's funny you should say that, the last time I saw Simon he was disappearing off to the toilets at half time, rubbing talcum powder in his hair to make it grey and mumbling something about "sorting that f'cking Baxter out". Didn't think anything of it at the time, but now you mention it......

*GalaKev (*Berwick): This will appear in a Question of Sport, 20 years from now. What happens next? It will stop when the ball goes out of play. Are they ever going to imagine that this 150-year-old with no arms, jumps out of his wheelchair, climbs over many a WW1 veteran and launches the ball with his catapult at a Cowden player. And then is seen running off rubbing the grey talc out of his hair and is in fact a 15-year-old Harry Potter lookalike. It could only happen in the Third Division.

Indeed. *Helicopter Dreams* has tried in vain to track down the Smokie Pensioner, even assigning a Cowdenbeath OAP with a free bus ticket to get an exclusive interview with the dastardly offender. It wasn't "auld Milne", who was in goal for the Bon Accord game in 1885 was it? There is an omerta in Arbroath. (Great line that, isn't it?) Yes, a wall of silence. It is as if the lieges know that if they reveal the name of the culprit, a smoked horse's head will be found in their bed.

There we must leave this crazed debate. Mind you, Simon does look a bit like Harry Potter. I wonder.....

******

The Blue Brazil Hall of Fame inductees for 1955-80 are as follows:

1955-80

John Dickson *(Inside right, 1968-72)* – John was a gifted player. Sometimes a prima donna but always liable to bring the fans to their feet with his supreme trickery and skill. 1969/70 saw him at his peak as Scotland's leading goalscorer with 31 League goals in 34 games for Cowden as promotion was won. 1972 saw him tempted away to St Mirren and later he played for Ayr United. Subsequently, he managed Elgin City and Dundonald Bluebell. He scored 98 League goals in his career – 61 of them for the Miners.

Andy Kinnell *(Centre half, 1964-72)* – Second cousin of the illustrious Jim Baxter. A native of Cowdenbeath, Andy was signed by Cowden in 1964, playing for the first team at the age of 17. He spent eight splendid years at Central Park. Never flustered, Andy was a class player who could mix it with the best of them when necessary. He was Cowden's player of the year in 1968. As captain, he led Cowden to promotion in 1970 as well as during their year in the top flight. In 1972, he realised his ambition to go full-time when Willie Ormond signed him for St Johnstone for £8,000.

Jim McArthur *(Goalkeeper, 1967-72, 1983)* – Jim was the youngest player ever to play in the Cowden first team when he made his debut at Hampden v Queen's Park in March 1968 at the tender age of just 16 years and 13 days. His breakthrough came in season 1970/71 when injury saw Alan Wylie sidelined. He took over for the rest of the First Division campaign and a star was born. Eddie Turnbull signed Jim for Hibs in October 1972 for a £10,000 fee at the age of only 20. Eleven memorable years at Easter Road followed. He is now a highly successful football agent.

Andy Rolland *(Right back, 1961-62, 1964-67, 1980-82)* - Andy signed for the Blue Brazil in October 1961, but was released after a few games. Two seasons later new Cowden manager Archie Robertson re-signed him for Cowden. Andy was one of the new breed of attacking full-backs and thrilled the Central Park crowds with his dynamic play and powerful shooting. In October 1967, Dundee United paid £10,000 for Andy. After 11 years at Tannadice, he returned to Central Park for the third time, eventually becoming player-manager. His commitment inspired the side in their promotion challenge in season 1980/81. No Cowden fan needs reminding of the fateful day in season 1980/1 that Cowden missed out on promotion. Andy Rolland's missed penalty, his first spot-miss in six years, cost Cowden promotion.

Davie Ross *(Outside left, 1969-76)* – Davie Ross was playing with his local club Kennoway United when he scored as trialist for Forfar Athletic. Forfar couldn't afford to pay him a signing on fee and once director Jock Gilliard slipped him £200, Davie was happy to join Cowden. He made a huge impact in his first season as Cowden shocked Scottish football and strode to promotion. He starred in the First Division and he went on to score 48 goals in 223 games for Cowdenbeath. His loyalty to the club was also remarkable and he stayed with Cowden for seven years until he was transferred to St Johnstone in 1976.

10. KEEPING THE FAITH

The evening before the Celtic match I had watched a TV documentary on Martin Luther King and I was moved by the man and his faith. It rubbed off on me because when I had my team talk I spoke of my faith in Dunfermline Athletic. I said that I too had a dream – to see the club back where we belonged. I made it funny, of course, by saying to the players just before they went out on the pitch, "Do you believe?" They roared back, "I believe! I believe!" – Jim Leishman, revealing the content of his team talk before Dunfermline beat Celtic 2-1, August 1987.

Socially, a journalist fits in somewhere between a whore and a bartender, but spiritually he stands beside Galileo. He knows the world is round. – American writer Sherman Reilly Duffy

Light up the incense. I am the official chaplain to Cowdenbeath Football Club. In the international ecclesiastical pecking order, this appointment ranks third, after (1) the Pope and (2) the Archbishop of Canterbury.   How did I arrive at this dizzy summit of ecclesiastical power? Well there's a long version and a short version. Let's avoid the scenic route and take the motorway.

As well as being reared on stories of Cowdenbeath FC, miners' strikes and West Fife radical politics, I was brought up in the Church of Scotland. Nowadays, that seems an eccentric statement to make, as if one were some kind of a freak. Back then it wasn't. Churchgoing wasn't regarded as odd. In the 1950s, the Kirk alone had a signed up adult membership of 1.2 million, out of a population of five million adults and children.

My father was a regular churchgoer, though his propensity to imbibe a few jars and back the horses precluded him, he felt, from being an elder of the Kirk. Although a believer of sorts, my mother's attendances at worship tended to be restricted to quarterly communion services.

At any rate, I was brought up in the faith. I went through Sunday School and Bible Class, and then, after a spell of rebellion and absence, I attended the youth fellowship. This had as much to do with hormones as religion; but in the process, I began to explore questions about meaning. As a "broad" church, Cairns provided a hospitable place for such questionings.

I underwent an evangelical conversion when a student mission came to town. Though it sharpened my Christian commitment, I eventually couldn't cope with the fundamentalism of the student group. Cairns parish church allowed me scope to develop an understanding of religious faith that didn't depend on a literalistic reading of the Bible. The Youth Fellowship trips to Germany also broadened our teenage horizons. When a German group came over to Cowdenbeath, we played them at football on the North End pitch on which the early versions of Cowdenbeath Football Club used to play. My subtle left foot was used to devastating effect, but Cowden's scouts inexplicably failed to recognise my latent genius. On one occasion, when the German centre forward celebrated too exuberantly after scoring a goal, our maddened goalkeeper, Davie Russell, rushed from his goal and kicked the astounded young foreigner up the backside. This fiery move was not calculated to promote international relationships, and Tommy Deas, the local firemaster who was refereeing the game – did he have a coin with no heads or tails? - had to use all his diplomatic skills to sort the situation out. Oh happy days!

By this time I was working as a cub reporter on the *Cowdenbeath Advertiser and Kelty News* (much to the dismay of the rector of Beath High School, who regarded journalism as lower on the social scale than prostitution). I also worked for an agency which provided news and sports reports for the national daily papers. Not only did I cover the greyhounds for the *Daily Record*, I did football reports from Central Park for the *Sporting Post*, the *Evening News* pink edition, the *Sunday Post* and the *Sunday Mail*. (I also used to travel to all the away games in the Cowdenbeath team bus, and would play the mouth organ for the players on the journey home.)

Say I was covering a game at Central Park in which Cowdenbeath beat Rangers 8-0. I would use the same basic facts, but doctor them to suit the readership of each paper. The Glasgow readers would read a version from a Rangers point of view, whereas the pink readers would get more of a Fife slant. I used to be amused on Sundays when people would say to me, "The Sunday Mail says that Rangers were a bit unlucky, but the Sunday Post says Cowdenbeath were brilliant." I didn't reveal that it was me all the time.

What I am saying is that as a young journalist it slowly dawned on me that all stories, including my football reports, are told with a particular audience in mind. They are doctored, either consciously or unconsciously. Yet once they become part of the approved oral "loop" or appear in print, they become authoritative – part of a canon, carrying a certain "weight". The stories my father told me were either tales which had been passed to him down through the years, or were versions of events which he had seen with his own eyes. But neither the stories themselves, nor his ears or eyes were neutral. He was one of the tribe, looking at events through blue-and-white tinted glasses without even knowing he wore lenses. The stories were designed to tell of (often exaggerated) triumphs, severe injustices, and heroic fightbacks against misfortune; they were tales of insubordination, set against a background of a declining mining industry.

Stories have power, but to get at the historic reality behind them, you have to be able to take off the particular lenses you are using. The problem is that you can only do that partially. You cannot escape your point and place in history. You are both blessed and imprisoned by your own story. That, in a nutshell, is what post-modern philosophy is all about. Ultimately, you have to make choices about what matters to you, without the benefit of proof.

Which brings me neatly to faith. The Christian story was, for me, a powerful one, and I had worked out a way of believing that didn't require me to commit intellectual suicide. At the age of 23, I left journalism in Edinburgh to study for the ministry. (When, in Baillie's Bar in Edinburgh, I informed George Millar, my great journalistic mentor at the *Edinburgh Evening News,* his eyes popped out of his heid and he shouted "Jesus Christ!") After eight years study of philosophy, history and theology, I became community minister in the huge Glasgow housing scheme of Easterhouse. Eight years later I was elected leader of the Iona Community, and after spell of writing books full-time, I became minister of the beautiful St Magnus Cathedral in Orkney. After 11 years there, I stepped down early to concentrate on full-time writing, still from Orkney.

So what are my duties as chaplain to the Blue Brazil? Well, I'm not very sure, really. In 1994, when Cowdenbeath were in the midst of their world record-breaking run of 38 games without a home win – it's hard to achieve that even if you're actually trying to do it - I was called down from Orkney to see if I could break the hoodoo. In the dressing room, I didn't speak to the demoralised lads about Moses or St Paul, but about Hooky Leonard and Big Ming. After my address, which could be described kindly as Martin Luther King Meets Jim Leishman - or unkindly as Complete Bollocks - a photographer from the *Sun* newspaper asked me if I would wear a clerical collar and kneel down at the centre spot, looking to heaven with hands clasped in prayer. I immediately sensed that this was an offer I could easily refuse, and told him I didn't have a dog collar. The man from the *Sun* immediately whipped one out of his pocket. (Maybe he did pastoral counselling on the side.) When I still declined, he offered me £50. I was insulted. Did he think I would sell my soul for fifty quid? It would have to be a lot more than that....

Ah, but did my ministrations in the Blue Brazil dressing room work? Not for that particular game, nor the next one. But prayers take a little time to filter through. Ten days after my pastoral visit, Cowdenbeath Football Club at last won a match at

Central Park – on Easter Saturday no less.

Let me tell you what happened next. I went to bed early that evening, because I had three Easter services the next day. Then in the wee sma' oors, the phone went in the St Magnus Cathedral manse. I presumed it must be an emergency. It might have been a Rangers supporter threatening suicide because his team had lost that day. On the other end was a slurred American accent with a Scottish burr. The caller was phoning to say that he had heard that Cowden had at last broken their hoodoo. He had been celebrating, and he felt he had to call me. Well, thanks a lot, pal.

It was Hooky Leonard's son, from California. In the course of the conversation, he told me some more details of his father's history. The legendary Hooky had apparently run away to Gretna to get married, fathered 11 children, moved to the States and died at the age of 54. His son had read *Black Diamonds and the Blue Brazil,* and been excited by the stories of his father's artistry with a football. He'd obviously been drinking - and, of course, Hooky himself was no stranger to the demon drink - but he was so moved by the immortalisation of his father in print that he felt this was the right time to call me. It was a surreal incident, but then I suppose Cowdenbeath's entire history has the air of the surreal about it.

Where religion helps in being a Blue Brazil supporter is that you develop a theology of suffering, fatalism, endurance or whatever. But you also learn to appreciate the humour that goes with supporting a club like the Blue Brazil. After decades of dismal failure punctuated by occasional ecstatic moments of success, you learn to be philosophical. Whereas some Rangers and Celtic supporters are ready to throw themselves into the Clyde if their team is denied its God-given right to lift at least two trophies in any given season, Cowdenbeath fans regard one league trophy in a millennium as a sensational gift from heaven.

Now here's an interesting theological question: does God take an interest in football matches? Does he influence penalty shoot-outs, or even football transfers? That question was raised in August 2003, when Marvin Andrews, Livingston's 28-year-old central defender caused weeping and wailing and gnashing of teeth on Tayside by saying that God had told him to turn down a lucrative transfer to Dundee United.

Here's how the scriptures recorded it:

And Marvin spake unto the Lord, and asked him, "Lord, what shall I do?" And the Lord hearkened unto Marvin, and saith unto him, "Marvin, whatever thou doest, don't sign for Dundee United." And Marvin saith unto Ian, son of Call, "The Lord hath forbidden me to join the tribe of the A-rabs." And Ian, son of Call, saith under hith breath, "Bugger it!" and rent his raiment, and wept and mourned for forty days and forty nights.

An engaging and enthusiastic man with the kind of build that would be useful for smiting Philistines, big Marvin worships three times a week at Zion Praise Centre in Cardenden, Fife. When faced with any big decision, he consults his minister, Pastor Joe, and prays to God. The one thing which makes me slightly suspicious here is that Pastor Joe turns out to be a keen Livvy supporter. Was his spiritual counselling as neutral as it should have been? Is it possible that the pastor's enthusiasm for Livingston contaminated what should have been disinterested advice? Was the preacher wearing a Livvy scarf when this decisive non-directive counselling session took place?

When Marvin Andrews was considering the extension to his Livingston contract, his then manager, Jim Leishman, was prepared to go to places where no football manager has gone before. Zion Praise Centre in Cardenden. "I went to one of Marvin's gospel meetings," said Jim. "Initially it was to see the gospel band, but Marvin was down the front with his fellow worshippers and I thought it was tremendous." Were the motives of Lochgelly's Poet Laureate entirely pure? Did it not cross the mind of Big Jim, a former Cowdenbeath stalwart who was once sent off for pulling down the shorts of a Dunfermline player, that Marvin would be moved by the sight of his eccentric boss singing his heart out at the gospel meeting? And that this might influence the player's decision to put pen to paper? Who can search out the depths of the human heart?

Actually, I find big Marvin's story refreshing. Football has become a sphere of such venality and cynicism that the sight of a player turning down a lucrative move for reasons which transcend sport and money is truly startling. Good on him. But if the creator of the heavens and the earth does take to do with football transfers, what I want to know is this: why does God not direct more good players to sign for Cowdenbeath? I am prepared to be his chosen vessel if he lines up a few players who are out of contract soon.

What I do know is that asking God for help with sporting matters is an ambiguous matter. When I was about eight, I prayed to God to let me win a race at a Sunday School picnic. The prize was a liquorice allsort. I came in last, and I was an atheist for about four years. One of the best examples of the crossover between religion and sport is that of the fastest–ever recorded goal, scored by the Brazilian forward Roberto Rivelino who was much admired for his powerful long-range shot and his "banana-bending" free-kicks. Apparently, Rivelino had been tipped off that the opposing goalkeeper always said a prayer at the kick off. When the whistle blew, Ravolino whacked the ball straight at the goal. Three seconds later the goalkeeper opened his eyes to find that the ball was in his net. Bloody hell! The poor sod had been praying for a shut-out! Who says God doesn't have a sense of humour?

****

The transfer window has swung shut. Berwick Rangers have released Bruno da Silva, the "New Thierry Henri" who, we were promised, would take the league by storm. He turns out to be a local fishmonger.

Going into February in troubled mode, the Blue Brazil certainly need to believe. Our normally reliable defence is still a bit shaky, and we are finding it harder to score goals. So far, Mikko Paatelainen has not been the scoring sensation we had hoped for. What better way to bounce back than to beat the league leaders?

February 4, 2006
Cowdenbeath 1 Stenhousemuir 1
Cowden edge the play in the opening period but it is the visitors who open the scoring after 34 minutes from the penalty spot. Three minutes from the interval the Blue Brazil get a deserved equaliser when Liam Buchanan fires home following a cross from Markus Paatelainen. For the third successive Saturday Cowden are reduced to ten men for the final five minutes when Darren McGregor is sent off for picking up two yellow cards in the space of five minutes.

February 11, 2006
Albion Rovers 1 Cowdenbeath 3
Cowden's bad habit of going a goal behind and then having to chase the game continues at a wet Cliftonhill. A lively Albion Rovers side open the scoring after only seven minutes. Cowden fight hard and miss several chances, but the breakthrough comes in 56 minutes. John Ward's header is blocked by the Albion goalkeeper, and Liam Buchanan, who is playing in his 100th game for the first team, nips in to score his 29th senior goal. Five minutes later we take the lead with a spectacular goal. Out of the left, Mikko Paatelainen lets fly and the ball hurtles past the astonished Rovers keeper. With ten minutes left on the clock Graham Guy scores with one of his trademark free kicks from 25 yards.

Because Stenhousemuir have beaten Berwick Rangers, Cowden move to within a point of second-placed Berwick. The Blue Brazil fans are jubilant. Though next Saturday's game against Queen's Park could well be a hard game.

February 18 2006
Cowdenbeath 6 Queen's Park 0
Mikko Paatelainen, who's found his scoring touch, opens the scoring after 23 minutes with a volley from 25 yards. On the half hour the Finn gets his second goal of the afternoon when he bangs home the rebound after keeper David Crawford had blocked a shot from Liam Buchanan. Two minutes into the second half the Blue Brazil are three up through Innes Ritchie. Liam Buchanan makes it 4-0 when he is put through by Mikko Paatelainen, then the Finn completes his hat-trick with five minutes to go when he slides in to score from close range. Three minutes later David McKenna completes the scoring from the penalty spot.

There are so many encouraging signs now. The flowing football is back. With Markus Paatelainen orchestrating the midfield and Mikko banging in the goals – and Mixu masterminding the tactics from the touchline – we're starting to look serious contenders again. But is the Championship a possibility? Cowden fan Colin Nelson and some of his friends have made a commitment that if Cowden do win the Championship, they will have Cowdenbeath badges tattooed on their bodies. Wives and girlfriends are apparently not best pleased. Colin says: "We would go to the tattoo place to get the badge tattooed on our bodies for life. This is how much the club means to us and how proud we are too display our affection for Cowden." Then he adds, "I hate tattoos personally, but this is something I will have to do."

Cowden's magic Markus picks up yet another award. For the fifth consecutive month Markus Paatelainen has been voted as Player of the Month by the fans. He has impressed fans across the country with his powerful and skilful running from midfield and has already secured 'cult status' at Central Park. Markus is so good a playmaker that opposing teams man-mark him very tightly and every week he ends up with bruises. Now after last week's great result v Queen's Park, Cowden are ready to make the long journey north to face an in-form Elgin City.

February 25, 2006
Elgin City 0 Cowdenbeath 4
Loan striker Mikko Paatelainen continues his fine form, opening the scoring after 35 minutes following a mistake by City defender Hugh Dickson. Cowden double their advantage after 58 minutes when a corner from Kevin McBride is headed home by Innes Ritchie. Mikko Paatelainen gets his sixth goal in three games when he is put through by brother Markus to score six minutes later. The scoring is completed for the afternoon in 68 minutes when David McKenna shoots home from a Mark Baxter cross. With 17 minutes to go, Markus Paatelainen, who has been tormenting the Elgin defence, has to go off after he is felled by a crude challenge from Hugh Dickson. Mikko Paatelainen is booked for remonstrating too strongly about the tackle.

One person who has good reason to smile at the end is young Aaron Tuson, son of Supporters Club chairman Dave Tuson. Dave and Hugh Alan had £2 each on Cowden winning 2-1. Aaron wanted to put his £2 on, but fancied 4-0. Dave tells me: "He was accordingly laughed at. He won at odds of 80 to 1. Even then we were looking for more goals. Makes you wonder."

There is drama later that evening, when Markus Paatelainen is rushed to Edinburgh Royal Infirmary. The midfield star suffers complications to the injury he sustained at Elgin. He is operated on immediately after haemetoma develops, amid fears that the leg may have to be amputated. Cowden boss and brother Mixu explains: "The family and everyone associated with the club are shocked by what has happened but Markus has been very fortunate. Such an operation should normally take place within six hours but Markus was not operated on until 3.30am on Sunday morning. But thanks to the expertise of the medical team, the surgery was a success. Markus will have a second operation tomorrow and will be sidelined for two to three months."

This is disastrous news for the player and the club. There is fury on Pie and Bovril. The thread about the injury to Markus has over 7000 "hits" and 349 posts.

CowdenCowboy: I am afraid as far as I am concerned Dickson's challenge was not a fair one. It was quite clearly needlessly aggressive as he was annoyed as Cowden were running rings around Elgin by then. Cowden were just starting to fire on all cylinders for the run-in and we couldn't have had a bigger blow. Hope Markus's injury doesn't turn out to be career-threatening. I would gladly pay money every week just to watch him play. The best player in the Third Division by a country mile.

Cityfan: Obviously this is awful news and I hope Markus all the best, but the abuse towards Dickson on here is a bit unfair. I have seen far worse tackles in this league, the fact the ref was right next to the challenge and didn't even blow for a free kick shows it wasn't a really dirty tackle.

Fudge (Stenny): I hope Markus is OK and is able to play again to the same standard, but from a completely selfish view it is a major bonus for us. I wish he was out with something far less serious though.

Debbie (Elgin): I don't think Shug is a particularly dirty player. The blood clot could have been caused by anything. One cause is a 'Recent trauma to the lower body, such as fractures of the bones of the hip, thigh, or lower leg'. Would that be likely? This kind of injury is as likely to happen in an innocuous challenge as a nasty one.

Bleubrazil (Cowden fan): Never in the 125 year history of Cowdenbeath FC will there have been a more determined bunch of players than when Elgin visit Central Park next Tuesday night. Markus will be in everyOnés thoughts from the first whistle. Let's pray he will recover from such a cowardly tackle.

Fudge: I always said when we played Cowden we should give Markus a bit of a boot early on to try and unsettle him, which is a great compliment to the player. Nothing nasty, but just let him know you are there. I presume that other teams try and do the same, only this time it turned out to be a bit more serious.

Francec Fabregas: Cowden have steamrollered teams that have beaten and sometimes outplayed us (Queen's Park and Elgin) and have the best player in the league in Markus, who adds that extra flair that is often lovely to watch. But we'll wait and see how they get on without Markus. I don't want to suggest that you're a one-man team, but everything good comes through him. Stenhousemuir will still win the league though.

The Cowden fans are shattered by this unpredictable turn of events. With their star player out for the rest of the season and their star striker set to return to Finland, the Blue Brazil could still be pipped for a play-off place, never mind the Championship. Arbroath, Elgin City, East Fife and Queen's Park are showing signs of resurgence, and there could be an almighty scrap which goes right to the last game of the season.

Old feelings of dread return to Central Park. Will this rollercoaster of a season end in tears?

****

The 1980-2005 era was a real up-and-down time in Cowden's history. It included some abysmal displays, the record failure to win at home for nearly two years, the emergence of one of the club's finest players and managers, Craig Levein, and the dramatic promotion-winning season 2000-1. Voting for the 1980-2005 era results in the following players entering the Hall of Fame:

Raymond Allan *(Goalkeeper, 1972-75, 1979-89)* – Quite simply a Cowden legend! Cowdenbeath born and bred, Raymond joined Cowden in 1972 from Glenrothes Juniors. He was freed after three seasons and re-joined Glenrothes, but eventually re-signed for Cowden in 1979. For the next decade, he was a fixture in the Cowden goal and was a familiar, popular, vociferous and dominating presence. After making a record 422 league appearances for Cowden, he left the club after a dispute with manager John Brownlie. He had made 620 Scottish League appearances in a 25-year career span.

Graeme Brown *(Centre forward, 1997-03)* – Born in Johannesburg, South Africa in 1980, Graeme was brought up in the rugby stronghold of Galashiels. He was signed at the age of 16 by Cowdenbeath. He is one of the few players to have scored a goal for Cowden whilst just 16 and still at school. The youngster was a hit with the fans from the start and as he developed his game, he became one of the most popular players ever to don a Blue Brazil jersey. He was Cowden's top scorer in 1999/00 and then was a member of the promotion-winning side in 2001. Cowden sold him to Ayr United in 2004. He is now with Alloa Athletic.

Craig Levein *(Centre-back, 1981-83, Manager, 1997-2000)* – One of Cowdenbeath's greats. He signed for Andy Rolland's Cowden side at the age of 17 in 1981, rapidly making the breakthrough to the first team. Following a League Cup tie with Hearts he was off to Tynecastle at the tender age of 19 in return for a £40,000 fee. He was a commanding figure at Tynecastle and his outstanding defending and distribution earned him 16 Scotland caps. His career was badly marred by injury, and in 1995 he had to give up playing, aged only 31. Two years later he became Cowdenbeath manager and built the side which went on to win promotion in 2001. He was an outstanding Hearts manager, but enjoyed a less happy time at Leicester City.

Innes Ritchie *(Centre half, 2003-06)* – After a senior career with a variety of clubs, in 2003 Keith Wright persuaded Innes to sign for Cowden. As team captain his leadership qualities have been greatly regarded both on and off the park, and is a great example to younger players for his professionalism and commitment. In his time at Central Park, Innes has twice been Players' Player of the Year and twice Supporters Club Members' favourite Player of the year. He has now made 296 Scottish league

85

appearances and scored 27 goals in his career.

Craig 'Toorie' Winter *(Midfield, 1994-2004)* – After spells with Hibs and Raith, Toorie joined Cowden and went on to become a real local hero at Central Park. He played for Cowden in some difficult times before enjoying the tremendous promotion success of 2001. Captain Toorie won the Cowdenbeath Player of the Year award a couple of years before that. After 10 years with Cowden, in his testimonial year, Craig was signed by First Division Brechin City and is now with Dumbarton. He made 286 League appearances for Cowdenbeath FC. Only two men have played in more matches for Cowden.

11. DUBYA AND THE COMING OF THE SPECIAL ONE

Reporter: *There's no negative vibes or negative feelings here?*
Gordon Strachan: *Apart from yourself, we're all quite positive round here. I'm going to whack you over the head with a big stick. Down negative man, down.*

Keep playing to the fat man.- Brian Clough tells his players to pass the ball to John Robertson.

Saviours come in all shapes and sizes, and the Special One is some shape and some size. Whoever would have believed that salvation would come to Cowdenbeath in the form of an overweight, unfit, six foot five inches black Frenchman who lives in Coatbridge?

In all of this historic season's amazing twists and turns, the signing of Armand Oné is in a surreal category of its own. The 23-year-old striker, whose parents are from the Ivory Coast, was born in Paris, and was on the books of Nantes for five years. His playing career in France did not fulfil earlier promise, and he crossed over to England, playing for Cambridge United, Northampton and Wrexham. Next stop was Glasgow.

From Nantes to Partick Thistle is not a great career progression. He started off well at Partick, but unpredictable form and fitness problems saw him lose his place. A reputed tendency to prefer drinking to training did his career no favours, and he was released by the Jags. He had a trial with St Mirren, but was not offered terms. After that he was out of football for some months due to shin splint problems. The inactivity did not decrease his bulk. At this stage in the Frenchman's downwardly mobile career, only a gambler would pin his hopes on Armand Oné.

Enter on left Mixu Paatelainen, the manager-entrepreneur who would have found gold in the coal bings of Lochgelly. With brother Mikko about to return to Finland, Mixu knows what he needs – a big target man. Well, target men don't come bigger than Armand Oné, so when Mixu is tipped off that the big Frenchman has turned out a couple of times for Albion Rovers, the Cowden manager gets into his car and heads for Cote-du-Brig, that well-known west of Scotland beauty spot. In Armand's home, Mixu spells out the irresistible attractions of Cowdenbeath. The French footballing nomad, who has lived a lot longer than his 23 years, is soon heading for Fife. From Paris to Cowdenbeath, via Coatbridge, is quite a geographical and aesthetic stretch.

Mixu Paatelainen is a bold man, confident in his judgments, the kind of person who attracts luck. He has his eyes on the prize, and he will take risks to claim it. Having seen Oné train at St Mirren, Mixu knows that even though the big man is unfit, he has skill. "I am very pleased to add Armand to the squad," he announces. "He has great technique and can play as a target man. I am sure Oné will score goals for us and will prove to be a good signing."

So the song has to be amended yet again: There's only Three Paatelainens and one Oné! As ever, the punters on Pie and Bovril have an opinion or three about the matter.

Albionrover: Is Fife ready?

6Boothy6: He really is utter waaaaash, he's also not fit. Not a finisher either He could prove me wrong but I think he's pish and it's a poor signing for Cowden.

Nelly: It def makes sense to sign a striker for Cowden as we are short big time and there ain't exactly a lot of free-agent strikers that Cowden can attract.

Fudge: I really, really, hope this is true!

Ach well. We shall see. Saturday will be a big test, against East Fife.

Two lads in France and Switzerland are planning to make the trip to see the derby game. It all began with a New Year visit Blue Brazil supporter Andrew Leonard paid to his brother, Gordon, who lives in the village of Voreppe, just outside Grenoble, France. Andrew and his son, Sandy, have been regulars at Central Park since November 2003, when Sandy, who was then aged nine, started to pester his dad to take him to a 'real' football match. Whenever Andrew spoke with his brother on the phone they would discuss the latest game and how well the team were doing, and whenever Andrew went over to France to see Gordon, he would take him a gift from the Blue Brazil shop.

Let Andrew take up the story.

"A mutual friend of ours, Stevie Smith, who lives near Lausanne in Switzerland was at Gordon's to spend New Year with us. Now, Stevie is originally from Thurso, but has lived in Switzerland for nearly 30 years and, as always when the drink starts to flow, the conversation turns to football and more specifically how well the Blue Brazil have been performing under the leadership of Mixu. As more and more drinks flow, Stevie announces that he has never been to a football match in Scotland."

A New Year resolution was made for Gordon and Stevie to come over to watch the East Fife derby on March 4th. Next day flights were booked: about 100 euros each return. A bargain.

"At the crack of dawn on the 3rd," says Andrew, "Gordon left on the 95 mile drive from home to Geneva airport, a two-hour drive over the mountains in pretty snowy conditions. Stevie had a more leisurely journey by train direct from Lausanne to Geneva Airport (48 euros return). As Gordon had driven he had to park the car in the long stay car park at the airport. (42 euros). In preparation for the trip I had also ordered t-shirts with the badges drawn by Cowdenbeath school children so that we could all wear them to the game (4 x £13 = £52).

"I picked Gordon and Stevie up from the airport at 2.00pm on Friday 3rd March and the sun was shining brightly, though there were still signs of lying snow in places as we drove from Edinburgh to Milnathort. As we approached Kelty on the motorway, we looked back over to Cowdenbeath and there was little sign of snow. Game on! Next morning when we woke, there had been no snow overnight, and we went out to the garden to test the ground for frost. It was hard, but not as hard as it had been over the past couple of days.

"Then breakfast in front of teletext to check the games that had been called off. Pitch inspection due at 11.00am. It's bound to be still on. Then cowdenbeath.net, 'Derby Game Off'! Shome mistake shurely, it's not 11.00am yet, the pitch hasn't been inspected yet! Check teletext again, no call off. Check bbc.co.uk, no call off. Must be a mistake. Then about 10.40am after reading P&B threads it looks like our worst fears are confirmed. Game is definitely off! Right guys, t-shirts on (over jumpers - we're not that hard!) and we'll walk down to the pub! Total cost of journey: approx 290 euros, plus £50 for the t-shirts (but hey, they're re-usable), plus beer money plus about 16 hours return travelling time and about 2500 miles return travel. Still, not totally wasted as we were when we eventually left the pub on Saturday! They have promised to come at a more clement time next season!"

And we complain if a match is called off at Larbert.

Markus Paatelainen posts a message of the official Cowden website: "Could you please pass my thanks to everyone through the web pages. I have received so many best wishes during the week I spent in a hospital that I would like to thank everyone who has supported me. It meant a lot to me and it has been great to see that there are so many people who care. It was very serious injury, but I am happy to tell you that I am feeling much better now. I got home last Friday and rehabilitation started right away. I hope to see myself practicing with the team after six weeks. Thank you for every warm thought."

Mikko wins the award of Bell's Third Division Player of the Month, while Mixu is Manager of the Month. Saturday's crunch game at Berwick will be Mikko's last game. Cowden need to win to put pressure on league leaders Stenhousemuir. With Cowden games postponed, Stenny are opening up an alarming gap.

March 11, 2006
Berwick Rangers 1 Cowdenbeath 0

Darran Thomson takes over from the injured Markus Paatelainen. Gary Fusco makes his 100th appearance for the club. Berwick take the lead in 31 minutes through Gareth Hutchison. Cowden's best chance of the afternoon comes midway through the second half when sub Armand Oné sees a powerful shot blocked by former Cowden Keeper Gary O'Connor. Mikko Paatelainen gets a standing ovation as he leaves the field in Cowden's colours for the last time.

Nelly tells me: "We saw Oné for the first time, like the black incredible hulk he is. Vince had heard a song that Partick Thistle fans supposedly sang to Oné. It comes from the Pizza Hut advert, and it goes ONé ONé ONé ONé ONé ONé ONé ONé PIZZA HUT HUT HUT !"

This is the third time that Cowden's have gone down 1-0 to their nemesis this season. To gain the title this young Blue Brazil side would have to win more or less all of their remaining ten games. Looks like Berwick and Stenny will fight it out for the Holy Grail, with Cowden settling for a play-off place. The Cowden fans are despondent.

StokeCowden: After today's result I think Stenny must now have it in the bag. I think that they have a good solid fan base and seem a good bunch of lads. Well done and I hope you have success in the Second Division. Anyway congrats and all the best for next season to you Akabusi Loyal.

6Boothy6: We already know we've won the league, no need to congratulate us. Good luck in the play-offs lads.

There is more discussion about the merits of Armand Oné. Dubya is keen to make a bet.

Dubya: Oné is shit by the way. I'd like to bet with anyone that he will not score for the rest of this season.

*Kierkegaard (*Cowden): How about a tenner, Dubya?

Dubya: I shouldn't have made this bet, he will score, but I don't want to lose face.

Kierkegaard: It's better to lose a tenner than to lose face, Dubya. It'll add a certain "edge" for you to watch the Cowden scores.

March 18, 2006
Montrose 0 Cowdenbeath 3

After spurning several chances we eventually open the scoring after 40 minutes. A corner from Graham Guy is headed against the crossbar by Liam Buchanan and Innes Ritchie converts the rebound. On the stroke of half time Ritchie gets his second goal of the game. The scoring is completed for the afternoon after 69 minutes when Liam Buchanan forces the ball past keeper Sandy Wood after his initial shot is blocked. Armand Oné has two or three good chances, but fails to score. Dubya breathes again, but he is clearly nervous about his bet, and at 4am he makes a plaintive plea.

Dubya: Updates should be placed here of any injuries, diseases etc. Kierkegaard, are we counting the playoffs? (Shit, we are, aren't we?) I have no money.

Kierkegaard: 1. I've a slight groin strain, but I'll make it along to the bank with your tenner, Dubya. 2. The season finishes with the last game of the season. I am without mercy. 3. The reason for the 4am wail about not having money is because you have poured several tenner worths of booze down your throat. Appeal rejected.

Blue Brazil Forever: The talk on the terraces was all of Dubya and, like our 5000th goal, bets have now been placed on the exact moment Dubya will shite himself.

The race for the title is hotting up with leaders Stenhousemuir losing 2-1 to East Fife at New Bayview. As a result, the Blue Brazil trail Stenny by only eight points with two games in hand. Second-placed Berwick move to within a point of top spot after their 2-0 victory away to Arbroath but have played three more games than Cowden. The climax to the season promises to be the most exciting battle for the Third division championship in years. Next game up is a rearranged fixture against East Fife, who are on a winning run and have an eye on a play-off spot.

March 21, 2006
Cowdenbeath 4 East Fife 1
Confident Cowden start off well, and open the scoring in nine minutes. The scorer? None other than the one and only Armand Oné! The Frenchman takes a pass from David McKenna just outside the penalty box before driving in a powerful shot. The Cowden supporters chant Dubya's name. This must have confused non-P & B-ers, who would wonder why Blue Brazil fans were chanting the name of the President of the United States. Would it be because it's Central Park? East Fife get an equaliser after 37 minutes when Gary Kelly scores from the penalty sot. This spurs Cowden on and two goals in a four minute spell from Buchanan and Mauchlen seals the win.

This is a critically important victory, with Stenhousemuir beating East Stirling 7-0. Mixu is pleased with his team's performance: "It was an excellent team performance. I was pleased to see Armand Oné score his first goal on his home debut. Armand's fitness is improving all the time and his first touch and link-up play has been one of the reasons for the improved midfield performances."

Poor old Dubya.

CowdenCowboy: I propose we should now establish the annual Pie & Bovril award to be known as the 'Dubya Trophy' - to be awarded each year to the poster who makes the daftest post during the season.

6Boothy6: Christ you would think you've won the World Cup lads. Share the tenner around the Cowdenbeath public for the sake of the kids, they need it.

Ivo den Bieman (Montrose): Oné is about as mobile as the scuttled German fleet at Scapa Flow, and in about as good condition physically.

Dubya: You'll get your money, dunno where it's coming from, but you'll get it.

Kierkegaard: Truth to tell, Dubya, I don't actually want your cash. But I do want you to honour your daft bet, so here's what to do with the £10: on the day that Stenny win the Championship - as they probably will - I want you to buy a pint for Boothy, Francesc and Fudge (and yourself), because your side will have deserved it. Alternatively, on the day that you lose the Championship, you can do the same to drown your sorrows. On either occasion, the toast is, "To Armand Oné, superstar!"

Fudge: Thanks Kierkegaard. Make mine a Tennent's, Dubya.

Armand Oné, Superstar, is now a cult hero at Central Park, and the big man is revelling in it. When he hears his own chant on the terracing, he does a little jig. Pure class.

Cowdenbeath Supporters Club, who are doing a superb job in marking this special year in Cowdenbeath's history, launch yet another initiative. They announce that they plan to re-establish the junior Supporters Club and are about to begin a recruitment campaign. As a first step they are approaching the local schools to talk to teachers and students.

Next game up is a home game against Arbroath – the first since the Smokie Pensioner match which ended in mayhem.

March 25, 2006
Cowdenbeath 4 Arbroath 2

The Blue Brazil open the scoring after 11 minutes when Armand Oné – who else? - fires home a left foot shot from 15 yards. The visitors grab an equaliser in 25 minutes through Swankie. Two minutes after the interval, the Red Lichties takes the lead through McMullan. Things aren't looking good for Cowden, but it takes less than a minute to get back on level terms. When David McKenna's shot is blocked, Liam Buchanan is on hand to score. Cowden's lead is restored after 73 minutes when keeper Mark Peat makes a hash of a clearance, allowing McKenna to roll the ball into an empty net. Arbroath are reduced to ten men for the closing ten minutes after Paul Watson - who was sent off in the first game at Central Park - is sent packing after on off-the-ball incident with Liam Buchanan. The win is sealed with two minutes to go when McKenna thumps the ball home from a tight angle.

The next game is a tough one. Elgin at home. This will be the first re-match since the game in which Markus Paatelainen was injured. Hugh Dickson, the Elgin defender who made the tackle on Markus, is out because he himself is injured. This will ease some of the potential tensions around the match, and make it easier for the players to concentrate.

March 28 2006
Cowdenbeath 5 Elgin City 2
Dougie Hill takes over from injured skipper Innes Ritchie. The home crowd become nervous when the visitors take the lead after 25 minutes through Martin Johnston. Four minutes later Cowden draw level when Armand Oné scores in his third successive game. More anxiety for the Blue Brazil fans when City take the lead through Booth after 33 minutes. Two goals in a minute from the break, however, swing the game back in Cowden's favour. A cross from Liam Buchanan in 44 minutes is met by a scoring first-time shot from David McKenna. A minute later Buchanan provides another cross which McKenna gathers before shooting into the roof of the net. Cowden extend their lead after 55 minutes through John Ward, and Iain Mauchlen completes the scoring eight minutes from time.

The result clinches a play-off place for the Blue Brazil. Now the team can relax and ask searching questions of the two teams ahead of them. Cowden face a huge challenge on Saturday – away to league leaders Stenhousemuir. With only a month of the season remaining Cowden, Stenny and Berwick all still have live title aspirations.

Mixu Paatelainen is aware of the size of the challenge. "We have put ourselves in a great position and the results over the next month will decide the destiny of the big prize. The game should be an interesting encounter between two attacking and in-form teams."

Interesting? It could be cardiac-arrest time on the terraces. Pie and Bovril is in a state of excitement.

Nelly (Cowden): I think Mixu and the boys deserve immense praise for the work they have done. Not only have they won games but they manage to entertain the Cowden faithful week in week out. If we can have one big effort on Saturday and get three points, great; if not then I won't complain coz the boys have worked their bollocks off.

6Boothy6: Really looking forward to this one. I had a dream last night that we won 4-0.....Let's hope this come true tomorrow.

BlueBrazilForever: Funnily enough, I dreamt last night that the Cowden fans on the terrace turned right towards Dubya and the rest and chanted 'Dubya, Dubya, Dubya' when Oné completed his hat trick.

MoreTeaVicar (Cowden fan): Saturday's game is so big for both teams that psychology and players mindsets, along with some good fortune, will probably be as important as any other factor. Which manager, if any, will "blink" and ask his team to play in an unaccustomed way? I suspect Des McKeown will. He'll bottle it cos he's terrified of losing. Scorecast - Stenny 0 Cowden 2. Stenny will then collapse like a lemon souffle at Berwick and Cowden will stroll to the title.

Gladstone (Stenny): We're at home, we're league leaders and have an excellent record at home. We have the experience throughout the team to help the younger players if needed and the goal threat to put Cowden to the sword.

So there it is. This is the Big Match. Am I nervous? N-n-n-n-n-o-o-o.

*****

Voting for the best managers/club officials in Cowden's history has put the following into the Blue Brazil Hall of Fame:

Andrew R Dick *(Chairman, 1910-31)* – Andrew Dick was one of the great names of Cowdenbeath FC. In 1886 he founded Dick's Cooperative. It was Andrew Dick who gifted Central Park (previously Dick's Park) to Cowdenbeath FC. A director when the club became a Limited Company in 1905, he was chairman for 21 years between 1910 and 1931, which included the club's golden era.

John Dougary *(Manager, 1934-38 & 1955-58)* – A headmaster, John was a leading figure in Scottish schools' football. In 1934, with Cowdenbeath FC broke and on the verge of extinction, he was asked to be manager at Central Park. He rapidly turned the club's fortunes around. The team he built went on a year later to win the Second Division Championship in record-breaking manner. After a spell as manager at Rhyl, he returned in 1955 to manage Cowden once more. Within two years took the club to within one place of promotion.

Scott Duncan (*Manager 1925-32*) – A former Cowden player, Scott became manager at Central Park in 1925. Cowden remained in the top flight throughout his seven years at the helm. His success was noted by other clubs, and in 1932 he was unable to resist the offer to become manager of Manchester United. He was manager at Old Trafford for five years, during which time United were Second Division champions. In 1937 he became manager of non-league Ipswich Town, taking them into the Football League. He was succeeded by Alf Ramsay in 1955.

Charlie Gronbach (*Chairman, 1964-81*) - The Gronbach family butcher's business has been prominent in Cowdenbeath since 1912. Charlie signed for Cowden in 1922 and endeared himself to fans on his debut by firing a 40-yard howitzer into the net of local rivals Dunfermline. Thirty years later he was to join the Cowdenbeath board, becoming chairman on 1965. Charlie introduced speedway and then stock car racing to provide a financial lifeline for the club. The highlight of his tenure as chairman followed in 1970 when a rejuvenated Cowden returned to the First Division after an absence of 31 years.

Andy Matthew *(Manager 1968-74)* A native of Kirkcaldy, Andy played for East Fife, Rangers, Raith Rovers and Dunfermline, before completing the Fife set and signing for Cowdenbeath. A highly successful five-year stay at Central Park produced 38 goals by the veteran Matthew in 145 league games for Cowden. In 1968, Andy was appointed manager of Cowdenbeath FC. Matthew's years in charge were a return to the halcyon days for Cowden fans, and he is fondly remembered as the man who built the team that took Cowden back into the top flight after a 31-year absence.

Skipper INNES RITCHIE and Manager MIXU PAATELAINEN hold the Holy Grail

MARGARET POLLOCK, founding mother

JAMES POLLOCK, one of the founding brothers

Cowdenbeath Ladies Football Team, whose matches raised money for the miners during the lockout of 1921.

ALEX, "Big Ming," MENZIES   Jennie Lee

Forward line of one of Cowden's greatest teams, 1924/5
l. to r.:– PATERSON, RANKIN, DEVLIN, LEONARD, WILSON – looking as if they
had just come off the back shift.

JOHN WARD gets his marching orders at Hampden

Cult hero ARMAND ONE holds off a small and bewildered Elgin defender

The scoreboard tells the story – while the fans mob the players

Jubilant players dance in front of fans

GORDON BROWN pictured in the stand during the Elgin game

MIXU holds up the trophy at Wee Jimmie's

GORDON BROWN hands over the trophy to the victorious Cowden team.

Proud chairman GORDON McDOUGALL holds the Holy Grail

Fans at Wee Jimmie's

Happy family at Wee Jimmie's – NEIL, SANDY, STEVEN, RON and FIONA FERGUSON

Historian DAVID ALLAN, Supporters Club Chairman DAVE TUSON and star player MARKUS PAATELAINEN at Wee Jimmie's

Front: Colin Somerville (Sommy), Alan Mayne; Middle: Scott Mayne, Callum Ferguson, Gary Moyles, Derek Neilson, Stuart Watson, Paul Murphy; Back: Craig Ferguson

Cowden fan DUNCAN STARK at his home in Boulder City, Nevada, USA

12. A LIE ABOUT MY FATHER

My father was the God of my childhood. His songs and stories and all that he believed in were gospel to me and remained so all my life – Jennie Lee

Sometimes I wonder how all those who do not write, compose or paint can manage to escape the madness, the melancholia, the panic fear which is inherent in the human condition. – Graham Greene, in his memoir Ways of Escape

John Burnside is a poet, a very good one. His nine poetry collections have won critical acclaim and big prizes. A high-calibre short story writer and novelist, he is regarded by literary critics as one of Scotland's finest living writers.

John Burnside is also from Cowdenbeath. He is very much on my mind as I write this, because I have been utterly entranced by his latest book, a memoir called *A Lie About my Father*. It is one of the most powerful and affecting pieces of writing I have ever read, and I'm not surprised that it's tipped to be among the prizewinners when the literary awards are given out this year.

What makes the story specially interesting for me is that the events he describes happened close to my own home near the top of Stenhouse Street in Cowdenbeath. Burnside was brought up in what were at that stage condemned tenemental houses in King Street, a few hundred yards from where I lived; then his family moved to prefabs in Blackburn Drive, a stone's throw from our back green. The strength of his writing and his observant eye evoked a lot of childhood scenes for me.

In his memoir, Burnside spells out the links between his strange upbringing in Cowdenbeath and his eventual descent into madness. His father, Tommy Burnside, told his son lots of stories about his own life: he had been adopted by a businessman, or a preacher, he had played for Raith Rovers and Queen of the South, and so on. They all turned out to be lies.

"He was himself a walking lie, and I knew that only because he contradicted himself all the time," says Burnside. "He would tell you one version one night, and then he'd be drunk another night and tell you a different version. There was violence too, and threats of violence. Harsh words and hurt feelings. Petty cruelties and minor tyrannies; inconsistencies, evasions and drunken denials. There was all of that. A life's worth, you could say. In truth, almost two. Maybe it was Philip Larkin who said it best: 'They fuck you up, your mum and dad.'"

The observant reader will recognise that this brings this book back to its starting point, or close to it. We have noted the power of ancestral stories in shaping our identities, in giving us a sense of who we are and how we fit into the scheme of things – whether they be stories about football, or mining or politics; or even stranger, shadowy "out of the box" tales of an unmanageable, disturbing God. But whose stories do we believe? And what if the trusted story-teller turns out to be an inveterate liar? This way lies madness. That is the core issue at the heart of this riveting book about a Cowdenbeath childhood.

Tommy Burnside was a hard man, the kind of man who radiates a simmering violence. He also had a vicious, hurtful tongue. There was a child before John – a girl, Elizabeth. The father used to tell his son that he wished John had died and his sister had lived. It wasn't till John was married with a son of his own that he found out, almost accidentally, that his father had actually been a foundling child – he had been literally left on a doorstep as a baby in 1926, the year of the general strike. One can only imagine the poverty and despair of that bitter time that led a woman to leave her baby, wrapped in a blanket, on a doorstep in Cowdenbeath. John learned from his aunt that his father hadn't been adopted at all, but had been passed around from family to family like a parcel that was barely wanted. Nobody's child. Hard circumstances made a hard, merciless man.

What do you do as a child when the stories you have been told by a parent turn out to be lies, and the father you rely on to protect you is a man of utterly unpredictable violence in his own home? Young John found solace in Beath woods, a matter of steps away from the back of the Council house where I lived. He was looking for magic, something to counteract the brutality of what was happening to him. "I thought Beath woods were magical: so close to home yet so dark and damp," Burnside writes, "they were haunted by tawny owls and foxes; haunted, too, by strange noises and movements in the dark that nobody could explain....This was the place where I learned the deep pleasure of being alone, of being out in the open with an angel-haunted sky over my head."

All this was happening at a time when Cowdenbeath had lost its major industry and work was hard to get. The family eventually left Cowdenbeath for Corby, the industrial boom-town in the East Midlands. Tommy Burnside's behaviour continued to deteriorate, and John, as a teenager, tried to find another "magical" world in binge-drinking and drugs. He left home after his mother died of cancer and he cut off all contact with his father; when word reached him that Tommy Burnside had died of a heart attack in a pub, the over-riding emotion his son felt was not grief but a sense of relief. Spiralling downwards, John Burnside crash-landed into a secure unit for mentally disturbed patients. Writing helped provide a way out of his personal hell; the lonely, bewildered child communing with nature and "angels" in the dark, dripping Beath woods found entrances into a different world that didn't depend on destructive hallucinogenics.

All this is to say the dark side of a coal mining town which had known heroic failures and sometimes desperate batterings claimed its own victims from time to time. It also points up the fact that the process of passing down stories from father to son is not always a benevolent one. In fact, it can be murderous. Yet Burnside is conveying a wider message than that. All our lives are, to a degree, fictional. "We are what we imagine," writes the native American writer N. Scott Momaday. We, all of us, create the myth of our own lives out of a mix of messages and responses to unmanageable happenings.

As that fine Scottish writer Alastair Reid puts it: "Words are only a fragment of what we really see. What we do is make what Borges called 'fictions', to try to make sense of this seething world we don't understand and put it into words – but the words are always a reduction. Borges says we are all *fictionados* – makers of fiction. We're constantly making fictions out of our own past, out of everything that happens." That is why John Burnside calls his book *A Lie About My Father.* His father was a congenital liar and fantasist, but John the poet and novelist understands that none of us ever gets a grip on the truth, the whole truth and nothing but the truth, and that his own account is partial. It must be. He is looking at his own life through his own lenses. Words on a page are seductive, and readers may give the printed word too much authority. His father would have given a different account of his days in Cowdenbeath.

So stories are important. So are the story-tellers. But even the best and most truthful story-tellers don't get it completely right. The great Orcadian poet George Mackay Brown used to work away at his poems even after they had been published; his view was that while we can never tell it right, we can learn to say it better. I like that. We need family, community and national stories in order to get our bearings in life; but we also need to keep a critical perspective on them. The freedom to stand outside the founding myths of our lives and ask questions about truthfulness is precious. It's like both playing in the game, and standing on the mound outside – Mount Killamanforhisgiro! – looking at the game with one quizzical eyebrow raised. As the great American theologian Paul Tillich puts it: "Don't give in too quickly to those who want to alleviate your anxiety about truth. Don't be seduced into a truth which is not *your* truth, even if the seducer is your church, or your party or your parental tradition."

When we are too embedded in one story and regard our personal or national or religious narrative as exclusively true, we become a danger to others. Too much uncritical story demeans anyone who is different. Taken to a national level with a strong ideological underpinning - and nuclear weapons thrown in - the situation becomes demonic. As the song in South Pacific puts it:

You've got to be taught, before it's too late
Before you are six or seven or eight
To hate all the people your relatives hate.

To reduce it all to a truly banal level: Can I honour and celebrate my own community without having to put down those who might be rivals? Can I be a true Blue Brazilian – loving the stories even while subjecting them to critique - and still love East Fife or Dunfermline? Gulp.

******

April 1 2006

April Fool's Day, and the crowds are rolling in to Ochilview Park, Stenhousemuir. The Akabusi Loyal are in good voice. The Cowden fans are in great voice, too. The air is filled with drink-fuelled anticipation, optimism, and dread. The Warriors know that victory over Cowden will, barring a complete Stenny collapse, put the Blue Brazil out of the title race. Cowden need to beat the league leaders on their home territory if we are to be serious title contenders. Team spirit and a hunger for victory will be important factors in the outcome of this football match.

By kick-off time, there are 781 fans in the stadium – not a bad crowd for a Third Division game. There is a blow for Cowden when captain Innes Ritchie fails a late fitness test. Young Dougie Hill again deputises for the experienced skipper. Cowdenbeath start the game very brightly, determined to take the game to their opponents. Iain Mauchlen goes close for the Blue Brazil on the half hour mark, when his cross deceives keeper Chris Fahey but clips the post. Seven minutes later, against the run of play, the Cowden fans are silenced. A Paul McGrillen corner is not cleared properly by the Cowden defence and Colin Cramb plays the ball back for Jim Mercer to head the ball into the net. This is a serious test for the Blue Brazil. They answer it five minutes later. The home defence struggles to defend a Graham Guy corner, and the ball falls to Dougie Hill, who fires home a glorious shot from 14 yards. The players' celebration shows how much it means to them.

At half time, the talk is about tactics. Will Stenny settle for containing the lively Cowden side? A minute after the break, the Cowden fans are singing again. Liam Buchanan surges into the box after the ball breaks to him from Steve Fallon's clearance and the little front man scores his 15th goal of the season from six yards. Soon afterwards Armand One has the ball in the net but the "goal" – much to Dubya's relief - is disallowed for offside.

The Blue Brazil are dominating the game, cheered on by an enthusiastic support. Twice the ball is cleared off the Stenny line. It looks like Cowden are going to win this crucial match. Then, deep into injury time, the Cowden faithful hold their breath as Stenny's Jim Mercer breaks through with only the goalkeeper to beat. David Hay is equal to the occasion and makes a superb save.

100

The final whistle sees the Blue Brazil leave the pitch to a standing ovation from the Cowden fans. There is much blue and white dancing and singing on the terracing for some minutes. The fans are celebrating a fantastic team performance in which a young and fearless Cowdenbeath side have gone to their more fancied rivals' home and comprehensively outplayed them.

Now we are in a serious title race.

Stenhousemuir fans are understandably gutted. What disturbs them is that their experienced team were so tentative and defensive. In the tactical battle, did Des McKeown, the Stenny manager, blink first?

Helicopter Dreams can reveal that there is something in this claim. At training in the week before the big match, each Stenny player was issued with a dossier, running to several pages, on Cowdenbeath's players. The document several times highlighted the danger of John Ward and Innes Ritchie at set-pieces, pointing out that Ward often headed the ball down for Ritchie to score. It also said that Liam Buchanan had to be watched all the time. Of course there's nothing wrong with good preparation before a big game, but the pre-match plans betray an undue nervousness about the opposition. Cowdenbeath seemed to sense the tentativeness in the Warriors' ranks, and even when they went a goal down, they remained the more assured and vibrant team.

Second-placed Berwick Rangers are on a roll, and Stenny's defeat gives them a great chance of winning the Championship – especially as the wounded Warriors travel to Berwick on Saturday.

6Boothy6 (Stenny): Enjoy tonight. I hope the rest of Cowden fans do, they have a team to be proud of tonight. I will still be wraaaaaaaaacked

*Dreamteamer (*Berwick): All we have to do is win our few remaining easy games, Cowdenbeath will lose to Queen's or Elgin or both, and hey presto, the title's in the bag..........easy huh????

QP 4ever 67: Cowdenbeath will win the league.

Jimmy Shaker (neutral)*:* Stenhousemuir's act of throwing it away has lost me nearly £700. Cheers boys.

It is announced that Cowden's assistant manager Michael O'Neill has been appointed manager of First Division relegation candidates Brechin City. Cowden's local rivals, East Fife, reveal the name of their new manager to succeed Jim Moffat. Who is it? Step forward Dave Baikie.

Suddenly, things are looking really good for Cowden in terms of the Championship. They are still third in the league, but they have the Big Mo. Hopefully this momentum will take them through Tuesday evening's game – another rearranged fixture – against bottom-of-the-league club East Stirling. That should mean another three points, which will take us to the top of the table for the first time this season. Mixu rightly warns against complacency. Nevertheless, top-of-the-league Cowden must fancy their chances against the team propping up the Third Division.....

April 4 2006
East Stirling 1 Cowdenbeath 1

Right from the early stages, there's a sense that this one isn't going to plan. The reason is obvious: Cowdenbeath are tired, mentally and physically. This heavy backlog of midweek games is taking its toll; not only that, Saturday's win-or-bust performance at Ochilview over Stenny dipped deeply into the reservoir of energy. It's no surprise when the home side take the head after 34 minutes through Tweedie. The vocal Cowden support, having gone to the game with an expectant air, become nervous. Surely Cowden won't lose to the worst club in the division after beating the team at the top? In 71 minutes, Cowden get a break. David McKenna picks the ball up 20 yards out and keeper Jackson spills his shot. Teenage substitute Paul McBride gleefully knocks in the rebound.

Cowden's failure to beat East Stirling encourages the Stenhousemuir and Berwick fans as they prepare for their big battle at Sheilfield Park. For the first time in six months the winner of the Fans Player of the Month award is not a Paatelainen. Coming out on the top of the poll for March is top scorer Liam Buchanan. Buchs, a product of the Blue Brazil youth system, made his debut for Cowden in the Second Division as a 16-year-old year old. This season, under the tutelage of Mixu Paatelainen, the young forward has really come of age.

To turn to less important things, a dead swan found in Fife is thought to have died of the dreaded bird flu.

Roy of the Rovers (Albion Rovers): Could have been what Cowden were suffering from on Tuesday at the 'Shire! Mask & white wellies for our visit to Cooden on Saturday I fear.

Igor: That is standard dress code for outsiders heading to Central Park anyway.

Fudge: Can we not just cull all Fifers?

Second-placed Cowden go in to the final four games of the season having picked up a remarkable 19 points from seven games over the last 21 days. This heroic run has reduced the gap on league leaders Stenhousemuir from 11 to a single point. A home fixture against Albion Rovers provides the latest hurdle for the Blue Brazil.

HOW THEY STAND

	P	W	D	L	F	A	Pts
Stenhousemr	32	21	4	7	71	31	67
Cowdenbeath	32	21	3	8	70	30	66
Berwick	32	20	6	6	48	26	66
Arbroath	32	13	7	12	50	42	46

April 8 2006
Cowdenbeath 2 Albion Rovers 1

For the fourth successive game Cowden find themselves a goal down when four minutes from the break Scott Chaplain scores. Cowden equalise in 73 minutes when a long clearance from Carlin deceives the Rovers defence and McKenna latches on to shoot past McGlynn. Three minutes later McKenna secures the three points when he converts a cut-back from Liam Buchanan. Cowden's Chris Hughes, aged 16, makes his first-team debut, coming on for Armand Oné.

Cowden move to the top of the Third Division for the first time this season, level with Berwick Rangers on 69 points after the Shielfield team's 3-0 win over previous league leaders Stenhousemuir. Cowden have a superior goal difference of 16. So with only three games remaining of an exhilarating league campaign, the destination of the Championship has moved into Cowden's hands! Cowden fans receive a boost with the news that Markus Paatelainen has made quicker progress than expected and is in line to make a comeback before the end of the season.

Interviewed on the Cowden website, cult hero Armand Oné is asked if he knows that a Stenny fan who had seen him play for Albion Rovers had said he was useless and unfit, and had bet the Cowden fans that he wouldn't score? "That's good!" he laughs. "I have scored and Mixu makes me work very hard. I will go for a hat trick tomorrow. "

Anyway, we should beat East Stirling on Saturday. Wait a minute: where have I heard that before?

April 15 2006
Cowdenbeath 5 East Stirling 0

The match begins with a minute's silence in memory of stalwart Cowden fan, 90-year-old Willie Anderson who passed away this morning. Willie was a lifelong supporter of Cowdenbeath FC and could remember sneaking in to watch Cowden by crawling under the fence when Cowdenbeath first won promotion back in season 1923/24. He was proud to say he had watched the Cowden side which spent a decade in the top flight before the Second World War. Away from football, Willie was a Labour councillor both on Cowdenbeath Town Council and Fife Region. He also worked for the National Coal Board for 51 years and was probably the only fan left who saw every Cowdenbeath promotion-winning side play. He was Provost of Cowdenbeath between 1967 and 1970, and it was Willie who in 1970 had the privilege of hosting a civic reception for the promotion-winning side in Cowdenbeath Town House. Even in his 90th year, he still travelled on the Supporters Club bus to virtually every match, including the memorable trip to Stenhousemuir. It was fitting that the hearse carrying Willie's remains drove around Central Park. What better way could there be to honour Willie than to win the Third Division Championship?

With nearly 600 fans – double the usual home attendance – Cowden score first for a change. They open the scoring after 17 minutes when Oné and Liam Buchanan combine to set up McKenna who scores from 12 yards. Two minutes after the interval Oné powers home a cross from Buchanan and goes on to bag a hat trick with a header from a Kevin McBride corner in 70 minutes and another shot from a Buchanan cross seven minutes later. Well, the big Frenchman said he would get a hat-trick, didn't he? For Dubya, with love. With 11 minutes to go McKenna completes the scoring when he lobs the on-rushing Jackson in the Shire goal. This is the fourth successive home brace from young David McKenna, who is in superb form.

There is even better news after the game, when fans learn that Cowden have moved two points clear at the top of the table, as rivals Berwick and Stenhousemuir have both dropped points. So with only two games remaining, the Blue Brazil sit proudly at the top of the Third Division, two points ahead of their nearest challenger.

One of the big talking points is what has happened to Stenhousemuir? For a long spell they had looked as if they might run away with the Championship. Their fans point the finger at their experienced players. The matter is made worse by an interview with Stenny captain Greig Denham in the Daily Record. Published under the heading A BUNCH OF BOOZERS AND BRAWLERS, Denham claims some players indulged in drinking sessions just hours before top-of-the-table clashes, and says that relationships in the dressing room had disintegrated to the extent that he believes it's cost Stenny the Third Division title. The Stenny fans are understandably depressed. They've followed their team all over Scotland, and watched them throw away a nine-point lead. Now they trail Cowden by three points with only two games left.

Only two teams stand between Cowdenbeath and the Third Division Championship – Queen's Park and Elgin City. Both teams are fighting for a play-off spot, so these matches will be tough. Queen's have just beaten a demoralised Stenny away from home, and are on a bit of a roll. The visit to Hampden will not be easy. The Cowden fans on P & B show their apprehension.

Blueminer: They say that most men think about sex constantly, but I'm bucking the trend at the moment! This week, I think I'm cracking up, two games away from winning the Championship, but it's hard to enjoy because the fear of failure is overwhelming!

*Hughj (*Gretna): Seems to me you are still thinking of sex, "It's hard to enjoy because the fear of failure is overwhelming!"

Dubya: I would really prefer Cowden to win the league so we don't have to go there again this season. I'm a wanted man in the shitehole that is Fife.

A member of the last Cowden team to win the league title gets in touch with Blue Brazil On-line to wish the current team good luck in their quest to emulate the success of the 1938/39 side. Eighty six-year-old Alec Gillies, who now resides in Alabama, proudly wears his Championship medal around his neck at all times.

The match at Hampden is huge for Cowden. If they lose and Berwick beat East Stirling, then Berwick go into the last game of the season knowing that a win will give them the coveted Championship. The climax to the season could hardly be more dramatic. There are rumours that Markus Paateleinan, our totemic player, will play, even though he is not match fit. Can it possibly be true?

Saturday April 22, 2006

Cowden fans descend on the national stadium in big numbers. Before the game I have a drink in the social club with *Andyboy* and *Attendant,* two Pie and Bovril regulars. Quite a number of Cowden fans from south of the border are here, and I meet Paul Jones, a Blue Brazil supporter from Wales. The imposing stadium, with its big scoreboards, lends further significance to the occasion. When the teams are announced, the Cowdenbeath fans are dismayed that experienced skipper Innes Ritchie is still absent. Markus Paatelainen is not in the line-up, but he has a place on the bench. You can almost touch the tension in the stadium, where the 1247 crowd has a majority of Blue Brazil fans.

Queen's Park are first to settle, and they take the game to Cowden. The big open spaces of Hampden suit the home team, and Cowdenbeath are on the back foot. It's no surprise when the Spiders take the lead through Ferry with only 12 minutes gone. Cowden fans are edgy, especially when John Ward is booked for a challenge on the keeper at a corner. The Cowden nerves are settled in 26 minutes, with Liam Buchanan getting his 16th goal of the campaign. The sense of relief among the blue-and-white fans is palpable – but only for one minute. Waterston races past two defenders before slotting the ball past Hay.

Queen's Park have dominated the first half, playing the more confident football. At half time, with the score 2-1, the Cowden fans are worried. Whatever Mixu says at half time galvanises the Blue Brazil. They attack Queen's Park from the kick-off, and within a minute the scores are level. McKenna's neat flick finds Armand Oné, and the big Parisian crashes in a shot on the half volley. It's QP who are on the back foot now as Cowden have a real go at them.

Then, with 60 minutes gone, a disaster for the Blue Brazil. Ward and Weatherston tussle for a ball on the edge of the penalty area, with both leaning on each other. The referee decides Ward is the villain, and the yellow card means that the big centre half is sent off. The decision is unfair, and Ward is distraught. He knows that he will miss the vital last game of the season. With the advantage of an extra man, the home side enjoy plenty of possession but struggle to penetrate the Cowden defence, in which Pat Scullion is outstanding. The word is passed around that Berwick have taken the lead against East Stirling. The tension levels are ratcheted up to even higher levels. All we are asking is that the ten-man Cowden team keep repelling the waves of Queen's Park attacks.

With 13 minutes to go, the visiting fans see the sight we never really expected to see this season. Markus Paatelainen gets a standing ovation as he steps on to the Hampden turf to replace David McKenna. Can he help us hold out? In the dying seconds, it's looking as if we will get the precious draw, until the referee penalises goalkeeper David Hay for time-wasting. A free kick for Queen's Park right in front of goal. Few Cowden fans can bear to look, as every player dressed in blue takes his place in the defensive wall. There is a hush in the ground as the Queen's player runs up and shoots….and the ball cannons off the wall to safety.

The Championship dream is alive. The news comes through that Berwick have won their match. We walk away from Hampden, blood pressure slowly dropping back to safer levels. With one game to go, it's in our own hands.

In a poll for the Hall of Fame five greatest Cowden teams of all time, the following legendary sides are voted in: the 1914 & 1915 Championship team, the fifth best in Scotland 1924/25 , the 1938/39 Championship team, the Miners 49ers - 1949/50, and Matthew's Miracle Workers - 1969/70.

Will the current Cowdenbeath side enter the Blue Brazil Hall of Fame as Champions? The mathematics are simple. Win next week, and we claim our first Championship since before the Second World War.

13. CHAMPAGNE BREAKFAST AND HELICOPTER DREAMS

Richard Keys: *Well Roy, do you think that you'll have to finish above Manchester United to win the league?*
Roy Evans: *You have to finish above everyone to win the league, Richard.*

To dare is to lose control for a while; not to dare is to lose a whole life.
– Soren Kierkegaard.

This is it this is it this is it. After 67 years, history beckons Cowdenbeath Football Club. This afternoon the Blue Brazil will either win the match and the Championship, or will lose or draw on their own turf and go into the history books as runners-up. (Mind you, Berwick Rangers can assist our cause by failing to win at home.) There is one Cowdenbeath hand on the Holy Grail, but the iconic trophy can still fall from our grasp. It is in our hands; it is ours to throw away. These are chilling words.

I wake early in Glasgow, where I've been for the last two weeks. Why is it that feelings of dread are amplified before dawn? You imagine that today's game is a step too far for a battle-weary Cowdenbeath side. You remember that at the end of the 1991/2 season Cowden lost out on the Championship on goal difference.

There's also the possibility of a Third World War, depending on what happens this afternoon. Now this is taking doom scenarios a step too far, isn't it? Possibly not. By quarter to five this afternoon, we may be living on red alert.

In talking about world war, I'm not using that as a metaphor for a wee bit of dancing and mayhem in the streets of Raith. I mean it for real. The facts cannot be disputed. Cowdenbeath's Championship wins in the 20th century have been followed by the outbreak of world wars. When the Blue Brazil won the Second Division title in 1914, the Great War broke out. Fast forward to 1939. Cowden won the Second Division championship with a record 60 points. Then Hitler marched on to centre stage.

After both world wars, the Scottish football leagues were reorganised, and on both occasions Cowdenbeath Football Club was denied its hard-won promotion. To have it snatched away once is unfortunate; to have it snatched away twice is west of Scotland conspiracy. So if Cowdenbeath beat Elgin City this afternoon, should we be heading for the nuclear bunkers? Is another world war a reasonable price to pay for a Cowdenbeath Championship? Mad Cowdenbeath Disease overtakes me at this point as I ponder these possibilities.

I am jesting, of course, because I am nervous. Soon, my family – wife, daughter, elder son, younger son and partner, plus two grandchildren, aged four and two – are piled into two cars heading from Glasgow to Cowdenbeath. We get a call from my daughter's car to say that there are some traffic problems near the Forth Bridge. Time to get a move on. Result? Done for speeding, fine £60.

Eventually we arrive at the holy city of Cowdenbeath on a gloriously sunny afternoon. As we drive along the thronged High Street, you can sense the anticipation. I honk the car horn as we pass Wee Jimmie's, one of the great drinking haunts of the Blue Brazil faithful. The Cowdenbeath Player of the Year event will be held there tonight – let's hope it will be a celebration rather than a wake. There are masses of blue-and-white people on the pavement outside the bar. They are singing and chanting in the sunshine. All this before a ball has been kicked in earnest. If a town can be high as a kite, Cowdenbeath has lost its moorings and is flying in the sky on this 29th day of April in the Year of Our Lord two thousand and six.

Inside Wee Jimmie's, the Cowdenbeath players are having their routine Saturday bonding meal of beans and toast. Whether the din outside makes them more or less nervous, only they can tell.

******

All week, emails have been flying between Cowden supporters, trying to keep panic levels under control. "We were all bricking it," Derek Neilson (*Vince Sinclair*) tells me later, "but deep down hoped Saturday would be our big day." Stephen Harley (*cowden_harley*) said on his weblog on Friday, "Oh how can I describe my feelings? Mmmmm, shit scared just about covers it. When I think about the game tomorrow I feel physically sick. Struggled to eat breakfast this morning….. Ahhh, it's dain ma heid in."

A message from Colin McCullie of the 1970 promotion-winning team reads, "Can't believe the mixed emotions I am going to have tomorrow when the results come through. As an ex-Cowden player in the late sixties and early seventies I still have a great affection for the team, but having lived in Stenhousemuir from the age of four till 30 and having been transferred from Cowdenbeath to Stenhousemuir you can imagine how my loyalties are stretched. The only consolation now is that I am a native of Forres and if I say that Forres people regard Elgin in the same light as Cowden fans regard East Fife you will know where my support lies. All the best for tomorrow and hope the present day players enjoy the feeling as much as we did back in 1970."

Today in Cowdenbeath, the sun has been splitting the sky since early on – just like the morning of May 5th, 2001, when Cowden beat Brechin to clinch promotion at Central Park. A good omen. Stuart Watson (*Blueminer*) tells me: "It's like the feeling you got years ago when you were young and you awoke on Christmas morning." Stuart had arranged to be picked up at 10am by Derek Neilson to go to the house of Colin Somerville (*Sommy*) in Lochgelly for a Barbecue Breakfast. "I didn't see much food on show," says Stuart, "but there was plenty of liquid refreshment. There were about 12 of us there, standing in the garden in the beautiful sunshine talking about the game ahead. I had bought two bottles of champagne with me. I'd been keeping them for something special, and this was it! Derek Neilson had brought a bottle too, so we decided to drink two bottles and keep one for after the game. When we got to Wee Jimmie's just after 12 noon, the bottle of champagne was put in the fridge for safe keeping for after the game." Another thing Stuart had brought with him was an inflatable cow head, which he had purchased on eBay. The cow is dancing about outside Wee Jimmie's in the sunshine, and thereafter is omnipresent.

Colin Nelson (*Nelly*) was at the famous Barbeque Breakfast as well. "I arrived a little late, and the guys are there already with three bottles of champagne and a big case of Tennents – so we tuck into our champagne breakfast, a couple of glasses of champers along with a couple of rolls, then heading off for Torley's for a pint before going through to the pub where we sit before every game – Wee Jimmie's. The pub is full, but we stand outside to get the rays and to speak to old faces who have come to the biggest party Cowdenbeath has potentially seen. The players usually go the Wee Jimmie's before games, so a few are making their way past us. This just sets us up: 'C'mon Bucks, give us a hat-trick', 'C'mon Mixu big man, you can do it today', and 'Innes, you are a fucking legend'. Derek has spotted Oné and brings him round the front where we all start that chant - ONé, ONé, ONé, ONé ONé ONé ONé ONé PIZZA HUT HUT HUT! The big man is loving it! This is us all hyped up now."

Champagne and rolls – a breakfast for Champions! Craig Ferguson (*CFC on the Cowden unofficial site*) is there too. He had been up since early. "My stomach was doing somersaults. I went for a walk with my black lab (Cain) to try and settle the nerves. It didn't work. I hung about till 12 and decided the best place to be was Wee Jimmie's beside my fellow Cowden fans. The place was moving, singing in the street, you could feel it was going to be a big day."

After passing the crowds outside Wee Jimmie's, we go on for lunch at the home of Margaret Graham, a lifelong Cowden supporter who is a Procurator Fiscal. When she is not prosecuting criminals, she is persecuting referees who have failed to give obvious penalties to the Blue Brazil at Central Park. Margaret and I were in the youth fellowship of Cairns Kirk. Some other Cowden fans are there as well, and there is plenty to drink. The talk is of what will happen this afternoon. Despite the bonhomie and the banter, intimations of dread keep breaking through into the chatter. This matters to us – and it's about more than football. It's about defiance. It's about a vulnerable community making its presence felt once more. The proud town has been struggling for years since the coal industry finished, and the football club is kept precariously alive by dreamers who are determined to keep on proving every week the continued existence of Cowdenbeath, at least on the world's football coupons.

Will there be yet another disappointment for the town? Or will there be another hurrah from a community which has known more moments of defeat than of glory?

****

Mixu is the man. When he was first appointed in the difficult circumstances of David Baikie's departure, Cowden fans weren't unqualified in their praise for the appointment. Although Mixu Paatelainen had coaching experience, he had never been a manager; and in this special 125th anniversary season, with high hopes of promotion, some fans had looked for someone with a stronger managerial CV.

After a stuttering start in which disappointed players were coming to terms with Baikie's departure and Mixu was trying to find his best formation, the Finn soon put his distinctive stamp on the campaign and the Blue Brazil went on a run which saw them win 10 games out of a possible 11. From then on, Mixu was the main man.

When he was growing up in Finland, his father Matti, a striker who had 50 caps for Finland, was his great role model. He watched his father train and play, and he determined to become a footballer. (If this failed to materialise, another strong option for Mixu was to become a sports doctor. His mother is a doctor, and Mixu was attracted to the notion of healing sports injuries.) Mixu showed early promise at soccer, and his father mentioned to a business associate when over in Scotland that his eldest son was looking the part. Weeks later Mixu became the first of Jim McLean's foreign signings at the age of 20, transferred from FF Haka for a fee of £100,000. He scored on his debut at Tannadice against St Mirren. A big, powerful centre-forward who scored some excellent goals, he finished as the Arabs' top scorer for the next two seasons. He was then transferred to Aberdeen for £400,000. Next he went south to Bolton and helped Wanderers win promotion to the Premiership. He then had spells with Wolves, Hibernian (twice), Strasbourg, St Johnstone, and St Mirren. He also won 70 caps for Finland, latterly being captain of his national side.

When Mixu was first approached by Gordon McDougall, he wondered about the advisability of going to a part-time Third Division club. "So I asked for help and phoned some experienced managers. All of them said that this would be a fantastic starting point because everybody knows Gordon McDougall is a fantastic guy and a fantastic chairman. In particular, Craig Levein and Alex McLeish persuaded me it was a good idea. All Craig could say about Cowdenbeath was positive. He said everything was run well and that it's a fantastic wee club."

110

Having been used to full-time football for all of his playing career, Mixu found that dealing with the part-time game was the most difficult aspect. "You lose the control of the players a little bit more than you get at a full-time club," he said. "A manager has to choose the players he can trust; the ones who live their lives in a professional way off the pitch because it's only two nights a week you have them. I wondered whether my ideas could be put across, but everything here is run professionally. From the chairman, down to the players and the back-room staff, everyone works exceptionally hard. Some players are in training every day - I can't ask for more than that. When I came here I decided that what I wanted was young and energetic players who were hungry for success; players who will listen."

The youngsters are certainly learning good habits from a man who has always been a consummate professional. A notice on the dressing room wall reminds the players that they are to be professional at all times. (Former Raith Rovers player Ron Hunter reminds me that there used to be a crude wooden plaque on the wall in the home dressing room at Central Park that read – burned in by a red hot poker – 'If you're a player, don't grouse – if you're a grouser don't play'. Ron adds: "It was a wonderful dictum and paraphrased what my dad – always scrupulously fair – inculcated in me from the earliest times, 'Dish it oot, take it back, an say nothing!'")

Mixu is convinced that too many Scottish players don't work hard enough at their game. He believes in discipline, even in the part-time game, and being ten minutes late for training will bring a fine. What has particularly impressed the fans is that Cowden have got to the top of the league by playing attacking passing football. Mixu's stated philosophy is to build from the back, playing through the midfield to strikers who can hold the ball up as well as score.

The stadium may not look beautiful, but that doesn't worry the Boss. "It's what the people do, that's the most important thing," he says. "Of course everyone wants to play in front of 10,000 supporters, and perhaps one day that will happen here. It sometimes works against us in terms of getting players. They want to play in a nice stadium, and we realise we don't have that. But we have spirit, and we have determination. Sometimes you go to a club and there is a nice stadium, but inside the people are dead inside their heads. That's not the case here."

Mixu has learned from many managers in his time, but he is his own man. "You can't copy someone else's management style, because it comes from yourself, your heart," he says. "You make decisions on your own feelings and your own judgments, nobody else can do it for you." One thing for sure is that the players will be well prepared for the game. Mixu attends to the details, and his confidence is transmitted to the players. They believe in Mixu. The fans believe in Mixu. Mixu is the man.

****

You walk along the High Street to the entrance to Central Park. On the right hand side is the building in which my grandfather and father plied their decorating trade. Opposite is the site of the old Arcade, where Margaret Pollock sold her antiques, and where Jennie Lee listened to some of the greats of the Scottish Labour movement.

This place is full of ghosts. They'll be dancing in the streets of Wraith tonight. Wraith Ravers. The hopping chatter in the brain is incessant. It's time to go into the ground and face what has to be faced.

However much I love the old Central Park, I have to concede that it's not a prepossessing stadium. In his book *A Season in Hell,* David Bennie puts it thus: "Imagine an Albanian Second Division ground in Korce, say, where the only concession to capitalist enterprise is a stock-car racing track. To stop the souped-up Wartburgs, Moskviches and Volgas careering all over the pitch, giant rubber tyres from Chinese-made giant tractors surround the inside of the cracked concrete track." You get the picture. As for the toilets, you really don't want to go there.

Today, though, the battered stadium is invested with a certain grandeur. The saltires and the Brazilian and Finnish national flags, fluttering in the breeze, transform the amphitheatre into a colourful jousting ground in which noble knights will contest for the hand of a fair lady. (Mad Cowdenbeath Disease kicking in again.) By kick-off time, the stand and its opposite terracing are full. The official attendance is 2646, but when you add in the complimentaries and those who sneaked in for nothing, there are more than 3000 people in Central Park – that's more than a third of the able-bodied adult population of the town.

What about the big group outside Wee Jimmies? Let Colin Nelson pick up the story. "A few of us are quite bevvied so we make our way to the game. It's scorching and another refreshment is required in the bar in the ground. After this we make our way round too our usual spot near the toilets in the terracing. We walk round and it's unbelievable. It's just covered! It really is a sight, one which will live forever. There is a great atmosphere but there's definitely a lot of anxiety."

The regulars, of course, are all there – some of them disorientated by being displaced from their usual spots. They're not used to crowds. David Allan looks on, hoping to see history made before his eyes. His son, Stuart, is very nervous, confessing to a fear that he'll end up crying on the terracing if the Blue Brazil don't win. He's far from being the only one. Peter Park (*Auld Pete*) is hoping that he'll see the helicopter in his 76th year.

More than 30 members of my extended family are in the crowd. As well as the Cowden regulars who follow the team every Saturday, I recognise people from the Cowdenbeath diaspora in other parts of Scotland, England, and Wales. I say hello again to Paul Jones from Wales. There are the "Doncaster Lads" - nine Cowden fans who manage up to games from time to time. Six of the "Mersey Beaths" are here – Blue Brazil supporters from Merseyside. The "Cowdenbrummies" aren't here because some months back they didn't think that Cowden would win the title outright and had booked for the second leg of the play-off final! David Welch, a keen fan from Ipswich isn't here because he can't get off his work – where he's glued to the internet for match updates.

Stuart Watson is busily texting his friend Alex Ross, who recently emigrated to Australia – Alex is in an Irish bar in Adelaide, and by kick-off time has persuaded most of the punters in the bar to root for Cowden. In Boulder City, Nevada, Cowden fan Duncan Stark, who has been in the States for nearly 40 years, is waiting anxiously for news. In Glasgow, Stewart Miller can't be at the game because of commitments, but he is frantically checking what is happening at Central Park. In their home in Valkeakoski in Finland, Matti and Marjut Paatelainen wonder if their elder son's team will rise to the big occasion, and how their younger son will perform on the park.

Gordon Brown, Chancellor of the Exchequer, is in the Alex Menzies stand, surrounded by security men with radios in their lugs and blue and white scarves round their necks. What fun! My four-year-old grandson, Olly, is here on the terracing with me, clad in his Cowden strip. He too will learn the stories. This afternoon may or may not provide one of the best.

****

Mixu Paatelainen makes two changes to the starting line up which drew at Hampden last week. With John Ward suspended, it's great news for the fans that captain Innes Ritchie has been declared fit and will play at the heart of the defence alongside Dougie Hill. The fans are also delighted that Markus Paatelainen has had no after-effects from his short time on the park against Queen's Park and is starting the game. Having Innes and Markus in the starting line-up feels like a good omen for the day.

COWDENBEATH: David Hay, Graham Guy, Kevin McBride, Innes Ritchie, Dougie Hill, Gary Fusco, Mark Baxter, Markus Paatelainen, Armand One, David McKenna, Liam Buchanan. Subs – Iain Machlen, Darren McGregor, Pat Scullion, Lukas Krobot & John Gilbertson.

ELGIN CITY: Keiron Renton, Paul Kaczan, Allan Dempsie, Stuart Easton, Hugh Dickson, David Hind, Jamie McKenzie, Adam Nelson, Martin Johnston, Chris Gardiner, Mark Booth.

REFEREE: John McKendrick

Right from the kick-off, it's clear that Mixu is going to end the season as he has done since he came to Central Park, by playing attacking soccer. The Blue Brazil make a bright, confident start, taking the game to their opponents and settling the nerves of the home fans. Then with quarter of an hour gone, Cowdenbeath take the lead! A diagonal ball from Kevin McBride is headed on by Armand Oné to Liam Buchanan, who ghosts in behind the Elgin defence to chip home his 17th goal of the season. The fans are very, very happy.

There is no way this Cowden team will seek to defend their lead for the rest of the match. They continue to press forward at every opportunity, but the Elgin goalkeeper is in fine form. The half time score of 1-0 is satisfactory, especially with Berwick drawing 0-0 against Queen's Park, but another goal would allow the Cowden faithful to breathe easily. Five minutes into the second half, a corner from Graham Guy allows Buchanan to shoot, and when keeper Keiron Renton blocks his effort, cult hero Armand Oné is on hand to score the rebound. Over to Colin Nelson: "I'm hugging so many guys that it feels a bit gay but I don't care, these guys are ma mates - they understand. Big Fergie plans a kiss on my face again. Who cares? Cowden are going to do it."

Rejoicing on the terracing continues, as the home fans become increasingly confident that victory is in their grasp, even though they are dismayed when Innes Ritchie has to leave. Not having played for a few weeks, Ritchie has understandably run out of steam. Then, in 68 minutes, the crowd are silenced. Elgin win a free kick just outside the penalty area, and Adam Nelson fires an unstoppable shot past David Hay. Colin Nelson goes into panic mode. "This is when me and Fergie kinda go into a trance. I can't speak or even watch at some points. The sun is beating down but my face is pure white."

Can Cowden survive the next 22 minutes? The nagging doubts return. The dread increases when the news comes through that Berwick Rangers have taken the lead. What this means is that if Elgin score one more goal, Berwick will win the title, not Cowdenbeath. This Championship is on a knife-edge, and the pilot of the trophy-bearing helicopter must have no idea whether he'll be flying to Fife or to Berwick. The Elgin players sense the tension in the crowd, and they pile on the pressure, with striker Martin Johnston causing a lot of problems. After all, Elgin might still win a play-off place. Some Cowden fans can only watch the game through the cracks between their fingers. Eight minutes from time Elgin's Chris Gardiner receives a straight red card after a clash with Kevin McBride.

Central Park has suddenly become an improbable temple of prayer. People who haven't been to church in decades are making their own private bargains with God. Even Protestants are crossing themselves. There is more religion happening here than in Westminster Abbey right now. Colin Nelson is praying. "I have to admit I'm not a religious person but I am praying, please God please, I keep saying. The anxiety is too much, I'm literally about shitting masel. I keep thinking we'll lose it."

The news comes through that Berwick Rangers have won their match. Oh no. We're now into injury time. All these Berwick boasts at the start of the season haunt the imagination. Will they come true with the last kick of the ball? Surely the

Helicopter dreams won't turn to helicopter nightma.......One of the Elgin players suddenly breaks through the tired Cowden defence in front of goal. He can see the whites of the eyes of the Cowdenbeath goalkeeper.

The crowd holds its corporate breath. It's all happening in slow motion. As the ball leaves the Elgin player's boot, David Hay, the Cowden goallie, is rooted to the spot, knowing that he is beaten. Time seems to stand still as the ball arcs towards the top corner of the goal.....and passes over the bar. The name of the Lord is invoked once more.

Incredibly, the referee refuses to blow the final whistle. This is not for the faint-hearted. It is the heightened, fearful time when all the bad memories come flooding back. All the personal inadequacies break through the barriers we have carefully constructed. We're not really good enough. We don't deserve victory. It was bound to turn out badly.

At last, after six minutes of injury time, the sadist in black blows his whistle and Central Park erupts. The Blue Brazil have won the Championship for the first time since 1939, and we have been there to see it happen! On the terraces and in the stand, grown men, unaccustomed as they are to weeping, weep. The women have to daub away the men's tears.

Boys and men scale the big wire fences – the stewards and police are helpless - and run on to the pitch to greet their heroes. Colin Nelson is among them. "Best moment as a Cowden fan by far, brings a lump to my throat to be honest. Me and my mates have travelled all over the place week in and week out hoping and dreaming this would happen. I have to get on that park to congratulate the boys. I climb that fence quicker than a monkey and quickly drop the full length before running like a mad man to the players. First person I see is Davie 'The Cat' Hay who has been outstanding all season, big hug to him. Then I see ma mates Derek, and Colin Young. Big hugs all round, couple of tears in my eyes, I don't care if I sound like a girl, fuck it this is the greatest day ever. I swap Hi 5s and hugs with Derek about 20 times. I go round as many players as possible to say well done. A wee bouncy is done here and there. Everyone is starting to go back to the terracing - but me, Derek and couple of other guys stay and hide in the dugout, so we don't get escorted off. The place is going mental knowing that the trophy is coming very soon."

In Valkeakoski, Finland, Matti and Marjut Paatelainen rejoice at the news. In Boulder City, Nevada, Duncan Stark is having a wee greet, overcome with emotion. In Ipswich, David Welch is screaming with joy at his computer, at work. The Irish bar in Adelaide erupts when Cowden émigré Alex Ross gets a victory text from Stuart Watson. Alex is crying, someone gives him a whisky, then the band in the pub starts playing The Proclaimers "500 Miles". In Glasgow, Stewart Miller's daughter throws him a box of paper hankies as her father, a Cowden fan of forty years, weeps tears of relief and joy.

Back at Central Park, the players are dancing and embracing, and come over to greet the jubilant spectators. On the last day of the season, on their own ground, before their own fans, they have pulled off what seemed impossible back in September. In the last ten critical matches after losing to Berwick Rangers, the Blue Brazil have won eight times and drawn twice. While we are waiting, we think about this stunning achievement by a young side which has simply refused to accept second best. Club secretary Tam Ogilvie comes over to greet the fans, clutching the coo heid. Auld Pete, having witnessed a lot of failure at Central park in his 75 years, stands with tears in his eyes.

Things are starting to happen now. The Bell's Scottish Third Division board is brought out, and Gordon Brown comes on to the park, ready to present the trophy. This is what we have been waiting for, dreaming about. Then there comes the most beautiful sound in the whole world at that particular moment – the whirring of helicopter blades. As a tatty Third Division stadium is magically transformed into a theatre of once-impossible dreams, a huge roar goes up, the throaty, coal-gravelly Central Park roar of defiant jubilation.

The whirling bird circles the old arena. It's not just carrying the blue-and-white-ribboned Holy Grail; it's bringing with it some wonderful presences – the likes of Margaret Pollock, John and James Pollock, Bob Law, Hooky Leonard, Willie Devlin, Jennie Lee, Charlie Gronbach, Alex Menzies, Andy Matthew and Willie Anderson. It's also bringing particular faces of glad remembrance. For me, they include Alex Ferguson, and Joe and Ina Ferguson. They kept the faith. *They that wait upon the Lord shall renew their strength; they shall mount up on wings, as eagles; they shall run, and not be weary; and they shall walk, and not faint.*

This beautiful bird, glinting in the sunlight, is not just the bearer of a Scottish Football League trophy draped in the colours of the kingdom of Blue Brazil: it is freighted with psalms and coal-dusted memories and technicolour dreams. Helicopter dreams.

116

14. BOTH HANDS ON THE HOLY GRAIL

*Despite the best efforts of Opus Dei agents, I have located the Holy Grail.
Here's how it happened. After I keyed in the code I found in the murdered
monk's pocket, I was given precise directions to the sacred treasure's
location. Accompanied by my comely cryptologist, I made my way through
dark labyrinths, ending up in a mysterious building with a painted sign
which read Wee Jimmie's Bar. Strange name for a crypt, I thought. Hearing
sounds of tumultuous cheering, I strode masterfully into the noisy room. Was
it Jesus and Mary Magdalene's wedding reception? There, right before me,
was the gleaming vessel. I had my hands on the Holy Grail at last.*

Or so Dan Brown might have written the story. The only difference between Mr
Brown and myself is about thirty million pounds.....

Wee Jimmie's is jumping. The energy in the room hits you as you walk in.
The bedecked fans raise the roof when Mixu and the team enter the hall, holding
the Championship trophy aloft. The players are in great form, despite the draining
exertions of the afternoon. Every so often they burst into singing "Championees!"
while Armand Oné, whose lug-to-lug grin lights up Wee Jimmie's, moves into a
peculiar kind of samba. The man is something else. Armand sprays everyone with
champagne – it turns out to be Stuart Watson and Derek Neilson's bottle which had
been stashed away in the fridge for after the game.

The manager and players are welcomed by Supporters Club chairman
Dave Tuson, who thanks them on behalf of those present for a once-in-a-lifetime
experience. Lots of fans then have the thrill of being photographed with Mixu and
the players together with the trophy.

Plenty of fans from elsewhere would like to have been there, but they're
not forgotten. As with other fans in exile, the poor old Cowdenbrummies

who couldn't be at the game because they'd made their travel bookings for the play-offs, are kept in touch with what's going on. Simon Pearson tells me that he had been emailed photos of the game and celebrations by 8pm. "Obviously we'll be up next year for the assault on Division 2," he promises.

I am touched when Innes Ritchie comes over and gives me the Blue Brazil jersey he wore on the park this afternoon. It's pretty sweaty, but I don the sacred garment right away. People give me a wide berth, but I don't care. It'll go up on my study wall, the nearest thing to the Turin Shroud.

Then it's time to hand out the trophies, ten in all. It's no surprise that Markus Paatelainen, who has had a dazzling season, wins the Supporters Club Player of the Year, the Willie Anderson Trophy, the Blue Brazil On-line Fans' Player of the Year Award, and the Eric Mitchell Trophy for Players' Player of the Year.

"I would like to thank the fans for all the awards I have received but also for sticking by me during my injury," says Markus. "Your words of kindness were really appreciated and the response I got coming off the bench at Hampden last week was special."

Next up is Liam Buchanan, who wins the John Finlay Trophy for Supporters Club Young Player of the Year, and the Hooky Leonard Trophy for the season's top scorer. Having joined the club's youth system from Hearts in 2002, Liam has flourished under Mixu's guidance, finishing as top scorer with 17 goals.

When Liam goes up to collect his award, his mobile phone goes off. He answers it, and it's Gary Fusco, who's only a few feet away. "I really enjoyed the season and feel my game has really come on," says Liam. "It has been great to score so many goals and I've really enjoyed playing under Mixu. After the disappointment of relegation a few seasons back this is payback for the fans."

Goalkeeper David "The Cat" Hay, who has had a great season with 12 shut-outs, collects the Willie Mercer Trophy for Blue Brazil On-line Player of the Year. Cowden fan Colin Nelson has been sitting at a table beside the players, and he tells me: "Davie Hay and Innes and Fusco were on top form with some of their banter. After every trophy was announced, Davie Hay would say, "Surely I've got to win this one!" I think he even said it for the TOP GOALSCORER!"

David Hay was certainly delighted with his award. "This award means a lot to me," he says. "I have never won a personal award before and this caps a great day for me. It has been a tremendous season and great to keep so many shut-outs, but thanks must go to the rest of the team for our defensive record, particularly Innes and Wardy." Then he adds modestly, "I deserve this!"

The Joe Ferguson Trophy (in memory of my father) for Blue Brazil On-line Young Player of the Year goes to Mark Baxter, the teenage full back or midfielder who was one of Mixu's inspired signings. Mark, of course, was involved in the notorious Smokie Pensioner Mystery, and when he goes up to collect his award, the players break into a song to the tune of the old Bible chorus, "If you're happy and you know it". It contains distinctly non-biblical but precise instructions for Arbroath supporters as to where to put their smokies.

John Ward wins the Junction Bar Star Trophy. Wardy signed for the Blue Brazil last July after winning pretty much every honour available with Junior team Tayport. The towering defender formed an impressive partnership with Innes Ritchie at the back and the two also found time to compete for the highest scoring defender award.

And the winner of the Pollock Shield for the best individual performance? Who else but the one and only Armand Oné? He literally dances up to receive his well-deserved prize. "I have to thank the manager," says the Special Oné. "He came to my house and showed faith in me. Three months ago I had no club, no team and no fans. Now I have a Championship medal and I am one happy man."

Mikko Paatelainen is the winner of the One Stop Mortgages Trophy for goal of the season. Mikko scored seven goals and nine appearances, and these goals were crucial in Cowden's push for the Championship. The Lord Ewing trophy for Supporter of the Year is presented by skipper Innes Ritchie to joint winners Sandy and Ron Ferguson. It is humbling to know that last year's joint winners were Willie Anderson and Jack Gilmour.

This special season, many players would fully deserve the Player of the Season title. Special mention must go to a number of players. Captain Innes Ritchie was superb again and was deservedly voted into the Blue Brazil Hall of Fame. Innes takes the opportunity to grab the mike and say a few words on behalf of the team. "I would like to thank Mixu and his coaching staff for their part in this remarkable season. I would also like to thank the fans for their magnificent support over the course of the season. The support at Ochilview in April was amazing and something most of us had never experienced before. I have never won the Championship before - you can't beat this feeling. It is great to see the trophy in here and see how much it means to these amazing fans and players."

Then comes the biggest roar of this memorable evening, as Innes goes on: "I would just like to add - take a look at Sky when the league table comes up and you'll see a little "c" in brackets after Cowden's name - that means......CHAMPIONS".

The fans are delighted with the players' acknowledgement of the fans' commitment. Colin Nelson – who will have to get himself tattooed now - tells me: "Guys like Davie and Innes and Fusco and Bucks all understand what the club means to fans such as myself, and this to me is fantastic, knowing that they acknowledge this."

Although there have been winners in special categories, the truth is that every single player in this great-spirited squad has been a hero. Graham Guy, who has been promoted twice before with Stranraer, played a vital role at both right back and in midfield and provided danger from dead ball situations. Graham comments: "It was amazing to see how much it meant to the Cowden fans, and that made all the

119

lads in the dressing room even more proud than we already felt." Dead ball sidekick Kevin McBride was also a vital part of a solid defence. Left back in particular has been a problem position for Cowden over the years so great credit must go to Kevin. Dougie Hill had to be patient for his opportunity but was a vital and star performer from the turn of the year at the heart of the defence as injuries and suspensions robbed Cowden of the regular paring of Ritchie and Ward at different times of the season.

Gary Fusco is another player who had to bide his time. Fusco struggled to hold down a regular starting place at the start of the season due to the form of Marc Millar (who made a significant contribution himself) but was instrumental in the 4-1 demolition of Stenhousemuir. Fusco returned to his favoured position in March and from them on he was absolutely immense. Fusco beamed "It is absolutely fantastic to win the Championship. I really enjoyed moving back into central midfield but it did mean I get no goals these days! It has been a great season and party with the fans tonight."

Iain Mauchlen, our longest serving player, came into form when it really mattered – after Markus's injury. 'Mauchie' offered drive and pace from midfield and scored two classic and vital goals against East Fife and Elgin City. Teenage loan signings Andy Jackson and David McKenna scored some crucial goals for the team. McKenna in particular was tremendous in the second half of the season Eleven goals in 16 games (including four consecutive doubles at Central Park) speaks for itself. Young forwards Ryan McCallum and Paul McBride also played their part. McCallum scored six goals before heading off to Glenrothes on loan to gain some experience, and McBride scored the critical equaliser against East Stirling. Other players who deserve credit for their contribution in Cowden's historic season include Pat Scullion, Darran Thomson, Darren McGregor, Lukas Krobot, Robert Downs (scorer of the 5000th league goal) and Andy Carlin.

Then comes the man everyone wants to hear from. The manager makes his way to the microphone to the song "Mixu is the captain of our ship". Typically, he passes the credit to his players. "The boys have been fantastic all season and fully deserve the title – enjoy the moment. We trailed Stenny and Berwick by double figures and it required immense focus and effort by the players to win the games in hand. First we caught Stenny, then Berwick to go top - and once we got there we stayed there."

Mixu goes on to praise the contribution of his backroom team and all those working behind the scenes. "This is a great club and is so because of the people we have working in the backroom. As Innes said, people like Tam Ogilvie and Bert Johnston make this club what it is. In addition, I would like to put on record my appreciation for the backing and hard work of Gordon McDougall. Without Gordon there would be no football club in Cowdenbeath."

Mixu finishes off with words of praise for the support. "Last but by no means least I would like to thank the fans. Today was fantastic but we will also remember those who travelled week in, week out to support us. We may not be the biggest club in Britain but that does not stop us having some of the best supporters."

A bouquet of flowers is presented to the glamorous Mrs Mixu Paatelainen, prompting an improvised chorus of "Only four Paatelainens" from the jubilant crowd. It's announced that it's been unanimously agreed that the Championship-winning team of 2006, along with Mixu Paatelainen and chairman Gordon McDougall, should become members of the Hall of Fame on the back of their fantastic achievement this season. By winning the Championship, these guys have deservedly become heroes in the pantheon, having brought honour to Cowdenbeath Football Club and to the town. They deservedly find their place alongside legends such as Hooky Leonard, Scott Duncan, Alex Menzies and Charlie Gronbach.

The blue ribbon-bedecked Holy Grail sits proudly on the table, and is touched or lifted high in the air by everyone present. Forget the Old Firm, we are the mighty Blue Brazil! This is not the time to recall historic failures or reflect on the decline of the mining industry. There is a proper time for that, but this is not it. This is an evening of insubordination, of jubilation.

A letter from Willie Anderson's son and daughter to the Supporters Club is read out: "We can't thank you enough for the help and friendship you gave to our father William Anderson. We joked about the hearse being used for an away game. Well Gordon McDougall gave him his last run around the park in it, he would have liked that."

Smile on, Willie Anderson. This is for you and all the other past and present heroes. Let Wee Jimmie's rock, because, in spite of our fears and doubts, the helicopter landed in Cowdenbeath on this memorable day, April 29th, 2006.

So let the dancing begin. Start to samba once again, Monsieur Oné. After 67 years, this is going to be one helluva party, because WE ARE THE CHAMPIONS!

HELICOPTER DREAMS

PART TWO

The Players, the Personnel and the Punters

1. THE MANAGER

A coach is like a winemaker. He must produce the best wine from the grapes he has available – Fabio Capello, Milan coach

He trains them the right way, and he gets them to do what they can do well. He merges them all together. They're all helping each other. It's a form of socialism without the politics – Bill Shankly on Jock Stein's methods

Given what he has just achieved, it's hard to believe that this is Mixu Paatelainen's first year in management. Mixu is an engaging and likeable man. I talked with him in the club boardroom, with the Championship trophy in full view.

How were you approached for the job?
I'd had two knee operations, and my contract had run out. St Mirren wanted me to keep trying to see if I could play again after rehab. They also wanted me to do more coaching. My knee was getting better, but it wasn't up to the standard. I'd had a long career and I was thinking, "Why play another season when I'm struggling?" Going into management was in my mind. I'd had a couple of offers before that, but I still wanted to play. Now there was a doubt in my mind about my knee. So when Gordon phoned and asked if I was interested, the timing was right. Everything went very smoothly, and I agreed. It was still in my mind to play if at all possible, but now my playing career is over. I had a long career, and enjoyed it, so I have no complaints.

You've been at big clubs, with great facilities; then you come to Cowdenbeath with a stock car tracks and piles of big tyres?
The surroundings don't bother me. It's what happens inside the club that interests me. How the whole club is run. I want to know about whether they are ambitious and enthusiastic people. Are they supportive of the manager?

125

It must have been difficult starting as manager just after the David Baikie business?

The players were obviously disappointed at losing their manager. I called the players in for a chat. I said it was very unfortunate, there was nothing they could do about it, but we had to go forward and concentrate on football. The players have a great attitude. From then on everybody was very enthusiastic. They made a good response. Team spirit is great. The place is absolutely bouncing.

When I came here I knew very little about the players, their mentality, or the way they played. It takes time, it doesn't happen straight away. To get the best out of the players you have to get to know them and you have to work with the system that suits the players you have. You have to experiment, to start from somewhere and then you find your way through, find the best way to play with the players you've got.

What's your football philosophy? What do you like to see?

My philosophy is to start with the defence. When I've got that sorted, I want to be very positive. I like to concentrate on how we go forward, how we pass the ball. "Positiveness" is a big word in my mind. You have to go for it. You don't win anything unless you go for it. If you're not ultra positive, you don't win leagues. No matter how much emphasis you put on defending, you're always going to concede goals. If you don't have a strategy for how you go forward, you'll never win. On the other hand, if you're positive and you have a strategy for how you go forward, even if you concede an early goal you're confident you'll score. You know how to win the match. That's first of all. I gave the players very clear guidelines how to play, what movements to make, how to link up with other players. Every player has to know his own role and how it links with other players. That's the area in which we improved most.

It was very noticeable that you were playing football from the back.

I like to be systematic. If you get your defenders on the ball, I want them to go into the same kind of passing every time. Every time the full back has the ball, you should see the players moving into the right positions. Everybody must know what they're supposed to be doing.

The fans really enjoyed seeing this passing game. There was also the confidence that even if we lost an early goal, we'd score.

That gives you confidence. You need to have a goal, and how to get there. You need to know what is expected of you. That doesn't just apply to football, but to life. If you know how you're going to that, and that, and that, it gives you confidence, and your confidence goes higher because you know exactly what you're doing.

How do you get it all over to the players?
You do it individually. The players are all different. What works with one player doesn't work with another. You have to know their personalities. Some need a more aggressive approach, others need a cotton-wool approach. How to get information across and motivate the players is what football management is all about. When a manager is on the sidelines giving instructions and somebody makes a mistake, maybe sometimes you're a bit aggressive, at other times not. You may say "Well done, well done". Some people watching this might think the coach isn't very consistent, but you are being consistent. It all depends on the individual player.

How did you decide on your formation?
The fans might be interested in how we got to our formation. When I first came in as manager, we only had one training session before the Queens Park game. So I played the 4-4-2 formation the players had been used to. We lost 2-0. After it, I said, "That's not good enough". The next week against Elgin I changed the formation to 3-5-2. We played really well. I thought "Fantastic". In the next game, away to East Fife, it was an absolutely shocking performance. We couldn't pass the ball five yards, and our movement was poor. The three at the back system didn't work. I more or less abandoned three at the back. You have to base your tactics on the players you have. So we went back to a back four, we were solid, we had clean sheets and defended really well. After that, I said to myself, "Now we have to go forward". 4-4-2 was too obvious, too easy to play against, so I thought "Let's really go for it and have three strikers – who are not midfielders pushing forward but out-and-out strikers. I knew that in some matches our midfielders would be under pressure, they would be outnumbered. But the way our midfielders played, we could cope with that. So we played 4-3-3, and we defended well and scored goals. I was really happy with that. When you're a new manager at a club it can take time to get your ideas through and find the best formation. It's not easy – it doesn't happen straight away. You have to use your imagination.

You brought in Andy Jackson.
When I was at St Johnstone, I worked with Andy when he was 15 years old and in the under-17 side. He was scoring goals for fun. He was so good I took him straight into the reserves – and he scored straight away – at 15! He wasn't troubled by the fact that he was playing against experienced players. He worked hard and was very enthusiastic. So when I came here and I wanted to change the system, I phoned Owen Coyle and arranged for Andy to come here on loan.

I remember vividly the goal he scored in the 4-1 victory against Stenhousemuir...
That was the first time I knew we were going to challenge for the league. Berwick

and Stenny were in the lead, but Des McKeown was quoted in the papers as saying "Watch Cowdenbeath". That gave us confidence as well.

Tell me about Markus.

He was with Aberdeen last season, and he broke his ankle. His season was finished, and Aberdeen released him. He did pre-season training at St Mirren. I asked him to come to Cowden. At first he was against it. He'd never been part-time before. But he came here and worked on his weaknesses and on his strength. He trained so hard. Any young player who wanted to be a footballer would learn so much by seeing how Markus trained. Technically he is so good. He has lots of tricks, he makes it look easy. His movement is so good. He's so fluent. That only comes from training, from practising and practising.

He's got gracefulness of movement, he ghosts past players.

My mother used to say that watching Markus play is like watching somebody waltzing. I made him a personal training programme. I was training with him every day. We had a handful of players training with me on Monday, Wednesday and Friday afternoons, so in addition to the Tuesday and Thursday team training, they were training like full-time players. That allowed me to concentrate on movement, and individual development. We would analyse why they did certain things, and work on that. Individual development of players is important. When I came here I didn't make promises about promotion, but said I would work on the development of the players.

Tell me about the Arbroath game, when we lost 4-1.

We were magnificent that day. We were absolutely fantastic. We should have been three or four goals up. Then we defended a punt poorly and we were 1-0 down. Even after that we kept creating chances. Then came the incident with Mark Baxter. Somebody threw the ball in his face and he obviously lost the place and he was sent off. Even after that I was confident that we would win. Unfortunately Mauchie made a reckless tackle and we were down to nine men.

What about the Elgin game when Markus was injured?

That whole period was worrying. Markus got that knock and I said to myself that he wouldn't play again for the rest of the season. Markus was a key player for us, so that was a big blow. I knew that Mikko had only a couple more games for us. He had been in very good form and scoring goals, and I thought, "This is really difficult now." I didn't know what to do, then thankfully we got Armand in. And the players who came in and played on the left hand side did very well.

What about your backroom staff?
Yes. Brian NcNaughton was a great help to me at the beginning, because he knew the players. He wanted to be a manager, and when the Arniston job came up, it was a good chance for him. Neil Bryson was a good help, and so was Stevie McLeish. So was Jock Martin. Then Michael O'Neill came in as my assistant, and it was good to have someone to share ideas with – then he told me about the approach from Brechin. I always knew that he was good managerial material, and he had to take the opportunity.

Tell me about Armand Oné.
I knew Armand because I played against him when he was with Partick Thistle. Then he came on trial at St Mirren, and though he wasn't offered a contract I knew what he could do. Joe Macnamara alerted me to the fact that he played a couple of games for Albion Rovers. I knew that Armand could be useful for us, he could be a focal point for the attack, so I decided to go for it.

He quickly became a cult figure. He was very difficult to get the ball off.
He's big and powerful and his technique is terrific. He'd been out for four or five months with shin splints problems. He wasn't fit, but the minutes he gave us were quality.

The backlog of postponed fixtures was a problem, wasn't it?
My job as manager was to make sure the players realised they knew it was possible, and to keep believing. The players showed great mental toughness, coming from behind several times.

It was remarkable how many times we went behind, and fought back to win.
You have to have that confidence that you will score. When we went to Stenhousemuir and beat them 2-1, that was a critical game. The first half was even stevens, but we went a goal down in the first half. Then before the break, Dougie Hill scored a great goal, one that any striker would be proud of. That gave us a great confidence boost. We knew that we had to win that game. If we lost that game it would have been really difficult. The performance of the boys was outstanding; we won 2-1 but it could have been 4-1. Stenny knew that they had been outplayed.

What about the second last game of the season at Hampden?
I was really worried about that game. Queen's Park were a very well organised team with really skilful and sharp players and a good manager. On their day they could beat anybody. I said to the players, "They can really hurt you". They were good passers of the ball, and I knew they could create chances. Once again we went behind, but then we equalised. I believed we could go on and win, but it was bad

to concede another goal so quickly. It was another mountain to climb. Then Oné scored a great goal. Before the game I would have been happy with a draw, because it meant that in the last game, it would still be in our hands.

And the last game was incredible, wasn't it?
The last game was all about nerves. We had beaten Elgin three times. I was confident that both teams would score. They had the league's top goal scorer. Thankfully we got a 2-0 cushion, and that gave us a breathing space. Before the game I'd told the players, "Stay calm, relax and pass the ball, just concentrate on your jobs." I thought we started too calmly! But we showed our goal-scoring ability.
The final few minutes were nerve-wracking, especially when they made it 2-1. Half an hour from the end, we lost Innes, our big captain at the back who keeps the team organised and together. It was a fantastic feeling when the final whistle went.

And the fans hadn't had a championship win for 67 years.
Our supporters have been fantastic. We may not have the biggest support in the world, but we have great, great supporters. The support they gave the players at away games was unbelievable. They were very vocal and loud – the alcohol at the away games might be a factor! At the Stenny game, the vital game, the size of the support behind the goals was great for our guys. I couldn't thank the supporters enough. The numbers are not what we would want – we would want double or treble that – but they ones who are there are great and they've played a big part in our successful season.

Well, Mixu, you and the boys have given the supporters a wonderful season. To play such good football, to come from behind so often, and to win the Championship on our own pitch on the last day of the season is very special. We know that when we operate at this end of the football market we'll have our ups and downs, so this is all the more precious.
That's right. You have to enjoy all the good times, and be prepared to keep working hard.

2. THE CHAIRMAN

In some ways we're all a little mad because there must be easier ways to earn a living. – Wallace Mercer, late chairman of Hearts.

Gordon McDougall is very much a hands-on chairman. He often works on both football club and stock car racing business from around 8am till 9 or 10pm. The day before I interviewed him in his office at Central Park his computer had crashed and having just got it fixed, he was trying hard to make up for lost time. The conversation was interrupted from time to time by phone calls, and his secretary coming in with messages. Gordon is a bit like a juggler – a multitasker, to use the modern jargon.

Would you reckon that this is your highest point as chairman?
(Still typing away) Yes, the Championship must be the highest point. It's the Holy Grail of any football club, the be-all and end-all. You're competing at a particular level and you want to do the best you can. To win the Championship at any level is tremendous. It definitely adds something when you have a backlog of fixtures as we did. It certainly took its toll and there were nervous times. To win something like ten games in a matter of six weeks – with only one draw at East Stirling and all the finger nails going! – is a tremendous achievement.

Were you optimistic at the start of the season? Did you think that in terms of the Championship this could be it in the club's 125th season?
I was quite optimistic at the start of the season. I'm never *too* optimistic. You've always plenty of things to occupy your mind. You always hope to do well in anything you do. Sometimes it works out, sometimes it doesn't. I though that we were fairly well set up to have a good season. The difference between a good season and a great season is a very fine line, as I'm sure Berwick and Stenhousemuir would tell you.

Yes, if you look at Berwick and Stenny's final positions they had a good season, but they ended up feeling totally flattened because they were so far ahead.
Yes, for them it ended up a disastrous season.

So you were well set up for a new season, and then there was the David Baikie business.
I don't want to go much into that. I regard Dave Baikie as a good manager. Dave had never had a conviction in his life, he was 51 years old. I had a good bit of sympathy for him, but I felt that because of the severity of the offence it was a decision that had to be made at the time. It's not something we discuss with people. These were events that were totally outwith our control. You can't legislate for these things – and it's within a week of the start of the season. It made life very difficult. After thinking we were well set up for the season, the manager was away and we were starting again.

What made you think of Mixu?
I'd been tracking Mixu for some time. It wasn't a spur of the moment decision.

I suppose that when Dave Baikie was first in court you had to have something in mind in case a change had to be made?
I was thinking about Mixu long before that.

And Mixu had the track record and personality for a manager's job.
Yes. It's worked out well, and I'm sure it'll work out well in the future. I'm also sure he'll go on to great things, at a much higher level.

Yes, you can see that in Mixu's vision and commitment and ability to get the best out of his players. A bit like Craig Levein, isn't it?
Very much. We spent the last four or five years saying there'll never be another Craig Levein, but it turns out there is.

I suppose that as the chairman of a football club, the most important decision you have to make – apart from all the financial worries – is the choice of manager.
Yes, it's taken me about 15 years to make me realise that's the most important decision you have to make!

That's come through some pretty hard experience.
Very hard experiences. I've made a lot of wrong decisions and a few good ones, but it's very, very clear that the best investment you can make is in the manager.

At this level in the game you're going to get some right and some wrong, because

132

*you're often dealing with rookie managers. You're looking at the potential in
somebody and it might work out or it might not.*
With the appointments of Craig and Mixu, the answer each time was staring me in
the face.

*The way in which these two guys conducted themselves, both as human beings and
as managers, has been very important.*
That's what I mean, it wasn't a difficult problem you were faced with, it was
simply: can you put together enough resources to employ these people? After
you've met them, the question then becomes: can we afford *not* to employ them?

Was it difficult to persuade Mixu?
People know that people here do it for fun. If we can't afford something, we say we
can't afford it. We won't push the boat out beyond what we can afford to do. They
know they'll be working within a budget, but they know they'll get all the support
and they won't get any interference – the only time there would be a problem
would be if the results were bad. Even then, you can live with it if you know you're
going in the right direction.

This is a good place for young managers to learn their trade.
Yes, I also think that will be fairly significant in other people's thoughts
now. Before Craig, some people might have thought, who'd be a manager at
Cowdenbeath? Now Cowdenbeath is a much more attractive proposition for a
young manager with potential.

*I remember talking to you a few years back, Gordon, and you said it was important
not just to live within your means, but to have a good youth set up.*
Yes. We have six youth teams from 12 years of age, and there's also a women's
team and a girls' team associated with the club. Mind you a youth policy is fairly
expensive, but having said that, can you afford not to do it? Only if you're prepared
to accept limping along at the bottom, which we had to do for a number of years.

*Yes, you had to balance the books, and when you look at all the troubles with clubs
going into administration -*
The game's in serious trouble, there's no doubt about that. Will it ever recover?
Who knows. Sometimes you despair. You think things are getting better, and along
come people like Abrahamovitch and Romanov. You look at one side of Edinburgh
and they're living within their means and producing good young players, and the
other side is gaining success by buying everybody. That's a biased view, of course.
I don't think even the Hearts fans would argue with it, it's not the way they want
to go. Everybody wants success, but even Hearts fans, if you asked them, would

133

much rather do it with young Scottish players. Hibs are bringing through some good youngsters, but they're bound to be a bit erratic.

This season's been a rollercoaster. Berwick were well ahead and we were far down the order, then Stenny were well in the lead, but we just kept plugging away and gradually overtook them.
Yes, the 2-1 victory over Stenhousemuir was the start of the run in. Then we dropped two points at East Stirling on the Tuesday night when we were expected to consolidate, then Berwick beat Stenhousemuir on the Saturday and that gave us a bit of breathing space.

The Stenny and Berwick fans thought that we would lose points with the backlog of fixtures we had. It's one thing to have games in hand, quite another to win them all.
With a tight squad. If you look at the other two teams, they had more "personality" players than we had. Ours was more of a team effort than high profile players.

We're moving up a grade. Apart from the financial aspects, are you confident that we'll cope OK next season?
I don't see one grade making a huge difference. I don't think it'll be a huge jump in quality. We could be in contention at the top of Division 2, we could be at the bottom, but I see it as being a very tight league.

It's a good chance for our young players to make an impression at a higher level.
Very much.

Looking at the global financial situation, you've got the gate money, which isn't very much, the income from the stock car racing rental, league sponsorship money, and merchandise. Is that about it?
Yes. The gate money doesn't bring in very much There's no league sponsor at the moment. You've just got to eke it out. We're always looking for people to come in and help – I wouldn't use the word "invest" because it's not really an investment. It always makes me laugh when people say you've got to invest in football. You normally expect a return on an investment! If you get your money back you're very lucky. Merchandise has been good this season, and the new official website has been a great help. The online shop has done well. Most football fans shop on the web now. But even so it isn't a huge part of our income. It would be good if we could expand it.

The main component is presumably the income from the stock car side.
Yes. Without the stock cars, the football club would be in trouble.

In terms of debt, is the club self-sufficient?
The football club doesn't have a huge debt to meet, but if anything happened to me…. At Central Park, we're debt free, between the two companies. One props the other one up. We need to have a succession plan, because I can't go on for ever. Our main concern is getting a new venue, a place that is worthy of the club. We don't have a site in mind at this stage. We're talking with the Council and we'll see what happens. What we want is a small modern facility with all-weather pitches.

Cowdenbeath Football Club has brought great publicity the town, especially this year with winning the Championship. The name of the town has been in all the papers, with photographs of the players with the trophy. The club puts the name of the town on the map. And the stock car racing brings business to the local economy. What price could you put on all of that?
Exactly. We get people from all over the world – Australia, Canada - showing an interest and writing in about Cowdenbeath. People follow the club through the internet. The Blue Brazil name is great – I don't know who thought of it, but it was a stroke of genius. But if we want a future for the club, we need a good venue.

Isn't it great that the Championship has been won in our 125th season? This is a good time to get things sorted out for the future of the club.
That's right. What a fantastic season!

3. THE CAPTAIN

In Scotland, the toughest defenders I've played against have been Willie Miller and Alex McLeish. I've broken my nose against both of them. – Ally McCoist.

When Cowdenbeath's inspirational captain, Innes Ritchie, lifted high the trophy on the last day of the season, it was the first Championship the 32-year-old central defender had won. Innes signed for Chelsea at the age of 16 but was homesick in London and signed for Motherwell, where he played for six years. Then followed spells with East Fife, Clydebank, Berwick Rangers (twice) and Arbroath. He works as a manager with Ikea. I caught up with Innes in Edinburgh and got his story.

Innes, tell me about how you came to Cowdenbeath.
In my second season at Arbroath, some of the best players left and the team broke up. We played against Rangers in the Cup, and that was fantastic. The club got £250,000, and we got £85 each bonus money. It was terrible. I didn't get on with John Brownlie, the manager, and I'd just been promoted at my work at the end of that season, so I just thought to myself, if that's what fitba's like I don't really need to play, so I packed it in. Right through the summer I was adamant I wasn't going to sign for anybody, but I kept training and kept fit, and I did pre-season with Berwick. Keith Wright had been at me and at me, and I used to see him at the gym. He said, "We need a good defender because Mark Yardley destroyed us at the weekend. C'mon and see what it's like." So I went along the first night. It was quite funny: I jumped in the minibus and there were all these young guys like Liam talking about what they'd been doing at the weekend and I thought to myself..... but I liked the training, I really enjoyed it. There were some guys I knew like Toorie, Broonie and Kevin Gordon. I loved it, it was great. I was playing in the Third Division after being in the First and I knew that these guys played because they really wanted to play football. I really enjoyed playing for Cowdenbeath and I've enjoyed it ever since.

So tell me about this season. Were you optimistic at the start that we'd do well?
We thought we had a chance. We knew Stenny had signed a lot of good players, and Berwick had just come down. It's funny we always we thought it would be between the three of us, plus Queen's Park. I've always rated Queen's being pretty good. They've got great facilities and a good manager. We had a brilliant pre-season. Dave Baikie and Mel (assistant manager Graeme Irons) were great. When they first came I was a bit wary because I'd really signed on for Keith Wright and I got on really well with Keith, but when Dave Baikie came in I really enjoyed it. He had a very positive attitude. We had a great pre-season trip down Durham way. Then when I was back in the house the text messages started flying in – "Have you seen the papers about the court case?" It was quite unbelievable. We played Partick on the Saturday and we got a bit of a doing. Between the Partick and the East Stirling game, Dave Baikie stands up in the middle of the dressing room in tears, telling us he's going and stuff like that, wishing us all the best. It was horrible. Then I got a phone call asking if I'd take training. It was a hard game against East Stirling. They had Diack and Ally Graham up front, and I thought Darren McGregor was brilliant that day. Then there was all the uncertainty. Mel said he was going to go, and the rumours were that the manager was going to be Campbell Money. Then somebody phoned me at my work and told me Mixu Paatelainen had got the manager's job.

We had the game against St Johnstone on the Tuesday night, and we were a bit unlucky. Darren Gribben scored a wonder goal for us. We matched St Johnstone that night. It's sometimes things like that that bring everybody together. Then we lost 2-0 to Queen's Park and I thought, "Here we go again, a bad start to the season", but we won the next week up at Elgin. Mixu didn't know the players and it was hard for him, but he came over really well. As you know he's a good speaker and his enthusiasm came over. I hit it off with him right away. The fact that Brian McNaughton (first team coach) stayed for a bit was good as well. It kept a bit of continuity. We adapted to a different way of playing and it was very positive, very attack-minded. We won the next game up at Elgin; the only downside was me and Wardy were having a nightmare playing three at the back. We managed to get away with it at Elgin, but the next week at East Fife we were terrible. We said to Mixu that three at the back wasn't working. We changed to four at the back, we ended up playing better.

The fans really enjoyed the way the team played. The moves started at the back, sometimes with Davie Hay's good distribution, and played through the midfield.
Duff (David Hay) has been brilliant, he's got the confidence to roll the ball out to the full backs. Keith Wright played a long game, Dave Baikie got us playing more of a passing game and now we've been doing it a lot more since Mixu came in. It's

really quite a family club. Everybody's together, everybody's there because they like it. You always get a good laugh, the team spirit's brilliant.

Who are the jokers in the dressing room, the special characters who stand out?
Other than me?! Liam's funny. Fusco's hilarious. Beaky (Mark Baxter) is funny. I'm pretty sure they'd all say me, because I'm always at it and mucking about. I like to have a laugh and a joke. Mauchy's good as well. Downsie was great when he was here. Meeting before the game for beans on toast and a cup of tea at Wee Jimmie's before the game is brilliant as well. We have sprints at training on Thursday and the loser brings the jaffa cakes.

That was a fantastic run, wasn't it? Ten victories out of 11. The fans had been thinking before that run that it would be hard for us to even get a play-off place.
That's right. When we beat Queen's Park 2-0 at Hampden we played them off the park. I remember coming back after that game, joking about doing well, but at that time it still seemed too much because you saw the two teams so far ahead. The most frustrating game for me in the whole season was the 2-1 defeat at East Fife at the New Year. I've never been so frustrated in my whole life. We made so many chances, and we lost two rubbish goals from set pieces, and we hardly ever lost goals from set pieces. Being East Fife as well made it all the worse for us. Coming off, the door was getting booted. The manager phoned me on the Wednesday to ask me if I was all right. I said no, I'm no all right, because I can't believe we lost that game. He said I've never seen you like that before. I haven't been that mad for years about a game. Mixu said I've been feeling the same, but it's over and done with and we have to move on to the next game. And it was fine.

When did you first think we might win the Championship?
I can remember being up at Elgin, and we beat them 4-0. Coming back after the game, I was talking to Fusco and Marc Millar, and I remember saying, we're going to win the league. I thought they might laugh at that, but Marc Millar said, I think we'll win the league as well. I said I don't know what it is, there's just something about it.

The run-in towards the Championship was fantastic. Several times the team came back after losing a goal ....
That was the times when I wasn't playing! I had a really bad injury. I've never had a bad injury like that before. I tried coming back and coming back, but it wasn't right.

Winning the 2-1 game at Stenny was crucial game, wasn't it?
I wasn't playing because I was still injured. They were panicking. We made lots

of chances. After we took the lead we could have won by a big margin. They just couldn't handle us.

That game knocked Stenny's confidence.
I thought it was a long time coming, to be honest.

What about Armand Oné?
He was fantastic for us. He really surprised me. I wondered when I first saw him, but his touch is unbelievable for a big guy. He must have been about two stones overweight – imagine what he'd be like when he's fully fit. He's great with his back to the goal, and he can turn you.

But you were back for the last game. The fans were hoping you'd be back, to settle the team down.
I can remember the gaffer saying to me I want you to play and settle everybody down. I never though of it like that, I didn't think anything other than turning up and playing a game of fitba and having a few laughs and doing what I do. I remember when we went to Wee Jimmie's for the pre-match meal and the fans were asking me if I was playing. When I said yes, they were all cheering and that felt really good. The gaffer said at half time we were maybe too calm! Fusco was absolutely brilliant. We created a few chances. If it had been 6-0 before I went off you couldn't have argued with it.

The fans were getting nervous as the game went on.
I don't get nervous when I'm playing, so it's easy for me. I said to Liam before the game playing fitba's no nervous, there are other things in life that make you nervous, like looking after your daughter, or you can't pay your mortgage or something like that. It's maybe just when you get older you see it like that, but I never batted an eyelid before the game, to be honest. At half time I was really struggling, and I thought, if we get another goal I'm going to go off. The game should have been over and done because we had so many chances. It annoys me when people say we were lucky at the end. We definitely deserved it on the day, and nobody can take that away from us. I was a bag of nerves watching the game after I had to go off. I thought I hope we don't give away a free kick, and we did and the guy goes up and bangs it into the top corner. At that point we were totally on top.

Then the final whistle....
It was great. It was unbelievable. The fans were on the park and everybody was going mad. I couldn't see some of the players and I went into the dressing room. Everybody's going mad and the champagne's popping – this was maybe about an

hour after the final whistle. It seemed to take for ever for the helicopter to arrive with the trophy. I probably did the worst thing I could possibly do by jumping on the Racewall. They expected us to stay in the dressing room but I thought there's no way I'm doing that, and I went out and everybody followed. I said I'm going over to see the fans because it's their day and it was great. Getting the trophy was fantastic and running round the park, it was great.

Then it was brilliant going over to Wee Jimmie's and the fans are all cheering, and singing the Pizza Hut song when Armand walks in. Then everybody singing Championees. It was great. You'll always hear me at the end of the season at Cowdenbeath say thanks to people like Tam (the club secretary) and Bert (kit man) because they are the people who make the club for me. After Wee Jimmie's we went back to the manager's house in Edinburgh then into the town to celebrate. By that time I was knackered. It ended up I was phoning everybody walking home at three o'clock in the morning, telling my mum how much I loved her and my sister how much I loved her and all that. The next day Fusco was having a barbecue and he was trying to get me to go out. I said I was going to see my daughter and I said, "I was nearly crying going home last night, Fusco." He said "I was in tears walking along the road when I started to think about it." The next couple of days were brilliant as well – loads of pictures and text messages. When I went into the work on the Monday night, they had big pictures on a big plasma screen at Ikea. The PR woman had emailed the Sun and got the pictures sent over. They had the cuttings on the noticeboard, so it was a massive buzz at work. The text messages are still coming in. All the players saying: "How are you doing, champions?" and all that. I think we'll be living on the back of that for a while.

How about next season?
I don't think we've anything to fear, no the way we're playing and the team spirit we've got. The only worry I have is other clubs trying to sign our players. Brechin and Peterhead wanted to sign Fusco, but he preferred to play for Cowden even though he would get more money. He loves it here. Other clubs will have noticed that Liam Buchanan scored 17 goals. He's got great attitude. I've never met a guy who eats, sleeps and breathes football as much as him. When Markus comes back fully fit other teams will be after him. He can certainly play at a higher level, at SPL. Mark Baxter as well. Graham Guy has come in and played different positions and has played really well. In fact you could go through the whole team. If we have a good start – and I think we will – other clubs will be looking at our players. That's my only worry for next season. But I'm looking forward to it. We'll go into the season with our confidence high.

4. THE CHANCELLOR OF THE EXCHEQUER

Being in politics is like being a football coach. You have to be smart enough to understand the game and stupid enough to think it's important. –
Eugene McCarthy

Gordon Brown, MP for Kirkcaldy and Cowdenbeath and Chancellor of the Exchequer, was proud to be invited to hand over the Championship trophy. Here he talks to Sandy Ferguson about the importance of football in the community.

Did you play football at school?
I played football as well as rugby.

What position?
I liked to play forward all the time. I was called Speedo!

What was the first team you supported?
Raith Rovers and then Cowden. My father told me that he attended matches at Central Park when Cowdenbeath won promotion in 1923/24. He was nine years old at the time.

Which footballer do you most admire?
Jim Baxter. Did you know that Raith sold him to Rangers for £17,000?

Who were the best Raith players you saw?
Willie McNaught. Ah yes Drummond, Colville, McLure, Young, McNaught, Leigh, McEwan, Kelly, Copeland, Williamson, and Urquhart.

Q. Any memories of Raith-Cowden derbies?
Ask me after next season's derbies!

Have you read Black Diamonds and the Blue Brazil?
Yes. I was particularly struck by the interplay of the history of Cowdenbeath
Football Club with the social and community aspects.

Before the Elgin match, did you think Cowden would do the business?
Before the match? Oh yes.

How did you feel handing over the trophy?
It was a really great day for the football club and for the Cowdenbeath community.
The atmosphere was special with so many fans there, men, women and children. I
was conscious of just how much it meant to the fans and to the town.

What are your feelings about how the club is run - no debt, youth teams etc?
Prudent! Gordon McDougall and the board are very sensibly building for the
future.

How important do you think the football club is to the local community?
Very important. This is the way ahead for clubs who need to engage fully with the
wider local community. Raith have very recently appointed a community director.

*Will your son John be the first Honorary Supporter of the Cowdenbeath Junior
Supporters Club?*
Oh yes I'm sure.

5. THE CLUB SECRETARY

After the match an official asked for two of my players to take a dope test. I offered him the referee. – Tommy Docherty.

Tam Ogilvie and I go back a long way – to primary school, in fact. After school, our lives took different paths. Following a couple of jobs on leaving school, Tom joined the police force at the age of 19, and he was a policeman until he had "served his time" and retired from the force. (When he was a policeman, Tam played at Central Park, for the police against the Cowdenbeath Royals.)

He has been club secretary since the 1991-2 promotion-winning season. The secretary helps to keep the club functioning – he handles player registrations, players' contracts, making sure match officials are contacted, etcetera: "all sorts of mundane things", as Tam puts it.

Gordon McDougall relies on Tam - who is now a director of the club - a great deal. When, in an interview for the club website, the chairman was jokingly asked how he had put up with Tam Ogilvie all these years, he replied: "Tam does a great job. Some boy, Tam - a real character with his heart totally in Cowdenbeath and football. He hates referees and loves his job. We do have our ups and downs but I could do with many more like him."

Whenever I meet Tam at Central Park he complains with characteristic humour to anyone who's listening that I didn't mention him in *Black Diamonds and the Blue Brazil.* I promised him that if I ever wrote a sequel, I would rectify that. So here we go, Tam.

How long have you supported Cowden?

Since I was about five years old. So that's about 61 years. My dad used to take me to matches.

When were you first associated with Cowdenbeath Football Club?

When I was 11 years old. I was a ballboy at Central Park from the age of 11 till I was 15. I did a bit of scouting for Cowden, and then I became announcer at Central Park. I was appointed secretary when John Brownlie was manager.

Tell me about your time as announcer.

In one game against East Fife, one of the Cowden players was having a terrible game. I said to someone, "We need to take that clown aff". I didn't know that the microphone was still on, and my words were heard throughout the ground. In fact the player was taken off soon afterwards. John Brownlie said to me after the game, "I believe you were criticising me during the game!" There was a bit about it in the *Evening News* under the heading "Sound Advice from the Tannoy."

So tell me about this season, Tam. Hasn't it been wonderful?

It was brilliant. Right at the beginning I wasn't sure whether we'd go up or not, but Mixu came in and got things into shape. He began to get the team to play in the way he wanted and I became more hopeful that we'd be promoted. We had that great run, winning ten games out of 11 and it made a great difference. There were lots of good things during the season. Mikko was a good signing for us, although he seemed out of touch when he first came over from Finland. Once he was fit he was really good. The horrific injury to Markus stood out as well. The referee was a joke that day, and I reported him to the SFA. When Markus was hurt in that tackle, everyone could see that he was in pain but the referee waved to him to get up and he ran up the field. When Mikko told him Markus was badly hurt the ref booked Mikko for dissent! It was an absolute disgrace. The players were fantastic through the season. They all enjoyed playing for Mixu, they played as one. That long run of games on midweek days as well as Saturdays was amazing.

One of the lowest points for me was losing to East Fife for the first time in years. Another low point was the draw at East Stirling after beating Stenny. I complained to Mixu about not winning the game, and he said to look on it as a point gained. The second last game of the season against Queen's Park at Hampden was a big result for us. In some ways we were fortunate, I suppose, because Queen's outplayed us in the first part of the game. The boys kept battling away, then big John Ward was sent off. My heart hit my stomach when the referee awarded a free kick against Davie Hay for time-wasting, but the boys held out. They were out on their feet at the end of the match. It's a great testimony to their fitness that they went through that long run and won so many games.

Now tell me honestly Tam, when it came to the last game of the season were you confident we would beat Elgin?

No I wasn't. I was nervous as anything. I hadn't slept for about two weeks worrying about what would happen. I was like a bear with a sore head. We'd hammered Elgin in the last game, but I thought they'd really be up for it this time. I kept thinking how flat it would all be if we lost - the players and the supporters would be shattered. The team played well, and when we went 2-0 up I thought we were home and dry. Then when Elgin scored I was worried again. I kept nipping out to look at the teletext to see the Berwick score. Then when yon Elgin boy broke through and hit a screamer just over the bar I could hardly watch. I couldn't believe how much injury time the referee played. It was like his watch had stopped. I don't know where he got all that injury time from. When the final whistle went it was just great.

And that helicopter.....

Seeing the helicopter coming over Central Park was one of the greatest highlights of my life. It was wonderful. And then the night at Wee Jimmie's, just great.

How would you rate Mixu as a manager?

I've known about twelve managers, and Mixu and Craig Levein have been the best. Craig did a really good job for us, really getting us promoted, and there's not much to choose between them – but Mixu won the Championship.

It's amazing to have almost all the squad signed up at this stage, isn't it? We're usually scrambling about at the last minute.

I know. I used to burn the midnight oil getting all the player registrations in.

How do you think we'll do next season?

I'm confident we'll stay up.

6. THE YOUTH TEAM COACH

*The players will receive only two-thirds of the extra bonus they were on for
entertaining, despite winning 6-1. There was some slackness and mistakes.*
                                                                    - Jim McLean

Cowdenbeath FC's youth set-up is the envy of many clubs in Scotland. I
asked Under-12s coach and Dundee United fan Grant Letham to describe
the season – especially the impact of the "Mighty Finn", who Grant used to
watch score goals at Tannadice…..

*I'm an Arab, I used to be proud to be an Arab but now I'm just resigned
to it! As I finished university I made the weekly pilgrimage to Tannadice
to watch Jim McLean's side in the days when we were feared throughout
Europe as a footballing side. We signed a young Finnish striker called Mixu
– he was 'no bad' but like many before him, he fell out of favour with Wee
Jum and was on his way to Aberdeen. Before he left, Mixu managed the
unthinkable. United were 2 – 1 down at Ibrox in the Scottish Cup. There
was five minutes to go when Alan Irvine (now Davie Moyes' assistant at
Everton) shimmied past Terry Butcher and put over a peach of a cross that
Mixu bulleted past Chris Woods in the goal. The top tier of the Broomloan
Road stand went mad as the players celebrated in front of us. Coming from
behind to get a draw against Souness' team that was beating all before
them!*
       *The next time that I saw Mixu was in the 1993 Cup semi final when
we beat Aberdeen in a replay, in no small part thanks to Brian Welsh's last
minute equaliser at Hampden. I suppose that's the reason for me writing
this. I met Brian Welsh on a coaching course at McDiarmid Park and*

offered him a chance to have a look at some of the players in the team that I coached. Nothing happened for months then all of a sudden and quite out of the blue, I got a call asking me to come along and help out the Under-12 side who were struggling for players. We did alright and as a result our whole team became the Cowdenbeath FC Under-12 side for this season.

At the start of the season, the first team staff had nothing at all to do with our team. After Dave Baikie's unfortunate departure from the club there was co-incidentally a youth coaches meeting before a new manager was in place. Gordon hinted at someone perhaps coming in who would have a high profile and would want to be very involved in the youth system. How right he was.

Cowden's season was about to change for the better and it was all thanks to the Under-12 side. Not unlike the first team, they had a good start to the season – going undefeated until well after Christmas when the size of the squad rather than the quality of our players began to take its toll. Just before the CIS Cup tie against St Johnstone, the club asked the boys to take on the job of ball boys at Central Park. The rest is, as they say, history. A spirited display against the Perth saints (not to mention one of the goals of the millennium by Gribben) was the beginning of the revolution. As I sat with the other parents in the stand, there was a big blonde guy that I recognised sitting in front of us. Little did we know how far the Mixu revolution would take us in such a short time.

The first thing that struck me about Mixu was that he appeared to be genuinely interested in all aspects of the club. He always had time to talk about the games and he would put himself out to make sure that we had everything we needed for the boys. His door was always open and he was always keen to share his ideas on how the game should be played – for me as an enthusiastic amateur, this is an immeasurable privilege and pleasure. We aren't talking about a guy who has flirted with senior football; this is a man who had played at the highest level in both Scotland, England and also in international football. Have you ever met anyone who has been marked by Laurent Blanc and Marcel Desailly?

I combined my season ticket at Tannadice with watching Cowden whenever I could. It is fair to say though, that I never got nearly as much enjoyment at Tannadice as I did at Central Park last year. Mixu encouraged the players to play attractive, attacking football – how many other teams played 4-3-3 like we did? The effect on our own team was amazing too – the boys saw how the first team played and tried to emulate them in their own games. It's amazing how motivated those 12-year-olds get when you tell them that the coach of their team has a bet on with Mixu that his team will score more goals than the first team at the weekend. He never did buy me that pint!

The Cowden season had a few memorable moments – with the highs thankfully far greater in number than the lows. From my point of view here are but a few....... The bruising encounter with Arbroath on a freezing cold Tuesday night in December, when the Cowden midfield were kicked more times by the Red Lichties than the ball was!.....The chairman's wife Lillian getting locked in the kit room under the stand by the ball boys one half time!......Getting on the minibus one Sunday morning and having to tell my group of 11-year-olds that Markus had been seriously injured the day before and had to have surgery to repair the damage done. They played like demons that day for him – Gretna paid the price for that tackle. I'm sure that they also sent him the best 'Get Well Soon' card......Standing at Hampden and hearing the welcome that Markus' return got from the travelling Cowden fans.....Seeing Central Park full of supporters for the final nervy game of the season and watching the ballboys planning their routes onto the pitch in order to celebrate with the team!.......The helicopter – it blew up so much dust that Gordon McDougall had tears in his eyes!

7. THE KIT MAN

Bert Johnston is one of the backroom boys who makes the club tick. Now aged 70, he's been helping out at Central Park since he was aged five. He used to live down the road from me in Stenhouse Street; now, still on a high three months after holding the coveted Championship trophy, he answers my questions about boots, characters and helicopters.

How did you first get involved with Cowden, Bert?
My father, Willie Johnston, used to help the Cowdenbeath trainer, Davie Stewart. I used to go down with my dad, and at the age of five I was scraping the players' boots. Davie Stewart encouraged my dad, who was a miner, to take all his certificates and he eventually became the trainer at Central Park. So I was involved one way or another. I was always a supporter and, as you know, we've had a lot of bad times as well as good. One day Eric Mitchell, who was a director, asked me to come in and help with different things at Central Park. Then when Jim Baxter, the kit man, had a heart attack three years ago, Gordon McDougall said to me, "You're retired, Bert. How do you fancy doing the job till Jim gets better?" Gordon said it would involve a couple of hours on a Friday, but it evolved into practically a full-time job! I do it for love.

What does the job of kit man involve?
You lay out the strips and boots in the dressing room for the home games, and pack them up for the away games. At Jim Baxter's funeral this week, his son gave the eulogy and he said that Gordon had told his father it would mean two hours on Mondays, Wednesdays and Fridays – and he ended up with the keys to the stadium! I recognised what he was talking about. Anything I could do to help the club, I would do. I get a lot of ribbing about Cowdenbeath from Rangers and Celtic and Hearts and Hibs fans, but I don't mind. Cowdenbeath's my home town and I've always supported the club.

At the start of the season, did you envisage winning the Championship?
No, we had the upset at the beginning of the season when Dave Baikie left. He had

153

signed the players, and then we had to have a new manager and I wasn't expecting anything. Then Mixu came in. He's a great lad, Mixu, absolutely amazing. He got the team playing the way he wanted to, and as a forward himself he believes attack is the best form of defence. Not only that, the atmosphere in the dressing room has been amazing, it was buzzing. When you've got 16 players five are going to be disappointed if they're not playing, and that can be a problem sometimes, but not with this team. They all back each other up and encourage each other, even if they're not playing.

Who are the biggest characters in the dressing room?
Wee Buchs (Liam Buchanan), he's a great character. Mark Baxter's a great patter merchant. Big Innes Ritchie is the calming influence. Davie Hay and Markus are quieter types, but they're all great lads. All the banter in the dressing room is good.

Tell me about the final game of the season.
Well, that was the icing on the cake, wasn't it? My grand-daughter – unfortunately she's a Dunfermline supporter! – was at the Elgin game and she was filming bits of it. She says to me, "You were running around like a banshee! You'd think it was the World Cup you'd won!" It was a great feeling when that helicopter came over with the trophy. There are so many highs and lows as a Cowden fan, and we all accept that. When Rangers or Celtic or Dunfermline aren't winning, the crowds drop. We're poor relations in Fife, but we have a loyal band of supporters who're always there, even in the hard times. So winning the Championship was special. We've won promotion before, but nobody ever remembers who the runners-up were. They always remember who the Champions were. I was only three years old the last time we won the Championship, so this was the first time I'd actually seen it. It was amazing. You see it on the tee-shirts and the strips, "Third Division Champions", and it's great. I've got all the cuttings, because Cowden have made football history and it was great to be there.

8. THE CULT STRIKER

The game's never over till the fat striker scores – John Robertson, Hearts

Without the inspired signing of French striker Armand Oné, we might not have won the Championship. Born in Paris on 15 March 1983 to parents from the Ivory Coast, Armand has played a lot of his football in the UK. When he first came to Scotland, he found that the game was faster and more attacking here. The Cowden fans were disappointed at the end of the season when Oné signed for Raith Rovers, but with a new baby to support, he needed to take the best offer he could get. I caught up with him when he was feeding the baby.

Armand, How did Mixu get in touch with you?
I think he got my details from St Mirren, and my agent got in touch with me.

Did you remember Mixu when you were on trial at St Mirren?
Oh yes, he was a very good coach. He was always telling me things to do to improve my game. Working with him was a good experience.

Why did you sign for Cowden?
Because Mixu wanted me.

When you first went to Central Park, what was your impression of the team?
There was great team spirit, like a family. I said to Mixu there's a good squad here, we could really do something.

Did you think we could win the Championship?
Yes. I'd played two games for Albion Rovers against Stenhousemuir, and they were top of the league. I knew the level of their play, and I thought we could do better than them.

Any particular goal you scored stands out in your mind?
I think the last one in the game against Elgin City, because that won the Championship.

Were you really nervous that day?
No, not at all. I was really confident we would win. The Cowden team really work for each other and give more than 100 per cent in every game. They never give up.

How do you think Cowden will do in the coming season?
I think they'll do well. They won't be relegated. They're a good team.

Any particular players you think will do well at a higher level?
Liam Buchanan. Lots of them. I think the defence is very good. Innes Ritchie is a very good player. Although the forwards were scoring goals, the defence did very well. We finished with the same points as Berwick but our goal difference was much better. If the defence hadn't been so good, that wouldn't have happened.

What are your ambitions now?
To get back into shape and score lots of goals and be the best striker in the league.

As long as you don't score too many against Cowden! Did you know Raith Rovers were our local rivals?
I didn't actually know that until after I'd signed for them! A Cowden supporter asked what I was doing, and I said I'd just signed for Raith Rovers. He said Oh no, that's our rivals. If I'd known that I might not have signed for them!

I'm sure you'll always get a good reception at Central Park.
I hope so!

Thanks for helping us win the Championship.
It's a pleasure.

9. THE LEADING GOALSCORER

If it was a straight choice between having sex and scoring a goal, I'd go for the goal every time. I've got all my life to have sex. – Andy Gray

Liam Buchanan is product of the highly regarded Blue Brazil youth system, which he joined from Hearts at the age of 17. He was a prolific scorer for the under-19 side. Liam made his debut in the Second Division against Fife rivals Raith Rovers and has made many of his appearances from the bench. Despite this, he has scored a reasonable number of goals and has established himself as a first team regular this season. 'Buchs' really came of age in the 2005/06 Championship-winning season under Mixu Paatelainen's guidance, finishing the season as top scorer with 17 goals from 31 (4 sub) appearances.

Liam, who is a plumber to trade, is not big for a striker – 5' 9" and weighing 10.4 stones - but he is an excellent penalty-box player and a hard worker. Now turned 21 years of age, big things are expected of him in the Second Division campaign. Sandy Ferguson interviewed him for *Helicopter Dreams*.

What was your week like before the game?
I couldn't sleep. I was very restless and was dreaming of scoring the winning goal. The week seemed to last for ever.

How was Mixu?
The gaffer was great. He kept everybody calm. We were all much sharper at training during the week.

What were the highlights of the season?
Obviously winning the Championship. Personally being able to score a few goals. Mixu showed belief in me by giving me a regular team place, which really helped my confidence.

How did you feel when you knew Cowden had won the Championship?
I thought the ref was prolonging the game and we had several near things. The game seemed never-ending and I just felt total relief at the final whistle.

And finally getting your hands on the trophy?
Absolutely great. Better players than me have never won a trophy or medal. The whole day was fantastic. To see the big crowd of fans with the flags and colours and how they reacted gave us all an extra lift.

How do you think you will do next season?
Mixu likes us to play positive attacking football and I expect to score a few goals. The team will not be satisfied with mid-table and I think we can challenge for a play-off place.

How has Mixu improved your game?
He has given me confidence and belief by knowing I have a regular starting place in the team. He has also helped me to improve my skills as a team striker and my goal-scoring abilities.

10. THE YOUNGEST DEBUTANT

Q: What do you call a Dunfermline supporter with a good knowledge of football?
A: Unique.

Chris Hughes, recently turned 17, is the latest product of the Blue Brazil youth system to come through to the first team squad, making his debut as a sub against Elgin City. Chris is an ambitious and focussed young man who is very mature for his age. He has recently started in a job with the Royal Bank of Scotland in Edinburgh. Mixu Paatelainen is confident the youngster has a bright future.

Sandy Ferguson interviewed Chris for *Helicopter Dreams*. With Chris living in rival town Dunfermline, Sandy starts with a question which makes Chris burst out laughing.

What is a Townie doing playing for Cowdenbeath?
At least I live at the right end of Dunfermline towards Halbeath! I was spotted by Bert Paton at the Fife school trials and signed up for the Pars for three years. I played for the under-12s and under-15s. I have also played for Inverkeithing, Rosyth and the Blue Brazil Boys Club. Gary Miller (under-15s coach) signed me up for Cowden last year on trial for the under 17s.

What is your favourite position?
I prefer centre back but can play centre midfield.

What was it like making your debut for Cowdenbeath?
The Elgin match away was the first time I was picked as a sub. I was very surprised. Mixu told me during training at Aberdour on the Thursday before the match against Albion Rovers that I would be making my debut as a sub. It was quite a shock. Mixu told me what to do and I was very excited to replace Armand One and make my debut. I was so happy that Cowden finished winners and got the three points.

Who do you model yourself on?
I watched Norrie McCathie as a young boy and he was my hero.

And Mixu?
Mixu said it doesn't matter how young you are. He is a really good man-manager and tells you what he expects of you.

What do you think of the youth set up at Central Park?
The coaching staff are great. There are more boys coming through than at Dunfermline and the set up is much better.

If you had to pick, who do you think will be the first Cowden youth player to be capped for Scotland?
Paul McBride.

How do you think Cowden will do in the Second Division?
All the players think we will do very well. I am excited and want to go on and play for a regular place in the squad next season.

Finally why do you have the nickname Duracel?
Because I was the fittest of the Under-17s.

11. THE LEAGUE'S STAR PLAYER

Marco played football like a ballerina, like Nuryev with a colossal body
– Rene Marti, Swiss specialist who treated Marco van Basten

Markus Paatelainen has star quality. It's no surprise that he was voted by his peers as the best player in the Third Division. He took a few games to settle at Central Park, but once he was match fit he became a stand-out on the park. His skills on the ball are a joy to watch, and his ability to drift past defenders as if they weren't there means that there is a sense of expectation every time he gets the ball. The standing ovation he received at Hampden after his recovery from a serious injury showed just how much the Blue Brazil fans admire this classy player. I asked him about his background, his impressions of the season at Central Park, the injury at Elgin, and his ambitions in the game.

Where were you brought up?
In Valkeakoski, 20,000 people, small town in the middle of Finland.

How many were in your family?
- Dad Matti, Mum Marjut, and brothers Mixu, Mikko, dog Kevin and cat Kidi.

When did you start playing football?
I started playing when I was four years old.

Are there good facilities in Finland?
Nowadays facilities in Finland are even better than in Scotland. There are a lot of very good indoor astro-turf pitches where you can train in wintertime, and a lot of good grass pitches at summer. When I started, winter facilities were not as good as now. Many times we had to train on ash pitches in the summer too and wooden surface indoors in winter time.

Tell me about your football career in Finland.

161

Started playing at four years old, went through youth ranks in Valkeakoski's top team FC Haka. After under-19s I moved to Helsinki to play for AC Allianssi (Finnish premier league). Spent there two seasons and then went on loan to another Finnish premier league side FC KooTeePee for one season. That season was good, I was first team regular, scored five goals and was named for the Finnish under-21s national team for the first time. After the season, in January I went on trial to Aberdeen and won a contract to the end of the season, and the next season signed for Cowden!

What did you think of football in Scotland?
Compared to Finnish football it's more tactical and quicker, I mean tempo is higher.

Was it an advantage or a disadvantage to have Mixu as a high-profile player ahead of you?
Being Paatelainen in Finland means that everybody expects goals from you because my father Matti and Mixu have played striker in the national team and scored lot of goals. I don't know if it's advantage or a disadvantage, because it's always been like that for me, you know. But when I came to Scotland, it was definitely an advantage, because Mixu knows about everybody here, so he has been able to arrange me those opportunities to go on trial - but after that it's all about myself doing well. I'm sure no one thinks I am a better player just because my brother was great. I don't really think that I need to beat Mixu's scoring record or become better than he was. I'm just enjoying my football here in Scotland and play as high as possible, with my own skills and attributes!

When Mixu asked you to sign for Cowden, what was your first response?
"I have to think about it." First I was a bit concerned is the football good enough in the Scottish Third Division because I compared it to the Finnish third division, which is poor, and would it be right decision to go down three divisions after last season with Aberdeen? We went to see that cup game against St. Johnstone at Central park at the start of the season and even though we lost that game 2-3 I saw that standard here is far better than I had thought. The other thing I wasn't sure was how it would be like to be the manager's wee brother in a team! But the main reason I signed for Cowden was the chance to improve as a player. Mixu said to me, "Come to Cowdenbeath for a year or two, improve your game and skills under my coaching and then move back up there." After a good chat with Mixu I decided to sign for Cowdenbeath and what a great decision was that!?

When you started playing for Cowden, did you think we had a chance of promotion?
Of course! Cowdenbeath finished third in the year before I came so I knew we had every chance.

When you were injured at Elgin, were you aware how serious it was?
First I thought it was just a heavy knock, but on the road back down the pain started to rise and in Edinburgh it was so horrible for me that I started to think something isn't right and went straight to hospital. That was the best decision of my life!

It must have been a shock to learn that you could have lost your leg.
It's not nice to hear there is a possibility that your leg might get amputated! Shocking.

What did you do to get back to fitness?
After all nothing was broken, so I was able to start running quite quickly after I got home from the hospital. Basically it was swimming, cycling, running and weights for four weeks. Just hard work.

Were you determined to play again before the end of the season?
All the time my goal was to be at least on the bench in the final game against Elgin.

In the last game of the season, were you confident we'd win?
Yes I was!

How did it feel when the final whistle blew?
Felt great! First time I'd won anything in football. And it was relief because the weather was so hot that day. Too hot for a match!

What are your ambitions in the game?
To play as high as possible, but the same time enjoy it as much as I do now in Cowdenbeath.

Anything you'd like to say to the fans?
Once more I would like to say a big thanks to every one of you who supported me when I was injured! You pulled me through!

12. THE NEWSPAPER EDITOR

Fans with typewriters – Daily Mail reporter JL Manning on Scottish football journalists.

Jim Stark is editor of the *Central Fife Times*, local correspondent for a number of newspapers, and announcer at Central Park. He explains how he got into journalism, and how he felt about the Championship season.

Where were you brought up?
Dunfermline.

How did you get into journalism?
A friend tipped me off about a junior reporter job at the Dunfermline Press.

When did you become editor of the Central Fife Times?
July 1989.

Do you cover the home games for other papers?
I cover Cowden home games for the Times, Sunday Post, Sunday Mail, News of the World and the PA teletext service.

When did you start as announcer at Central Park?
During the 2003-2004 season.

Were you optimistic about Cowden's chances of promotion at the start of the season?
I was hopeful of a good run under Dave Baikie but did not expect the climax to the season which transpired.

What did you make of the Dave Baikie business?

I was very surprised because the man seemed unruffleable. Even the 8-0 home defeat from Gretna did not seem to upset him. Clearly what happened that night in Dundee was one of those things that can occur when feelings are running high.

How did Mixu impress you when you first encountered him?
Mixu immediately struck me as one of those guys who are larger than life. I would imagine he has a few things up his sleeve which will leave the Second Division gasping.

What, for you, were the definitive moments of the season?
The arrival of Mark Baxter and Markus Paatelainen set the tone. I suppose there were a few pivotal moments such as the 4-1 home win over Stenhousemuir, the 1-1 home draw with Berwick - the only point off them - then the 2-1 victory at Ochilview, followed by Paul McBride's late equaliser against East Stirling. It turned out to be such a vital goal.

When Berwick, then Stenhousemuir, took big leads, did you still think we were in with a chance?
To be honest I was thinking purely of a play-off place by the beginning of February and take it from there. I was so wrong.

Tell me about the big day - 29th April.
It was a day which stood alongside the Brechin match when we won promotion in 2001. Everything about the day was so special and I only wish more of the people who turned up would do so on a regular basis. What a difference it would make. Not many clubs, even Man U, have the Chancellor of Exchequer on hand to present the league trophy!

How do you think we'll do next season?
It will be tough but as I indicated earlier I feel Mixu will have a few surprises in store for the opposition. I see sixth or seventh place a real possibility

13. COWDEN FANS

This section gives an understanding of what winning the Championship means to the Blue Brazil supporters who have kept the faith during lots of dark times. I issued a general invitation to supporters to let me have their reflections for *Helicopter Dreams*. Parts of the contributions have already been woven into the narrative of the season. What follows are edited extracts of what remains, along with biographical information about the contributors. Where they have been posters on Pie and Bovril, I've given, with their permission, their posting names.

Some of the contributions are fairly short. In a few exceptional cases, I've used a longer reflection.

(a) Local fans

Stuart Watson *(Blueminer):* Stuart is a 42-year-old operations technician in the petrochemical industry at Grangemouth. Has supported Cowden since he was five or six, and was a ballboy at Central Park.

The final whistle was something else. I forgot my age and invaded the pitch, but I felt like a youngster bounding across the Central Park surface. We had to come off for the trophy presentation, so I was back on the terracing when one of the sweetest sounds I've ever heard reached my ears. The sound of the helicopter bringing the trophy gave me as much of a buzz as the sound of the final whistle going. Watching it circling Central Park is actually my most vivid memory of the whole day and will be hard to beat! After the trophy presentation it was back onto the pitch once again and I was lucky enough to be passed the trophy by one of the players, but when I turned round there were no players near me. I had my Cowden top on, so maybe he thought I was one of them! I did pass it back eventually, but holding it for what seemed like an age was a most exhilarating experience.

Stuart Allan *(The Minertaur* – surely one of the classiest names on P & B.): Stuart, son of club historian David, has just finished his Highers at school.

The last day of the season ended up being one of the best of my life. From the moment the game kicked off to when I left Wee Jimmies with my Dad - what a night that was! My Dad was slighty drunk as he went around the house singing "Oné Oné Oné Oné" at half past one in the morning at the top of his voice! (Please put that in!) He claims he was just very happy - the term "drunk" is how I would describe it!

The game that stood out for me the most was the Stenhousemuir game at Ochilview when we won 2-1. That was the game when I started to believe we had a great chance of winning the league. The way the fans and the players united was unbelievable and I will never forget Dougie Hill's thunderbolt. It was heading straight towards me and I haven't jumped about so much in a long time! This season has had so many great experiences for me - Dubya and Oné, the Arbroath OAP, but the best moment was obviously seeing the helicopter circle around the ground. My Mum and Gran and their neighbours were all out in the streets waving at it as it flew over the town and I will never forget how proud and happy I felt when I saw it fly over.

David Allan (*Cowden Cowboy*): David is simply the best historian of Fife football ever. Forty nine years old, he has supported Cowden since 1966. He is treasurer of the Supporters Club.

Firstly, I believe my son has alleged I was suffering from a degree of inebriation on 29 April - this I admit is true (my late night phone calls with associated lusty choruses to my brother in Preston and elder son Steven in Aberdeen were perhaps somewhat incomprehensible) but it was not as bad as my infamous 10-hour memory blank when the Supporters Club hosted Hooky Leonard's sons' (Ed and Tony) visit to Cowdenbeath a couple of years back!

I was in an internet cafe in Vienna when I heard of the departure of Dave Baikie and would never have believed at that moment the season would have turned out like it did. A highlight for me has been the way, as the season progressed, you could see and feel the momentum building and how remarkably for once the board, management, players and all the fans began pulling together for a shared goal. That's what made the success so much more enjoyable - everyone played their part and believed in the dream! A dream that didn't need Brooks Mileson to bankroll it. Cowden walked the walk while Stenny and Berwick talked the talk. Never once did Cowden fans crow that they would win the title. Even in the last game v Elgin when we went two up there was a brief chorus of 'Championees, Championees' which was rapidly shouted down with those involved being quickly told to shut up.

Numbers swelled remarkably to join us as the season developed. They came because Cowden played thrilling attacking football, there was a greatly admired and respected charismatic manager who delivered the goods, the players had a pride in their jersey, ability and flair and never- say-die spirit, and every time the club got a knock back during the season (and there were many) they refused to give up the quest. There were many new young fans (not just the CCF!) as the season went on, plus families plus long lost fans who discovered or rediscovered the great joy of sharing in your community's club's success rather than the sterile, much-hyped, commercialised televised version of the beautiful game.

The Supporters Club I believe has done much in the last few years - The Fife Shield Quiz bringing together fans from clubs from all over Fife, the 125th Anniversary Badge Competition with Beath High School, the Honorary Supporters Scheme, the 5000th goal competition, a bigger and better Player of the Year function with 11 awards (only 2 awards some 5/6 years ago), the Supporter of the Year award, pioneering hospitality for visiting fans which is now often reciprocated, the Cowdenbeath Hall of Fame with the assistance of the Club website and Jim at the Central Fife Times, running a bus to every single away game in all three seasons I have been involved, looking at the re-formation of a Junior Supporters Club, Meet the Manager meetings, and many other initiatives.

Other random recollections from the season, leaving aside the well known Dubya/Oné, Arbroath OAP and other well-ventilated matters would include: Sheer brilliance of Markus Paatelainen - a throwback to the old style player who excited crowds by taking men on. Worth the admission money alone to see him play. Much- kicked player who doesn't kick back.

I recall too the fantastic run in to the title with 10 games undefeated and one defeat in 15. The quiet confidence that Mixu exuded was so crucial. The game at Stenny on April Fools day when we gave them the 'hunty gowk' was a key turning point. What a following we had that day and the emotional commitment by fans and players was tremendous. It was a triumph of the will (if I can be forgiven for such terminology). Final whistle - pandemonium and the players doing the Soccer AM 'Easy Easy' act. Left the ground and huge volume of Cowden fans doing 'the bouncy' out in the street - it was an amazing scene.

Last day - a day of dreams, drama, and drams. As Lou Reed sang 'Just a perfect day'. My dad saw the 1939 title, his dad the 1914 version. To share this special day with my son was unforgettable. Never heard a cheer like that for a helicopter in my life. The scenes on the pitch and that evening will live with me

169

always. Stuart and I's photo with the trophy is on my living room wall where it will sit for all time. My mother and her neighbours were out of their houses waving to the helicopter as it went over. She had flags out for us when we returned home.

Craig Ferguson (aka Fergie, and *cfc* on the unofficial Cowden site forum). Craig, aged 40, has been supporting the Blue Brazil since 1976. He goes to games now with his nephew, 12-year-old Calum – "He loves it, his room is a shrine to Cowden."

On behalf of myself and the rest of the Wee Jimmie's crew, this has been the best season ever if you follow Cowden, for the quality of attacking football and the amount of goals. The game against Elgin was a bit of a blur, I was too nervous to enjoy it, but I'll never forget that feeling when the ref blew for time up (awesome), or the helicopter over Central Park – been waiting most of my life for that. I couldn't stop the tears at that point. I'd like to thank the players and management of Cowdenbeath FC for making this season unforgettable for us Cowden fans, and to Mixu, who will forever be a Cowden legend from now till he dies.

Dave Tuson Dave is the chairman of the Cowdenbeath Supporters Club, which has done a fantastic job in marking this special anniversary season. Apart from winning the Championship, what does he remember most?

Above all, it's the banter. I'm sure that all supporters will say the same for their team, but to stand in the terracing at Central Park and to be with the loyal few at away games is both a privilege and a pleasure. Saturday afternoons are priceless and I always look forward to Tommy Thomson telling me exactly how many "Away tae buggeries" I've directed at the unfortunate referee (the poor soul was just wandering round Woolworths when someone asked him to referee a game).

Colin Nelson (*Nelly*): Aged 21, Colin was only seven when his brother took him to Cowden's promotion party at Alloa – "I remember thinking I'm going to follow this team all over. When I was 14 I used to see the guys at the back of the bus singing the songs, having a beer and supporting the team passionately. This is what I wanted, and now I'm living it." Colin works in sales and production planning for local company Todd and Duncan which has customers all over the world. Even his Hong Kong agent asks every week whether Cowdenbeath have won!

Me and my ETB and Tea and Scones buddies are proud of the club and fans, mainly proud of the effort the players have put in all season. We have to take a reality check and say these guys are playing for very little money. They are part-time, and most have day jobs. I know our fans take stick on Pie and Bovril, but I think the fans are a credit to the club. We have a far bigger fanbase than our average attendances show, but for the diehards like myself, Derek Neilson, Craig Ferguson, Stuart Watson, this season has been the greatest we have ever seen. When the trophy eventually was in the hands of big Innes who raised it high, at that moment I couldn't have been happier. I don't know if I will ever see Cowden win a Championship again. I certainly hope so but don't think anything will compare with the season just past.

Stuart Juner (*BlooCoo*): A lifelong and passionate fan, Stuart is a 40-year-old IT support manager – "The technology equivalent of Dear Deirdre".

For all the years that I've followed Cowdenbeath there has been a veritable drought in the ocean that is known as success. Depending on how you look at it, success can be measured in different ways, over long or short periods of time. In relationship to football clubs of similar size Cowden aren't the worst but are a way off those who have the luxury of a trophy cabinet or an area of the clubhouse where 'the spoils of war' are displayed with pride.

There were loads of experiences from the season, from the Geoff Capes wannabe pensioner at Arbroath to the assault by a Dunfermline fan on a Stenny fan at the East Stirling-Cowden match. The signing of unfit Frenchman, Armand Oné, one of **the** biggest players to ever have a Cowden jersey stretched over his torso, was viewed as comical by our rivals. They would mock his size and inability to run, but a plateful of words would come back to haunt them when the big man started hitting the back of the net with a great deal of regularity.

The final match day will be something that I will cherish for a long time. I had a gut feeling that we would beat Elgin, we'd won every encounter against them that season. This was by no means arrogance, far from it. I knew what could happen – it was just a gut feel. On the morning of the Elgin game I took my four year old daughter out for the morning papers and nipped into the ground to show her where her dad would be going in the afternoon. This was my field of dreams. As a child I stayed directly opposite Central Park over the railway line, I knew when training or reserve games were taking place as I could hear the players shouting to each other. I'd see the wall that I used to climb over as a kid and saw knocked down in the 70s when gale force winds destroyed the cowshed. Those were the halcyon days to me, still starved of success but something I remember fondly. I looked at the terracing which I knew would be seriously crowded with supporters from near and far who would make the pilgrimage to the Fife Maracana. I looked over at the old stand where my father used to sit with me when I was a kid and I could still visualise some of the 'old faces' that I'd grown up with at Central Park. Working men, no better or worse than the next man – just good honest working men who like to watch a game of football at the weekend. It would've been great if some of them had been there to witness what would unfold during the course of the day.

On leaving I bumped into Gordon McDougall who, to put it in layman's terms, was shitting buttons. He was in a pessimistic mood, but had too much on his mind to organise for the game. I tried to allay his nerves, telling him my gut instinct, but he nervously laughed and grabbed a handful of flags to place around the ground and was off. If our illustrious chairman was in doubt, then could I be wrong? I began to psychoanalyse my thought - Cowden win, league champions, Elgin have never won at Central Park. During the course of the season when Cowden scored first they went on to win the game, Elgin conceding first went on to lose every game. All we had to do was score first. OK - reality check complete. Returning to my car, Mixu, Markus and the physio appeared – I mentioned that I looked forward to having a celebratory drink with them later. Mixu gave me an icy stare and responded with a wink, saying, "Well let's hope so!". He was certainly not taking things for granted, a wry Scandinavian smile to my daughter and both he and Markus went into the ground.

After consuming a hearty breakfast, I made my way to the Junction Bar to meet up with comrades, grabbing the 'Coo Heid' and 8ft Brazil flag from the garage. We would fill the bloodstream with alcohol to keep us going for the remainder of the day. The jukebox was turned off and 'The CooBell Polka' was sounded from the stereo followed closely by 'Una Paloma Blanca' with a few other anthems thrown in to boot. Yes, the atmosphere was building nicely. Leaving the JB at after 1pm we sauntered down the road to Wee Jimmies and met up with a few more hardened disciples of the Cowden cause, and a few 'new' ones as well. The pub was bursting at the seams, we resorted to staying out in the sunshine and having shifts of going to the bar for drinks. The fantastic weather and the opportunity of seeing some history being made certainly dragged a lot of what some people called 'glory hunters' out of their usual Saturday haunts. The number of brand new Cowden t-shirts and replica jerseys were there to prove it. The club shop must've gone like a proverbial fair. Central Park was going to be busy and blue, royal Brazilian blue. After an hour of drinking and singing we began the march to Central Park; 30-odd souls in our band which grew with every pub and street corner we passed. Following Cowden is something that is a more spiritual phenomenon and certainly not something that draws large crowds. Many a Cowden supporter has broken into a cold sweat standing in a queue of a dozen people at Woolworths, never mind the 2500+ that would make the Central Park turnstiles *squeak more than a mouse on viagra.*

The game itself turned out to be excellent, not just from the scoreline, but from the attitude adopted by the players. Mixu had instructed them to go at Elgin, and go at Elgin they did from the first whistle. Even when they were 2-0 up, many managers would have tried to kill the game off. Not Mixu, Cowden went looking for more goals and playing some neat football in the process. Bearing in mind that Elgin could still sneak a play-off place, something that was an ambition for us at the start of the season when Dave Baikie had left the club. We were going for a bigger prize and a win would guarantee it. Even when captain Innes Ritchie left the field of play to a standing ovation we looked solid.

When the final whistle blew the area of terracing where I stood literally erupted. Throats that had been dry from lack of drink for just under two hours and voices that had sung, cheered and roared were now cheering and singing with relief and joy. I stood for what seemed an eternity with my arms in the air, Brazil flag aloft with a smile that could only be surgically removed. Grown men looking around for someone to grab hold of and celebrate. Some tears also flowed but I'm sure that was from the wind changing direction. We had done it - as Innes said in his speech at the end of season dance: "When you look at the league table on Sky, there will be a small 'C' next to Cowdenbeath. That stands for CHAMPIONS." A legendary comment from a great guy and the man can spell as well - not something you'd expect from a Third Division player. Mind you he wasn't a Third Division player any more.

Peter Park *(Auld Pete):* Pete, who has supported Cowden off and on since the 1950s, is 75 years old. It's been a particular delight for him that Cowden have played such flowing, attacking football in this special year.

Without doubt the highlight of my time as a supporter was the sight of that helicopter hovering over Central Park at the end of last season. I do not think of myself as being over sentimental but when that league winners' trophy was presented to the boys the tears came to my eyes followed by a big lump in my throat. I am still floating on cloud nine.

Derek Neilson *(Vince Sinclair):* Derek is a 30-year-old civil servant and a committed member of the Tartan Army as well as a passionate Blue Brazil supporter. Here he talks about 29th April, 2006.

Up at 6am absolutely buzzing. I'd seen us get promotion on the last day of the season against Alloa and Brechin, but this was for the Championship. It was a cracking sunny day. Went through to Cowden and picked up a few Cowden boys. We all met at Sommy's after 10.00am. Watson and me had bought some Champagne which didn't last long. The short walk to Torley's for a pint, then the taxi through to Cowden about 12ish. We just beat the rush, as shortly after we arrived you couldn't move. The atmosphere was unbelievable, the beer was flowing, however most were still nervous. What we'd give for 1-0. When both goals went in it really was party time. I was on the pitch celebrating, couldn't believe we'd done it. Lump in the throat holding back the tears. Only a diehard football fan from the lower leagues could experience this. This was for us and the players, the management, backroom staff and board. I'll never forget the sight then cheer when the helicopter circled Central Park. Can't find any words to describe Wee Jimmie's at night. I'm almost in tears writing this, the hairs on the back of my neck sticking up. Can't wait for next season.

Brian Fraser: Brian is webmaster of the unofficial Cowden website (www.cowdenbeath.net). Brian's father, Ian, is a director of the club and former webmaster of the official Cowden site (www.cowdenbeathfc.com). Father and son have been dedicated Blue Brazil fans for many years. Brian talks about April 29th, 2006.

Scenes of wild jubilation on the pitch, the trophy-bearing helicopter circling the ground, the players performing a lap of honour, these are the memories which will live on forever in the minds of all those present. We had triumphed in winner-takes-all promotion battles against Alloa and Brechin but this was something different - Champions!!! Obviously Mixu must take most of the credit for Cowden's success. His signings proved inspired and he must be applauded for deploying an adventurous three-pronged attack for much of the campaign. Liam Buchanan, Mikko Paatalainen, Andy Jackson, Armand Oné....all these guys grabbed goals galore. We were fortunate to be able to play a settled back four for the entire season and Innes Ritchie and big John Ward were a watertight pairing in central defence.

Mixu said something very shrewd in his speech at the Player-of-the-Year dance. He pointed out that the main reason for lifting the title was the mental toughness shown by the squad as they notched up win after win during the gruelling run-in as the Blue Brazil caught up with their postponed fixtures. I wholeheartedly agree with this point. It's easy to sit back and say, "Oh, we have x amount of games in hand", but winning those games is a different matter altogether. Markus Paatalainen thoroughly deserved his Supporters' Player of the Year award but special mention must go to Liam Buchanan. The Wee Man has really blossomed under Mixu's tutelage and is now an all-round attacker who worries defences constantly. There were many more players whose contributions were invaluable. Midfield playmaker Gary Fusco, goalkeeper Davie Hay....the list is long. I'd like to thank every one of them for making this the best season of my life, although I do hope to still be around in 67 years time for the next one!

Sandy Ferguson *(Blue Brazil Forever):* Big brother of the author, Sandy went straight from Beath High School to the Foreign Office in London. He served in Rangoon, Kuwait, Macao, Beirut, Yokohama (scored 49 goals in one season for the local side and captained them when they beat the South Korean national side), Brazil, Georgetown, Fiji, Baghdad (HM Consul during the Iran-Iraq war), Lisbon, Kingstown St Vincent, before retiring in 1996. His latest assignment is Vice-chairman of Cowdenbeath Supporters Club.

I attended all the Cowden fixtures home and away - many highlights including Downsie's 5000th league goal at Cliftonhill, the unexpected implosion at Gayfield when Beaky met the Smokie Pensioner, the despair of Markus suffering a career-threatening injury at Elgin, the daft goal at Berwick when Davie Hay was adjudged to have carried the ball outside the area, the 6-0 dismantling of Queens Park.

The week before the Elgin game was a sweaty one. Like Liam Buchanan and others from the Cowden squad, as well as a goodly number of the Central Park faithful, I couldn't sleep. However by midweek I had calmed down. Gordon Brown emailed to say he would be attending the game. When I phoned the news through to the club it was Mixu who answered the phone and I like to think that, like me, Gordon's willingness to attend gave him confidence (I heard that he too was suffering). On Friday night I went to Edinburgh Airport to pick up my son Steven. I was totally surprised when not only my boy but my other son Robert and all wives and three grandchildren were waiting. I went early to the game with my two sons and with Holly and Jake my two older grandchildren. It was a lovely late spring day, a large crowd of men, women and children with a carnival atmosphere and the old stadium was bedecked with Scottish, Brazilian and Finnish flags. The final whistle, the scenes of total jubilation and the hair rising again on the back of my neck as the helicopter circled the ground. Finally, finally Gordon Brown presents the Trophy. I was thinking of my dad Joe and grandad Sandy, of Willie Anderson and of the many, many Cowden supporters before them. Truly, the realisation of a dream as my brother and sister and three generations of Fergusons celebrated. The Supporters Club Player of the Year party that night at Wee Jimmies turned into a total celebration. It was an emotional moment for me to give the first ever Joe Ferguson Shield to Mark Baxter as the young website player of the Year. But I was almost completely overwhelmed when the Supporters Club awarded the Lord Ewing Shield as Cowden Supporter of the Year jointly to Ron and myself. As I write, I can see the Shield and the accompanying medal. Also in my study I can also look at the huge framed picture of Mixu and myself clutching the Championship trophy. I have I suppose supported Cowden for over sixty years. I always knew in my heart that The Day would come and I will forever remember it. To all lower league club supporters: keep the faith and your day will come too.

Andrew Mullen *(Cowdenbeath):* Co-editor of the Cowdenbeath football programme, Andy is a very committed fan who does a lot of work behind the scenes.

After spending the last 30 odd years watching Cowden, to finally see us win a league Championship has been nothing short of amazing. I thought winning promotion in 1992 and 2001 was great, but to actually win a trophy was really something else. Looking back now it is quite funny thinking about almost 3000 people getting excited about a helicopter, but when we heard the noise we finally knew that the Championship trophy was going to be ours.

It was really against the odds that we won the title; well being Cowden, nothing is done the easy way. Firstly losing your manager at the start of the season then losing your star player half way through, but we did it in the end. I remember being in Wee Jimmies after the Scottish Cup defeat after spending the morning with a round 20 or so diehards clearing the snow, and I said to Stuart Watson if we won the championship I wanted my photo taken with Mixu and the Cup. Maybe I was being optimistic at the time but I'm glad to say I now have my photo. In my view the thing that got us past the final hurdle was team work. Our boys worked well for each other and when the going got tough they stood up and were counted. Also Mixu is so professional in his whole attitude and it rubs off on the players. Thanks Mixu and all the lads for making my dream come true. It has been a long wait but it has been worth it.

Stewart Miller (farmer from Clarkston in Glasgow)

I have followed Cowdenbeath FC for about 40 years, including the good times and bad and even worse. Following a team like Cowdenbeath and living in the west of Scotland is not the easiest of pastimes and I have had to have a fairly thick skin to try and deflect the amount of abuse I get, although I have to say it's all fairly good- natured. A good sense of humour is an added advantage. I started following them around 1966/67 when Andy Matthew was the manager, followed by Archie Robertson who, by coincidence was a former BB officer in our local company. It was a real joy to witness the halcyon days of 1970 when we led the league all season only to be pipped by Falkirk near the end. It was a real blow when Johnny Dickson and Jim McArthur were sold.

I could only ever get to watch the team when they came through to the west and I remember chatting to Jim McArthur as he stood in his goal one evening at Lesser Hampden, such was our dominance in that game. I can also recall the league cup semi when we were horsing Rangers until Quentin Young sneaked a goal, but then again, I am maybe wearing my rose-tinted specs. There have been a few dark days over the years as well such as 1976 (I think) when we could only draw against Montrose and allowed Queen's Park to sneak promotion in our place.

I also have a group of friends who check our results each week, merely to fire abuse in my direction. Isn't it strange there has been a deafening silence from them this season. Can't think why. One of my friends is a former goalkeeper and subsequently a former chairman of Queens Park and I told him in the middle of February that if we were to win all our remaining games, we would be Champions. He thought this was a very bold statement to make and I had to help him up off the ground as he fell about laughing. He ain't laughing now! It was a bold statement to make at the time as we were 12 points adrift.

I dragged my son along to Hampden for the penultimate game against Queens Park hoping to witness Cowdenbeath actually winning something. Going into the break 2-1 down wasn't exactly encouraging and seeing Wardy sent off, mistakenly in my humble opinion, didn't help matters. We thought the point might just secure us the title until a girl sitting next to us told us that Berwick had scored near the end of their game. Oh well, we would just have to do it the hard way.

The date of 29th April will live with me forever. I really wanted to be there but church commitments prevented it happening. I couldn't even be in the house that afternoon and I have yet to receive my phone bill as I was forever phoning my family for an update on our progress. I was ecstatic when I was told we were 2-0 up and I got home with five minutes left to play. I think they were the longest five minutes of my life.

On a personal level, I am married with three long-suffering children and, as the final result eventually came through, I don't think they have ever seen me in such a state. The tears were streaming down and I don't think anyone could have chiselled the smile off my face. My daughter even threw the tissue box at me to dry my eyes. It was a day to compare favourably with our wedding day or the birth of our children. Forty years of suffering jibes and abuse. Forty years of depressing results including that horrendous record of consecutive home defeats were all forgotten and forgiven. The joy and happiness of that day was immense. We could eventually call ourselves Champions.

I have a lot of friends who support Rangers and Celtic and I am sure they cannot possibly know the depth of our happiness as they expect to win something each year, and with that expectation they have become somewhat blasé when they win. I could almost feel sorry for them. Aye, almost. OK, next season we might not win much, we may even get relegated, but at this time, who cares, we have won a Championship at least once in my life and I loved it. In fact I could get used to it. Bring on next season and we may even follow the previous Third Division champions, Gretna; but I think I'm getting carried away again.

(b) Cowden fans in exile

Alex Ross (Adelaide)

I grew up in Lumphinnans and went to school with Stuart Watson. As a lad I used to hate seeing all the buses leaving Fife every Saturday morning full of people going to support the Old Firm, and decided then that I would be a Cowden fan and I have been ever since. After waiting all my life to see Cowden actually win some silverware, I couldn't be there for the last few weeks of the season. At the beginning of the year I was offered a job with the South Australia Police. (I was a police officer in Fife, based, where else, but Methil. It was quite difficult to remain professional when you are on duty and Cowden take the lead at New Bayview).

At that time my mind was on other things but it certainly didn't seem that Cowden would achieve anything more than perhaps a play-off place, if that. As it was, I accepted the offer and flew to Adelaide on the evening of Tuesday 28th March, one week after my last Cowden game, the 4-1 win over East Fife. As the weeks went on Stuart kept me updated by text on Cowden's remarkable progress to the top of the league. I then managed to get some internet access and it was thrilling, but quite surreal, being on the other side of the world reading about the Cowden.

On that memorable day I was of course 8.5 hours ahead of the UK. I actually spent the afternoon attending my first Aussie rules match, Adelaide Crows v. Western Bulldogs. I proudly wore my new Cowden strip to the game, a leaving present from my mates, only to find that the colours were virtually identical to the Bulldogs. Fortunately there isn't the same kind of trouble at matches as there is in Britain. Stuart and I were texting back and forward, keeping me updated with his day, starting with his 8 am barbie. By kick-off I was in an Irish Bar, having had a few, with a load of other UK recruits, who were all rooting for Cowden by this time, as was half the rest of the crowd in the bar.

Stuart managed to get a text through that it was 1-0, but then it seemed like an age before I finally got the simple words "We won 2-1". We all erupted, I was crying, somebody bought whisky then bizarrely the band started playing The Proclaimers' "500 Miles". Absolutely magic. I managed to speak to Stuart on the phone a few hours later, before he went to Wee Jimmies, which was quite emotional.

Funny enough, I'm not the only Cowden fan in Adelaide. Stuart found a guy on one of the websites and I began e-mailing him. His name is Bill Davidson and
*he left Cowdenbeath for Australia in 1947. When he was five his dad took him to Cowden's last Championship-winning game in 1939. I have kept in touch and hope to meet up with him soon. I am waiting on the DVD being sent out and I will give him a copy. (*Helicopter Dreams *has since heard again from Alex: "I had a visitor today, Bill Davidson, the other Cowden fan in Adelaide. Nice old*

178

guy, 72 but very sprightly. He worked in the Holden car factory and used to race motorbikes all around Australia. His last Cowden game was New Year 1956 on a visit home. He sailed here in 1947 with his parents and wee brother and on the boat were about 900 orphans from the war who were being sent to Oz to be adopted by Australian families.")

David Welch, Ipswich *(Cowden123).* David, aged 40, is a security supervisor for a large insurance company in Ipswich.

What might surprise you is that I am English and I support Leeds United. Now why should I have any feelings towards Cowdenbeath? Well it started about nine or 10 years ago when I started to collect Scottish football programmes. Cowdenbeath were the first club I wrote to and since then my love affair with the club has grown.

It wasn't long before I was wearing my first Cowdenbeath shirt to the darts matches on Monday nights, I play in the local league. My mates would often take the mickey out of me and this would lead to other people in the pub joining in, but the more they took the mick the more passionate I became. It got to the point when I got just as upset when Cowden lost as I did when Leeds lost. I now have over 1000 Cowdenbeath programmes and other bits of memorabilia and have just ordered a Championship shirt and framed shirt to put on my wall at home. I consider myself a true Cowdenbeath fan and I would love to set up an East Anglian branch supporters club, of which sadly I am the only member so far. Due to the fact that I work most Saturdays and have a family to support I have yet to visit the ground but I hope that will change soon and I will at last be able to visit the Mecca of Fife.

I get very angry when people say you can't be a fan if you have never been to see them play. Well I may not be there in person but I sure am in spirit and I care very much about the club as much as the next fan does. You might think that because I didn't attend any of the games this year that it couldn't have been as exciting as it was for those who did. Well you would be wrong. I would read all the reports in the papers, visit the P&B and Cowdenbeath web sites every day and tell my mates just how great the Blue Brazil are. It got to the stage when my mates started to take an interest in the results of Cowdenbeath and they would often rib me when we lost.

As for the day itself, I was sadly once again working. I would have loved to have been there but despite the fact I had a row with my boss about getting the weekend off he would not budge and I had to work. I sat at my desk with the internet on waiting for any news to come in. I didn't sit for long, up and down like a yoyo, with my nerves jangling. I just couldn't do anything but drink buckets of coffee just to give me something to do until the goals stated to flow. I didn't have to wait long - 1-0 to the Blue Brazil. I shouted for joy only for the other workers to

179

look at me as if I was a looney. Half time 1-0 up. Could this be the day of all days, the day we win the league? The second half starts and it's not long before I scream out again in joy - 2-0. I can't believe it, and despite the fact that Elgin pull a goal back it doesn't bother me for I know the good Lord won't let me down. I prayed the night before. The results are coming in but for some reason Cowdenbeath's is the last one to come up on my internet. I start to panic. What's going on? How much injury time is he playing, I shout at the screen. Then deep joy as the result pops up. We have done it. That little club from Fife are the proud winners of a title for the first time in 67 years. Could it get any better? Yes, I say to myself, watch us go next year.

Duncan Stark, Boulder City, Nevada, USA. Duncan was a ballboy for Cowden in the 1950s.

I remember in early November 2005 when I walked into the only bar in Las Vegas that regularly shows both Scottish and English football matches. Rangers were playing Celtic that day and I knew several of my new-found acquaintances would be there to support the "big teams". Immediately I was met with a few snickers and laughs, followed by "Eight Nil, your team played well on Saturday" – reminding me that Cowdenbeath had suffered the humiliation of being the victims of Gretna. Having moved to Boulder City, Nevada (just over the hill from Las Vegas) only a few years ago after living for three decades in California, I had made it clear to everyone who would listen that the only team I really cared about was from my hometown of Cowdenbeath and let everyone, who was still listening, know that it was only a matter of time before they would rise to their rightful place among the elite in Scottish football.

Since Cowdenbeath didn't start the past season on the best of notes, my expectations were - how should I say it? - not very high, which led to me keeping a low profile around my friends about their results. As the season progressed and the Blue Brazil started their climb to stardom, I took great pride informing all the locals, and many of the visitors visiting Las Vegas, about the Blue Brazil's rise to the top of the league, usually followed by "Who?". Nobody believed that I would really follow Cowdenbeath's fortunes. As the season wound down and the Championship loomed ever nearer, my cell phone would be inundated with messages asking how they were doing and wishing me luck. I was wearing my Blue Brazil shirt with pride. I was saddened when I heard of the death of Willie Anderson and his son Bill. I had been a close friend of young Bill's prior to emigrating to the States, but then I figured, they were probably in a place where they could put in a good word for Cowden, us having to wait so long for

180

a Championship. That last week leading up to the final match was spent without much sleep, reminiscing about all those times at Central Park, even sneaking in when Paddy (some may remember our local policeman of stature) wasn't looking. I remember the night Celtic came visiting and me, the ballboy, going crazy when "Basher" Murphy scored, even though the score was sort of lopsided by then.

On the last game of this season, when the final whistle went, and Cowdenbeath had won, I couldn't help but sit down and have a wee greet. I don't think anyone else here in Boulder City, or Nevada for that matter, knew or cared about the Great Event that had taken place half way around the world, but I did. The so called "big teams" get their Championships and medals, go to countries that had a different name only a few years ago, but Cowdenbeath ...... "Champions!" It doesn't get any better than this, and they can't take it away from us. PS We had our first USA Blue Brazil Supporters Club Convention last week. Since I am the only member, my wife took a picture of me in my Cowdenbeath shirt.

Stephen White (Organiser of the Mersey Beaths)

There are quite a few of us who keep an eye out for the Beath's score. We first went up in March 2004 when we were staying in Edinburgh for me mate's staggy. We went to see the game against Albion, the ref was called Hardie, and while there were only 258 at the game (we were the eight) he took unbelievable abuse & we felt obliged to join in. One lad Fozzer has talked about Cowdenbeath being his second team for years, mainly because of their nick name "The Blue Brazil" and the rest of us just followed suit. Anyway, it beats the usual crap of one half supporting Celtic or Rangers depending on their religion. We now call ourselves The Mersey Beaths and we will try and catch a game or two next year. Anyway only six of the lads managed to get up to watch the title decider, but they all enjoyed it and it was fantastic to see them lift the Championship for the first time in 67 years. They managed to get their pictures taken with the captain and the cup.

Ian Barrett (Organiser of the Doncaster Lads)

The story of how I became a Cowdenbeath fan began a long time ago, when I was a lad of about eight years old. - I am now 43!! - and a boy from Scotland came to our Junior School. I mated up with him but he wasn't with us for long, about a year, as his dad got a job back up in Scotland. I don't know exactly where it was, just somewhere in Fife. This young lad was a mad football fan so when he left I looked at the map and chose a team in Fife to follow. It was Cowdenbeath.

The years went by and when I was about 18 years old I got a computer with a Football Managers game which I could play on it. The team I picked to play as was Cowdenbeath, and I took them all the way to the European Cup Final !! From then on I seemed to become more interested in them and followed them from afar, watching the results on the TV every Saturday afternoon. All that changed in the 2004/05 season. By this time some of my work mates had also become interested in the fortunes of Cowdenbeath and nine of us decided to have a trip up to Scotland for a game. We went to the home game Cowden had against Peterhead in March 05 and Cowden won 4-1 against all the odds. Since then we have been up to a further three games. The hospitality and reception we have received from everyone in Cowdenbeath has been second to none. Our fan club consists of Ian Barrett, Barry (Duggie) Dudley, George Ingle, Nicky Wilson, Baz Burns, Keith Thompson, John Booth, Bob Wortley, and Paul Rumney. My wife, Anne, is also involved with the fan club as she is the Social Organiser and sorts out all our travel arrangements for the matches we go to. The promotion this year was fantastic and we actually managed to be there at the final game. It was great!!

Steven Ferguson (Ronaldincoo): Steven is a son of Sandy Ferguson. He lives in Bedfordshire.

My name is Steven and I am a Cowdenbeath supporter. There I've said it. Not for me the shame-faced confession at a hushed meeting of Football Fans Anonymous. I am also one of the multitude of Scots that live and work in England, who continue to run Britain. For various reasons, for which I entirely blame my father and his perpetual wanderings around the globe during my formative years, I don't sound Scottish (a source of much interrogation about my ancestry by English friends) yet cut me open and I bleed blue. In a similar vein, not for me the plastic allure of a Manchester United or Chelsea or indeed the two 'get out the Scottish league ya bastards' unmentionables from Glasgow. My great grandfather was a Cowdenbeath man, my grandfather was a Cowdenbeath man and my father is a Cowdenbeath man. The torch has passed to me. I am currently indoctrinating my son, a four-year old, to fulfil his footballing destiny – to be a Blue Brazilian. He owns two Cowden football shirts, which he wears with pride. He catches my whoops of delight at 4.45 on a Saturday afternoon, after Cowden romp to yet another magnificent victory. The time will soon come, when he squares his shoulders, looks me in the eye and says "What's the Cowden score, Dad?" Paternal tears will flow at the accomplishment of a mission. It will be a difficult road though. He announced that he wanted England to win in the World Cup. Dear God. "But you are Scottish, son, like your dad." "No but I like England...." "Who's been telling you this stuff?" I enquired. "Nana," came the reply. Ah, perfidious Albion. Like some demented cultist, my English mother-in-law has been filling his impressionable head with the most insidious of propaganda. The England *underpants and socks I have accepted with good grace. The underpants are worn next to the only part of him that might be English, namely his bum. This latest, and alarming development means, of course, War.*

*Anyway I digress. Running the country doesn't pay as well as it used to, say in 1880, when Cowdenbeath FC was founded. A round trip to Cowdenbeath to be with the 300-odd hardy souls who watch Mixu and the boys play on Saturday is prohibitively expensive. Not being able to attend matches, I have become an avid internet videprinter watcher. Thanks to the technological marvel that is the internet, I can be drawn away from looking at porn by whiling the long, lonely hours staring at the BBC Live videprinter as it updates every two minutes. Just Waiting. Then it chatters: 15.36 SL3 **Cowdenbeath 1 (L.Buchanan 36)** East Fife 0. Get in there my son! I share the agony and ecstasy of every Cowden fan who is actually there, every minute that ticks by. One of the Stenny fans accuses me of not being a real fan 'coz I'm not attending matches. Away and play wi' yersel' ya eejit.*

Berwick fans are crowing. They thought they would win the league at a canter before a ball was even kicked in anger. Early season appears to prove them right. Eleven points clear at Christmas. All over bar the shouting. Oh ya bloody well think so? Stenny second, Cowden third. We lose to both teams. I swear at the videprinter, at its mute indifference to my suffering. But Cowden keep winning their other games and hang on to the coattails. 2006 starts well for both Cowden and Stenny. Cowden thrash Queens Park 6-0. First signs of panic in the Berwick ranks. By March, Berwick have blown it and the videprinter chatters away merrily dispensing good cheer. Stenny now 11 points clear. Berwick now second, plucky little Cowden still third. Big gap to fourth. We lose Mixu's brother Mikko, an on-loan striker from the Finnish league who had acclimatised and was banging in the goals. We also lose Mixu's other brother Markus, our star player to a thuggish tackle from Shug Dickson, a neanderthal from Elgin City, which puts him out for six weeks. Like some expectant father, I suffer agonising sympathetic pain in my calf. In a stroke bordering on the genius Mixu signs a gigantic, fat, unemployed striker, Armand Oné. I immediately shell out 30 quid to sponsor him. Not a real fan, indeed. Stick that up your pipe, Waldo. Oné starts scoring despite the predictions from, notably Stenny fans, in the Great Oné Betting Scandal, which merits a chapter all of its own.

It is the Stenny fans' turn to crow. All over bar the shouting. Oh ya bloody well think so? With the finishing line in sight, Stenny lose their bottle. The Markus-less Cowden keep putting in the results. The videprinter runs red hot, but not for Stenny, and is my friend. We go to Stenny and thrash them 2-1. The Akabusi loyal, the Stenny stalwarts, go into collective meltdown. They have never won a Championship and I sense tears. I would like to say that I feel their pain but it

183

turns out to be only wind. I crack. I must be there for the last game. A Wednesday night. East Stirling v Cowdenbeath. An easy win against the basement team. Like hell. The videprinter sits mute for endless minutes. It chatters into life. East Stirling 1 Cowdenbeath 0. Oh no, please no. I sit hunched in front of my screen in abject misery as the minutes tick away. Who cares how many Rochdale have scored against Hull – what about bloody Cowdenbeath? The videprinter operator must sense my anxiety for he doesn't tell me that Cowden have had a player sent off. Eventually, young McBride scores late on. Final result 1-1. Cowdenbeath second, one point behind Stenny. Four games to go. Saturday, Cowden 2 Albion Rovers 1. Stenny slip up at Berwick – Cowden are top on goal difference. Ohmygodohmygodohmygod! History beckons. We thrash East Stirling at home, followed by a 2-2 draw away at Queens Park. Markus re-appears. Still top on goal difference from Berwick. Beat Elgin at home and we are the champs! My airline tickets arrive. Oh boy....talk about sweaty Saturday.

It arrives – Saturday 29th April 2006 – Destiny day. Three generations of the family are there to watch the match. The atmosphere is enervating. Groups of fans huddle together in nervous anticipation. I'm standing outside the main stand, chain-smoking an endless succession of cigarettes. I see a man behaving furtively, trying to sneak behind us. He is wearing a jacket even though the weather is warm. I see a flash of black & white. "OY YOU, THE ELGIN FAN TRYING NOT TO BE NOTICED, YOU'RE DOWN IN THE OTHER STAND WITH THE OTHER ONE." Official attendance 2600. My arse. 500 kids have leapt over the wall. I reckon at least 4000 are there (and two Elgin fans). I meet Blue Brazilians like me. A bloke up from Oxford. Some from Brighton, Doncaster, even Dublin. The videprinter brigade have turned out in force!

The game itself is a nervy affair. Cowden don't play especially well but goals from Buchanan and the magnificent fat Frenchman Oné make it 2-0 to Cowden. It's all over bar the shouting. Is it hell. Elgin score from a free kick. 2-1 with 20 minutes to go. I feel the onset of a panic attack. The Chancellor of the Exchequer sits 10 feet away from me, white as a sheet. Another videprinter man. At this point I can now disclose the part that I played in Cowdenbeath achieving immortality this season. With five minutes to go, an Elgin player strikes a thunderous volley from the edge of the box. I am behind, right in line with that shot. I will swear to my dying day that the ball was flying, at speed, straight into the top corner of the net, an arrow to shatter the hearts, dreams and hopes of Cowden fans everywhere. The videprinter starts to chatter into life. I lend a hand. My gasp of outrage, dismay and horror flies from my lips, scoops up the ball and lifts it over the bar at the last moment. I feel sick. I'm told later that a referee's assessor sits in the crowd. He describes the ref's performance as the most one-sided officiating he

184

has ever seen in his life. You can take it from me that he wasn't pro-Cowdenbeath. The knob plays six minutes of extra time. Six! I age about 30 years in that time.

The videprinter chatters into life one last time.
16.51 SL3 Cowdenbeath 2 Elgin 1 Cowdenbeath Champions Div 3. I didn't see it. I was there. I saw the helicopter.

14. HOW WAS IT FOR YOU, DEARS?

Though fans of teams in the lower leagues routinely take the mickey out of each other's sides and controversies often become heated, there is an underlying camaraderie. Supporters of lower league sides spend time and money following their so-called "diddy" teams all over Scotland, hoping that at least once in their lifetime they will see the trophy-bearing helicopter land near their ground. Following an unfashionable club which rarely wins anything is not for "glory hunters"; it requires high levels of commitment and willingness to suffer, as well as large dollops of wishful thinking and black humour. So behind the banter, there is a great deal of fellow-feeling.

Blue Brazil fans know from bitter experience the disappointment of missing out on promotion at the death and of losing a Championship on goal difference, so while it would be an exaggeration to say that we cry ourselves to sleep at night over the plight of our rivals, we do, in our noblest moments, have pangs of sympathy. In this spirit of comradeship, *Helicopter Dreams* set aside its triumphalist mask and issued an open invitation to fellow Pie and Bovril fans to comment on the season from the perspective of their own club. These are edited extracts from the responses.

ALBION ROVERS
RangeRover1 (Eric Sim, a 48-year-old machine operator whose son plays for Albion Rovers.)

Got to admit I didn't see the start of the season as my boy, Andy, just joined in January, but what I have seen since then I have been impressed with. We have good players, maybe a bit lightweight, but play the game well, The teams I have been impressed with were yourselves and Elgin City. In the other games we could have won most of them if we had a finisher. As I said, my boy just joined in January and in his first two games scored two goals and got two man of the matches and then East Fife crocked him in the third game, which put him out for about eight weeks. I'm just looking forward to next season as I genuinely think we will be up there challenging.

ARBROATH
farflunglichtie (Allen Armstrong, based in Buckhaven)

Flying high in Division 1 in what seemed like only a few moments ago, two relegations in three seasons, Arbroath returned to grim reality at the start of 2005-6 for their first lowest tier campaign in eight years. Nobody had great faith in Brechin-minded (an oxymoron) manager, Harry Cairney and assistant Sorbie. But an opening draw at the Stade de Cliftonhill, closely followed by defeat at Firs Park and exits from both Cups all by the end of August meant even our exceedingly modest expectations were lowered. We had a great deal to be humble about. In an unaccustomed humanitarian role, Cowden came to our rescue with a one-sided 0-3 game at Gayfield in October which thankfully forced Harry's resignation.

The AFC Committee – soon to be transformed into a private company – saw sense and appointed a fans' favourite and former player, the all-action John McGlashan. Hope and interest revived and, quite soon in November we hit a purple patch. The positive vibe saw about 600 Lichtie fans travel to Easter Road for the third round of the Scottish Cup, where they outsang the Hibees. Even my wife came to her first game in many years though mainly because her family had been Hibees. We ran rings around them for 40 minutes but went down 6-0.

I was unfortunate enough to witness three of the four Cowden-Arbroath encounters over the season where there was quite a high body count (five sendings-off), though I can't say they were particularly ferocious. The 0-3 at Gayfield was a blessed relief from our manager and the 4-1 thrashing at Gayfield a delight, but that was all we took despite coming close in both games at Central Park. Returning to Central Park for the first time in nine years was like an East European refugee returning to his Stalinist past. The crumbling stadium, where fans are so far from the action, now had a strange chainlink fence to further enhance sightlines and the occasional stone lobbed by young neds outside to keep visiting fans on their toes... I had thought Gayfield fans were the most biased, but defer to Cowden fans – just no decision by the official seemed to satisfy them. But Cowden did impress with their expansive playing style and the flying Finns so we didn't really begrudge them.

Gayfield assumed the title of Scotland's Home of Hurling. A variant on Ireland's national sport took place in a January home game against Cowdenbeath. Inflamed by the promising football of the away team, Arbroath's crack pensioner hit-squad was mobilised after half-time. Short-tempered Mark Baxter was targeted and when the ball went out of play, it was returned with the velocity of an Exocet to the slow-witted Cowden defender. Demonstrating his complete professionalism, he took umbrage and threw it back. Quite rightly the referee had no option but to dismiss the offender. It's only fair – there's an unspoken compact in football that if we, the crowd don't attack the players, then they shouldn't attack us. Thanks to Eric

188

Cantona for clearing up this tricky point of law. Cowden were beaten by a better team and outsmarted by a better support. This pilot will be rolled out next season for our assault on the Division.

We finished fourth eventually, not a bad showing - indeed almost a triumph given the dire start. Strange days at Gayfield. For the first time in living memory, all home games throughout the winter were played in balmy and windless conditions. Normally it takes a major effort to stand perpendicular in the teeth of the wind, and where goal kicks frequently go directly out above the keeper's head for corners. This is more or less scientific proof that global warming and climate change is upon us.

Arbroath fans follow the adage – 'damn few and they're a deid', and only a few actually live there any more. I combine stays on the Costa Fife with regular working trips aboard. Though a season ticket holder (and thus now a shareholder since we turned private during the year), I miss maybe a third to half the games due to regular working trips abroad. It's not easy picking up a poor BBC World Service radio reception trying to catch results in remote parts of south Sudan, northern Kenya, Gaza strip, Lebanon, Bangladesh India, Nepal, Jordan which is where I spent Saturdays over this last season. Thank goodness for internet cafes even in remote places so you can catch up. Thank goodness for the Arbroath and Pie and Bovril websites to stay in touch with the buzz and the zeitgeist. Onwards and upwards. New season, new hopes – at least until the end of August.

SimonLichtie (Simon Reynolds, recently turned 16, from Dundee. Simon has supported Arbroath for seven years and hardly ever misses a game.)

For me as an Arbroath fan, the games that stand out are the derbies against Montrose, one of which was basically the start of our season (yes, our season started in November!). After the sacking of Harry Cairney, John McGlashan had come in and things had looked to be improving ever so slightly, but we still looked like a bottom four side, until the 5th of November, when we played the best 45 minutes the fans had seen in months and beat Montrose 2-1. The next Saturday we were at home to East Stirling, and the Lichties scored seven goals, the first and probably last time I will ever see this!

Onto the Cowdenbeath games. I think every single Cowden game this season has been a big game for Arbroath. The first game, which ended 3-0 to Cowden resulted in Harry Cairney resigning. Thanks Cowden! The second was the 3-2 game at Central Park in which we had a man sent off in the 20th minute but pulled back from 1-0 down to 2-1 up, only for Cowden to score twice in two minutes to win. The next game at Gayfield was big win for Arbroath, 4-1 against promotion-challenging Cowdenbeath, who had two men sent off, one for an assault on the park, and one for an assault off the park. One of the highlights of the season

189

was this game, a fantastic 90 minutes worth of entertainment! Whoever said Third Division football was dull eh?! The last game at Central Park was the game which me and many other Arbroath fans thought may be the end to our push to get into the play offs. A 4-2 win to Cowdenbeath, with Arbroath again having a player sent off, making it five sending offs in four games between the teams that season.

BERWICK RANGERS

Berwick till i die (Ian Gregory, aged 19, has been supporting Berwick Rangers since he was dragged along as a six-year-old by his dad.)

I felt we had a very successful season considering we had just been relegated and had a very poor pre-season. At the start of the season I certainly would have taken what we did achieve. Our start to the season was awesome, but we always knew it wouldn't last, with the size of our squad. As soon as the injuries hit we had major problems and threw away a seven point lead. You have to give credit to the manager and the squad for getting us back into the title race and in the end we were very unfortunate.
I was gutted to lose the title on goal difference as we had taken 10 points from a possible 12 against Cowden and were far the better team in those games. I felt the team were very tired in the play-offs, which caused us to get hammered at Alloa. Overall a very good season.

Djn (Doug Newton. Doug has been supporting Berwick since the late 1980s. Doug's father, John Newton, a former statistics lecturer at St Andrews University, has been an unpaid steward at Berwick for the last 16 years. In honour of his service to the club, he has a plaque on the gate he mans at Berwick!)

Possibly the best (and maybe the worst) season for a long time. To understand the season you have to appreciate where we were this time last year. Relegated as bottom team, onto our third manager in just over six months, not a lot of hope around the place. When Berwick win things we tend to still be bitter, cliquey and fragmented, so you can probably imagine how strained the place was when we went down. So whilst Cowdenbeath finished third the previous season (and Stenny were spending a few quid), we had no expectations of anything grand.
The cup game at Spartans was possibly the worst I've attended in almost 20 years of watching Berwick. Not because we lost to a non-league team (first time I've seen it happen though), not because of the poor performance, but because

Spartans looked like the club of tomorrow whilst the Third Division felt like relics. The two games with Stenny at the end of the season were great, but summed up one trouble with the Cowdenbeath games. I don't think either side has particularly bad fans, but we were segregated from each other, which was a great shame. The Stenny lads were frolicking around, high visibility waistcoats, congas etc. It's a shame that Cowden fans weren't given a bit of freedom to enjoy themselves. If we wanted a soulless ground with segregation and "thou shalt not" stewarding then visit the First Division (or Hampden!).

Finally we played Alloa in the second leg of the play-offs. Northumbria police decided to send the police helicopter over Shielfield (wary of trouble at the Alloa Arbroath match maybe?). After waiting on the helicopter a few weeks ago, one turned up for the wrong reasons. It didn't even land....

Oliver Tobias (Chris Sanderson, Sunday Mail Division 2 and 3 reporter and Berwick fan)

Being a fan of a club that plays its football in the lower echelons of the Scottish game and being privileged to be able to report and give your views on a game of football and get a bit pocket money into the bargain is something I've always wanted to do. Anyway – most of the past season was spent in the company of the fairytale unfolding at Gretna, and Morton's desperate attempt to thwart the Raydale Park dream. So most Saturday afternoons I'm out covering Berwick's rivals whilst getting updated on events of the respective 90 minutes wherever or whoever my team are playing. The funny thing about the season just gone is that I have covered Cowdenbeath perhaps just as many times as I have watched/reported on Berwick. Now when you're covering a game for the Sunday tabloids you really need enough eventful action that enables you to fill the required wordage with a deadline which is more than likely as soon as the referee blows his full-time whistle. So I wonder just how many times had I been cheering Cowden on to kill a game off, racking up more points and even more goals, which a number of months later would have me propped up against a nightclub bar in Berwick – gutted and green with envy over the celebrations taking place at the other side of the Forth Road Bridge.

As I was notified my first assignment was to be East Stirling v Cowden on the opening day of the season, added spice was poured onto the game with the shock news that Dave Baikie had quit his post amidst circumstances away from the pitch.. A number of players seem unhappy with the club's decision to allow Baikie to depart. I get the feeling he's jumped before he's pushed. By the next time I'm appointed to cover the Blue Brazil, Mixu has arrived as new manager and, living in Paisley, I'm well aware of the brilliant job he has done with the Love Street youngsters. I'm informing my Berwick buddies it's a good appointment.

191

The performances of Markus Paatelainen by now have caught my eye and a word to a chief scout of a League Club in England I know leads to him asking me to take in the midweek match at Hampden Park. An impressive Markus once again puts in a polished performance as Cowden help my fixed odds coupon come up and another three points I'm left to regret come May. My advice to the chief scout is come up and have a look at Markus.

On the final day of the season. I've asked the Mail if there's any chance they can send me to Shielfield Park. If we win I want to be there. I was too young to understand or remember the last time we won the league back in 1979. Our game finished a good six or seven minutes before your game and I kept ringing the Mail's Sportsdesk to see if Elgin had managed the unthinkable so at least I could file my copy whether we were champions or runners-up. What could have been a night to tell the grandchildren about turned out to be the biggest anti-climax of all. It's a blur from about 11pm, but I can remember stating to the boys that at least we had been pipped for the title by a very competent side, unlike the last time we had conceded the title to QP back in 2000.

I'm nevertheless pleased for Big Mixu – a real gentleman. There were no ill feelings or jealousy because we lost the league to a footballing side that played the game the correct and entertaining way. I enjoyed Black Diamonds and the Blue Brazil *and am looking forward to reading this one - even though the painful memories will no doubt flood back.*

EAST FIFE

Igor (Matthew McLean, aged 22, lives in Glenrothes, and is a greenkeeper at Ladybank Golf Club. Matthew has been deeply involved in the campaign to oust Derrick Brown, East Fife's chairman. "I've been supporting East Fife since the 1993/94 season when Steve Archibald took over. My great Uncle David McLean was the manager of our 1938 cup winning team.")

Sadly, matches themselves have been a bit of a side issue for us this season. There were one or two points where I thought things might have come together and we could have mounted a challenge, but those optimistic hopes were put to rest probably before the half-way mark. My biggest disappointment was that though our protest toppled Moffat as manager with ease, it still hasn't shifted Brown. I certainly think Moffat had exhausted his capabilities and could do no more for us, but Brown staunchly defended him weeks before, only to fire him when the heat turned up to save his own skin. I feared that would take the "edge" away from our cause. It didn't right enough, but I am obviously unhappy that he is still there as I won't enter Bayview again until he is gone.

EAST STIRLING

Gull (Ian Ramsay)

I've often said that `Shire are in a league of their own in the Third Division and have been since our chairman's controversial decision in 2002 to cut players wages from £30 plus bonuses to a flat £10 rate. Our fans are realists and nobody was under any illusions that we wouldn't struggle badly from then on. Sure enough we have finished bottom of the division every season from then on. We hold our chairman, Alan Mackin, responsible for the continuing crisis at Firs Park and we can only hope he gets bought out or tires of the hassle before our club sinks completely.

We know we will probably lose a lot of games but we will give even some good teams a problem on odd occasions. Our attention is focused on the bottom end of the table and the chances of getting above someone else after 36 games - I think it's fair to say we approach the season with a different mindset to all the other nine clubs in the division!

6th Aug, `Shire 0 Cowden 1: At the start of the season I list Cowden as 'a strong contender for promotion' but we fancy our chances of taking something from the game as we know the Blue Brazil play a fair bit of proper passing football and that usually lets our team get into the game. As it turns out it's a decent, close game with several chances at both ends and we are just edged out by a team with better finishers.

22nd October, Cowden 5 `Shire 1: `Shire's record at Central Park has been pretty poor for years now, even before our wage cap was introduced. However what you don't want to happen is exactly what did happen in this game - Cowden scored within 34 seconds of the kick off. We had to be playing at our best to get something and this was one of our poorest performances of the season to date – definitely a game to forget.

Tuesday 4th April, `Shire 1 Cowden 1: We were not expecting much and considered our season effectively over – so what happened was as much a surprise to the `Shire fans as it was to Cowden's. The game itself was obviously a pressure game for Cowden considering how tight things were at the top end of the league and this played its part in making their play very nervy in front of a bigger than usual crowd. To everyone's surprise `Shire came out and played with a determination and hunger that bottom of the table teams are not supposed to have in what was arguably their best performance of the season. There was some annoyance afterwards that if `Shire had put the same effort into the Saturday games things may well have turned out differently come the end of the season.

15th April, Cowden 5 `Shire 0: A real `end of the season` feel about this game and a return to the usual routine as Cowden made sure there would be no

193

shock result this time. In my opinion Cowden deserved to go up and good luck to you.

ELGIN CITY

Debbie

My reflections of the season? Well, my season was ruined when Kenny Black's bid to take over at Elgin fell through and I haven't been back to Borough Briggs since then.

Elgin 06 *(Sean)*

I think the Kenny Black takeover bid was probably the biggest event in the club's history, so maybe that should be the main point from Elgin City point of view. I think also a mention to Brian Irvine as well for the change of fortune in the results and to Jamie Mackenzie for keeping things on track after the resignation of Davie Robertson and Kenny Black. We also broke our points record in the SFL and Martin Johnston broke our record for most goals in a season.

MONTROSE

C'WAY THE MO (Gary Duncan, aged 37, nurse in a Minor Injuries Unit. Gary has supporterted Montrose for 30 years.)

Throughout my time as a Montrose fan the highs have been numerous and the lows, well even more numerous. Even so I still find it difficult to understand the Celtic or Rangers supporters' buses leaving the town for their respective games on a Saturday when we have a team here in the town. Most of these Old Firm fans would have watched Montrose during the high points of the club's existence and surely nothing the OF can offer can replace the joy of beating a Premier League side in the Cup or seeing your home town team win the league.

Memories of the season past are basically unhappy ones. Posters on the P&B on the whole had Montrose in the top three or four when asked to predict the league table for the forthcoming season. Maybe this was our year. The rest is history. After a half decent 0-0 away draw to Elgin in the season's opener, Montrose quickly lost their tag as one of the favourites for the league.

Notable highs from the season – Beating Arbroath 1-0 in the first derby and ending Berwick's 100 per cent record with a draw at Shielfield. Lows from the season are too many to mention, we took some hammerings from Stenhousemuir

194

and lost all our games against Cowdenbeath. Midway through the season Henry Hall's reign was over and after a couple of weeks of name-dropping ex-player Eddie Wolecki took over. This was a new beginning, he was going to take us to the play-offs THIS SEASON. The squad was quickly dismantled in the January transfer window and a new crop of young players were brought in. We plummeted down the league. Eddie had grossly under-estimated the task in hand and had over-estimated the ability of players playing in Junior football. At the time of writing there are once again signs of recovery. The addition of businessman Kenny Black to the board and a possible initial £100,000 investment looks already like it is going to draw a higher class of player to the club. So, for the tenth consecutive year, maybe, just maybe, this will be our season.

Ivo den Bieman (Jon Blackwood, 33-year-old lecturer in art history at Duncan of Jordanstone Art College in Dundee. Under the name of "Steeplejack" he has been running a blog for the last two seasons. It gets 2,500 visits per month and has generated a bit of interest in the club from all over the UK. It's one of the best and wittiest football blogs anywhere, and can be visited at http://gableendgraffiti. blogspot.com.

Montrose against the 'Miners' (I'm a fan of the old fashioned nicknames for teams) was an entirely unproductive experience for us Gable Endies. Four clashes, four defeats, no goals, eight against. And, to be honest, we were rather fortunate to keep the Miners' total at just eight. The first game in September saw the sequence begin as it went on; an awful Montrose performance, as Cowdenbeath coasted to a 2-0 win, in second gear. Things didn't get any better when Cowden visited Links Park in November. They won 1-0 going on 10-0. In late January another 2-0 defeat at Central Park, although this time the game was much closer. New manager Eddie Wolecki had brought it many new players and they gave a very good account of themselves for an hour. Mixu admitted to our manager afterwards that the better organisation and quality of our new players had made this game much harder than his first two clashes with the Mo.

That wasn't the case in March, in the last game at Links Park. Cowden, with their front line anchored in the ample frame of Armand Oné, strolled to a 3-0 win, whilst smoking a pipe and wearing carpet slippers. Cowden's promotion push was gathering an unstoppable momentum around this time and the gulf between the two sides was embarrassing. The Miners were very worthy champions, guided by an astute young manager, and I feel that their first season back in Division Two will go much better than many fans expect. All the best Cowden!

QUEEN'S PARK

Andyboy (Andy is aged 15, and has been supporting QP all his life.)

Two matches against Cowden stand out.

Cowdenbeath 6 Queen's Park 0. I felt we were unlucky to go into the break 2-0 down at half time after acquitting ourselves well. Cowden scored an absolutely stunning goal through Mikko Paatelainen and they took the other half chance that fell their way in the first forty five when Davie Crawford and Paul Paton got their wires crossed. The half time team talk went out the window straight away, though, with a stupid goal from a corner and we just buckled from then on.

Queen's Park 2 Cowdenbeath 2. Great game of football and very enjoyable I'm sure for both sets of supporters. I think the sending off killed us, because Cowden's Ward was having a howler, he was missing the ball completely, over and over again. Big Oné was dreadful but still managed to score a goal using his size to hold off the defender. If we had a player like him this season, the playoffs would have been secured. Hope you enjoy next season in Division Two and here's hoping we meet you there at the start of 2007/08.

STENHOUSEMUIR

Dubya (Paul Wilson, aged 18. Paul is studying Sports Science at Forth Valley College. He's supported Stenny for two years – "My first game was Gretna away. I only went along with a friend, we lost 7-0. I was hooked from that day forward. I'd never really followed any particular team and only moved to Stenny a couple of years ago. This season was my first full term, and to be honest I'm far too emotionally involved in my team now. It can't be good for my health!")

Unsurprisingly enough, the stand-out games for me mainly involved the ones which separated the Champions from the mere contenders. We got an absolute doing at Central Park the first time around, a game I missed (thankfully). The game when we beat you at Ochilview on the 17th of December is another stand-out because we had just beaten Berwick at their place and it gave us a great lead (one that, in all truth, I though we would keep). We then drew with your mob on my birthday (4th of Feb) at Central Park, a game with few efforts on goal, but it was important as we left unscathed, still with a lead intact. The definitive game of this season for me however was at Ochilview – Stenny 1-2 Cowden. We took an undeserved lead through Jim Mercer (possibly the worst player I've seen in the flesh) and for, oh, about five minutes, I was in dreamland, already thinking about Division Two. Then after a scramble in our box, Douglas Hill slammed home the equaliser shortly

196

before half time. My heart literally sank. We looked lost. And then Cowden took the lead, and that was (for me anyway) our season doomed from then on. And for Cowden it showed that they had fighting qualities that our lot simply didn't have any more. Earlier on in the season we scored late goals so many times, but that day I just sensed it was never going to happen. So many times after that game we needed a big effort after falling behind, and it never came. That's why that game was so important.

Heart-stopping moments: in our last two games against Cowden we led for a short space of time, and that feeling was pretty great. Had we held onto those two leads, Stenny would be Champions. But, alas, it was not to be! Also, seeing David Templeton play for the first time was an experience I will look back on if he goes onto greater things.

Francesc Fabregas (Craig Telfer, 20-year-old student. Craig has been supporting Stenny for over two years.)

Highs of 2005/2006- Looking back, in a season that promised so much yet delivered so little, all the highlights seem hugely insignificant compared to the eventual failure to win the league or attain promotion. That said, however, one of the most glorious moments I have ever witnessed at a game of football was down at New Bayview in the middle of November, when David Templeton made his first team debut against East Fife. We had been told about the boy's ability by an old guy, Auld Donald, on the bus through to Methil. He told us that the young lad had been released by Aberdeen on the account that he was "too wee", and so Campbell Money managed to sign him for us. We saw him warming up with the rest of the team – a boy. He looked tiny. The game itself was a hugely shocking affair from our perspective – some shocking defending gifted them a goal after half an hour, and they hit the post in stoppage time. Even worse, they scored soon after the restart. 2-0 down, and I was convinced, with Berwick winning that afternoon, that we had blown the league. But, two goals down, I reckon that Des thought that he might as well thrown on wee Davie. The words "tactical masterstroke" are banded around far too often in football, but to describe Templeton's introduction as anything less would be hugely churlish. It was the most incredible half hour of football I think I've ever been witness to. After we drew level, Templeton received a pass out on the left flank. He used his pace to knock the ball past the full-back and galloped one-on-one with their keeper. He curled a fine shot round him, but it hit the inside of the post and the ball was cleared to safety. In the final minute, Joe McAlpine found Templeton on the left flank and once again, the boy made his way into the penalty area. With only their keeper to beat, he placed a fine shot round him and straight into the net for the winner. It was an astonishing performance. I celebrated so hard, I thought I was going to pass out. I raced down the concrete steps, jumping in glorious abandon. Man, I wish you could've been there to see it. His dad was there, he had tears in his eyes. Magical. Incidentally, this was also the first appearance of the Akabusi Loyal's flag.

    Low point of the season: pretty obviously, the lowest point I have ever been watching football in my lifetime was the final month of the season when we lost three consecutive games, thus blowing our chances of winning the Championship. To see our lead cut from eleven points to four was brought about by some nerves, but to blow it when the finishing line was in view was heartbreaking.

    The defeat to Cowden, when we lost 2-1, was the lowest point of the season, the biggest disappointment ever at a game of football. I usually go to Ochilview about 45 minutes or so before the kick off for a few beers, but that day I went nearly two hours before the match started, and the place was already buzzing. We had fans up from England, some as far south as Bristol, I believe. I had never been so excited about a game of football in my life. The first half went pretty well until big Slim Mercer flicked a header into the net. I never celebrated so hard. The place went mental. I'm not kidding, I damn near lost my breath. However, Cowden came right back. Hill's goal was well-taken sure, but he should never have been given so much space to shoot. In the second half, quite simply, we were steam-rollered. Even more horrendous defending allowed Liam Buchanan in to score pretty much straight after kick-off, and from then on, we were raped over and over again. Cowden's tactic was to play big long balls in big Armand, so he could play in Bucks or McKenna. I swear, if you threw a football out of an aeroplane, Oné would kill the thing stone dead. He's fat, slow and grossly unfit, but by lord, his control is awesome. It was 2-1 going on 6-1 to tell you the truth. We nearly stole a point at the end, but we didn't deserve it. I cried at the end of the game. It was the beginning of the end. Even worse was when I had to take down the flags, the Cowden players were doing their warm-down, their fans were in a double-decker bus and they could see the players, and both began celebrating with clenched fists. It was pretty heartbreaking stuff. The definite low-point. Your players wanted it more.

POSTSCRIPT: SO HOW ARE YOU, MRS POLLOCK?

Scottish Third Division

		P	GD	PTS
1	**Cowdenbeath**	36	47	76
2	Berwick	36	27	76
3	Stenhousemuir	36	40	73
4	Arbroath	36	10	55
5	Elgin	36	-3	52
6	Queen's Park	36	5	51
7	East Fife	36	-16	43
8	Albion	36	-21	29
9	Montrose	36	-28	28
10	East Stirling	36	-61	23

Life can only be understood backwards; but must be lived forwards
– Soren Kierkegaard.

I expect to live long enough to hear 'They fuck you up, your mum and dad' chanted by Girl Guides in the Albert Hall.' – Philip Larkin

I can't stop looking at that league table. It's still hard to take it all in. The season has been such an emotional rollercoaster, all the way from unpromising beginnings, through flirtations with play-off places, through to the drama of the last game of the season. I'm an emotional wreck, knackered. Following the Blue Brazil fair takes it oot ye.

Granny Pollock, do you realise what you started? I hope you're feeling good. That thirteen shilling football was the best purchase you ever made. Worth every penny of fifty-two quid. Costs you all of that for a meal out for a couple of people these days in a high-class Cowdenbeath restaurant. What an investment! Even my two grandchildren – who are, of course, proud to be related to you even though the full significance hasn't dawned yet, but it will, it will – are learning the old, old, stories.

This league campaign has delighted more than Blue Brazil supporters. St Mirren, for whom Mixu was a player-coach – and who provided us with one of our young strikers, David McKenna – won the First Division Championship, gaining deserved promotion to the Scottish Premier League. It seems that their fans have been following Cowden's fortunes, and there is a response on Pie and Bovril:

Skull (St Mirren fan): Old Firm fans, no matter what trophies they win, will NEVER understand that feeling. To them, failure is to win only one trophy in a season, and for obvious reasons, they cannot celebrate as long, loud and openly as supporters of 'provincial' clubs do on the rare occasions that success comes our way! We pick our team when we are knee-high, it lives with us until they are screwing the lid down, and any success between times is a bonus! I am fortunate that I have seen three First Division titles and a Scottish Cup: fans of some clubs would say that's not a great return for 38 years of devotion, but I am grateful for each of them, and if I see no more then I can't complain! Your experience will live with you forever, and every time you think of it you will have a lump in your throat! Enjoy it, there ain't much can beat THAT feeling!

I email Mr Skull to get his story, and he turns out to be Matt Canavan, a 44-year-old cabinet-maker by trade, who is currently working as a postie. He is a Buddie born and bred, and has supported St Mirren since 1968. "I am the black-and-white sheep in a family of Celtic fans! My family always indulged my 'eccentricity'; my father and even more so my mother, were more than willing to fund my visits to Love Street, and when I was slightly older, away trips on the 'juniors' bus. With hindsight, I reckon that (having no truck with bigotry themselves), they were quietly pleased that I had chosen to follow St. Mirren, and would therefore be less exposed to the madness which prevailed at certain other west of Scotland grounds in the slightly-less tolerant 60s and 70s. The 38 years between my first match and now, have been for the most part enjoyable, occasionally wonderful, and sometimes unbearable, but moments like the 2006 title-winning day, I wouldn't swop for ANYTHING!"

Thank you, Matt. Another post is from Celtic fan who was at the Elgin game:

Bhoy4life: Having seen Cowden a couple of times this season (when Celtic weren't playing) I feel they definitely deserved the title. I was at Central Park the day they clinched the title and their fans were brilliant. I don't know how many adults I saw with tears in their eyes that day, and if I ever see an atmosphere like that one at a Third division game again I'll be shocked!

So who is Bhoy4Life? I decide to find out. He is William O'Neill, aged 15,

200

from Dunfermline. Whenever Celtic and Dunfermline are away, he and his pals go to Central Park "to see some real football where there are no prima donnas, just honest pros trying 100 per cent." Ten of them went to the Elgin game (six Celtic fans, two Dunfermline fans, one Aberdeen fan and one Cowden fan). "When Elgin scored that free kick it was nail-biting time, and when the full-time whistle went we were all on the pitch celebrating with the players within minutes. After we were all chucked off the park I looked around the terraces and saw whole families from grandads down to kids in their prams, and saw the tears in their eyes. That was when I thought that this day was important to them, and being a Celtic fan I would never experience the feeling that they were feeling at that time."

Good luck to you, mate, and do come to Central Park more often. That applies to all of the 3000+ people in the old ground. Now, if we could get 1000 people at every home game......

******

The play-offs. Ah, yes, the play-offs. Blue Brazil fans yawn. While once we yearned for a humble place in the play-offs, we now look down on the lesser tribes who compete at that lower level. Stenhousemuir entertain Berwick Rangers in the first leg. Mixu Paatelainen takes in the game, and when he goes to his seat in the stand he is applauded by the Stenhousemuir fans – a gesture of graciousness. (That's what keeps lower league fitba still an arena of courtesy, and of generous acknowledgement of honest achievement.) The game is really scrappy, played out by two tired teams whose common currency is disappointment.

One distraction from the poor soccer occurs when a strange sign appears on the terracing. It has blue lettering on a white board. The words read: COWDENBEATH FC DIVISION 3 CHAMPIONS 2005-6. Just in case they had forgotten.

The brains behind the sortie into enemy territory is our old friend *Blueminer* (Stuart Watson). He and his friend Sommy wanted to make a statement to those Berwick and Stenny fans who had poured scorn on Cowdenbeath's promotion chances. Stuart made a big sign with four inch high blue letters, and two heavy pieces of concrete were attached to ropes. Colin Nelson came along to help. They arrived at half time, and once the game had started, they scrambled up the wall with the sign and put it in place. "I was busy wrapping the rope around the pieces of concrete," says Stuart, "when I heard Nelly and Sommy shouting to me. They were already back in the car and I was meant to be the getaway driver! We headed off up the road and the normal route would be to turn right, but the police were doing some sort of spot check in that direction. Paranoia had set in, so I turned left and took the long route home!"

This is what winning a Championship for the first time in your life time does to sane people who support a team which is not normally garlanded with honours. Good on them.

By the way, Berwick beat Stenny over the two leagues, while Alloa, second

201

bottom in Division 2, overcame Arbroath. Alloa beat Berwick in the final, to retain their place in the upper league. But that's all a bit boring, really.

******

More silverware is on its way to Central Park after it is announced that League sponsors Bell's have named Mixu Paatelainen as the official "Manager of the Year" for the Third Division. As both a journalist and a minister, I have had dealings with many people in all walks of life, and it takes a lot of impress a cynical hack. Well, I am impressed by Mixu Paatelainen. You can tell the best soccer managers not by the statements they make to the press but by the results they produce on the park. Think Jock Stein. (The only mistake Stein ever made was to turn down the first and best offer of a manager's job he ever had – the hot seat at Central Park. But the boy done good.) He had the gift of getting the best out of an unexceptional group of players, turning them into heroes filled with self-belief, as at Dunfermline, Easter Road and Parkhead.

Mixu Paatelainen is not just a good manager. He is a natural leader. He has charisma, authority, a sense of purpose, clear goals, and an ability to communicate his ideas to those he works with. He is self-confident without being arrogant. He has a sense of where he is going. It would not at all surprise me if Mixu goes to the very top as a manager. I recognise that this is a foolhardy thing to say in print on the basis of one season in the Third Division of the Scottish Football League. I'm also aware that just as injuries can cut short a wonderful playing career – just ask Craig Levein - so events can happen in football that derail even the best of coaches, and once-promising careers can end on the scrapheap. Nevertheless, I will back my hunch about this man.

It is not a question of if we lose Mixu, but when. Every Cowdenbeath supporter and player knows that. And when Mixu does go, he will do so with the heartfelt good wishes of every single Blue Brazil fan. You see, he delivered the Holy Grail to Central Park, Cowdenbeath on 29th April, 2006. It was he who coaxed the bird from the sky. He is already a Blue Brazil legend, secure in the pantheon. I don't believe that Mixu will ever forget managerial his roots – his affection for the Blue Brazil is palpable.

Ah, Mixu, he will go to bigger places, and good luck to him. Helicopter for Paatelainen?

On the 1st of July, the Cowden players display the Championship trophy from an open-topped bus as part of the Civic Week parade. It's a brilliantly sunny day, and the streets are thronged with cheering people. This Championship win has brought great cheer to the town. Chalky Whyte, originator of the Blue Brazil nickname, is pleased to note that everything in the parade is on the Brazil theme.

Pie and Bovril holds its annual Five-aside tournament. *Dubya* reports an interesting happening. "Armand Oné was playing five-a-sides nearby and when he saw the Akabusi Loyal strolling past he shouted, 'Hey, Stenhousemuir! Championees, Championees!', accompanied by a strange dance. Also said something about a tenner!"

Yes, Dubya, the Pizza Hut dance. What a guy! The Special Oné played only ten games for us, but he will always live on in the Blue Brazil corporate memory.

Clubs in the First Division of the Scottish Football League meet together to discuss radical change. They are worried about the fact that as yet no new sponsor has been found for the SFL. There is even talk of a breakaway league – SPL2. They want to establish a pyramid system, allowing progressive clubs to enter the Scottish Football League through the Third Division. They also want to get a bigger share of the money available to the Scottish game (which means that lower clubs will lose out). It reminds me of the proposals made by the breakaway Scottish Premier League clubs which so enraged the First Division clubs – who are now involved in a similar tactic!

The trouble with all these so-called "radical" proposals for change is that they come from the top down, with no consultation further down the footballing food chain. The top teams always wish to break away from the rest and grab most of the available cash – whether it's in the interest of the Scottish game or not. When the SPL was set up, Willie Miller, himself a former great defender-cum-referee, urged the smaller clubs to "set aside self interest" and vote for these changes.

Excuse me, Willie. Self interest? Are you suggesting that the top teams are acting out of idealism? One is reminded of Ralph Waldo Emerson's comments on a politician, "The louder he talked of his honour, the faster we counted our spoons." The wee clubs are not destroying Scottish football. It has been brought to its knees by the already failed pursuit-at-any-price of a European chimera. Millions of pounds were spent on foreign players instead of being invested in youth. Only now, when big clubs have been driven to the edge of bankruptcy, is proper attention being paid to youth academies.

Cowdenbeath Football Club has a much better youth system than many of the clubs who're seeking change to suit themselves. This has been confirmed by the SFA, who have awarded Cowden Performance League Status. The Blue Brazil are the only part-time side in the country to be granted the elite status. As a result, next season the under 13, 14, 15 and 16/17 squads will compete alongside the 12 SPL sides as well as First Division Hamilton Accies, Livingston and Ross County. The under-19s will continue to play in the SFL league during the season. Lowly Cowden's ambition to develop its youth programme is underlined by the signing of Gary Smith, who was playing last season for Hibs in the Scottish Premier League. Gary's experience will be invaluable for the young players, and in addition to playing for the first team, he will coach the under-19 side.

This recognition of excellence in the youth coaching set-up is a big boost for the club. Delighted chairman Gordon McDougall says: "It has taken a few years to reach this level but all the hard work has paid dividends. This is quite an achievement for a part-time club like ours."

Under-12 coach Grant Letham tells me: "When the season ended we thought that things couldn't get better, then we learned that the youth development set-up at Cowden has been given Performance League status. We really are punching well above our weight now and will be endeavouring to compete against the biggest clubs in Scotland. This is in no small measure due to the commitment to the cause of youth development that the chairman has, not to mention the infectious enthusiasm of The Mighty Finn. If others shared their passion and commitment, we would have been watching Scotland in Germany this summer. We all pay the price for such short sightedness."

It certainly is a tribute to the vision and tenacity of Gordon McDougall. And herein lies a problem the club has to face. Gordon McDougall is 61 years old, and can't go on forever. In this book, we've shown how Cowden have always had to have another source of income – greyhound racing, pony trotting, and stock car racing. The club's fortunes – survival even – are linked to the success of the stock car venture. Cowdenbeath FC needs a clearly mapped-out succession strategy.

The fact is that Central Park is dilapidated, and is not worth spending any more money on. As it stands, it is a deeply unattractive prospect for a buyer. What is needed is a new, small, low-maintenance stadium for the football club and a new base for stock car racing. This could be achieved by selling Central Park to a supermarket or property developer and using the funds for a stadium on a new site. If a synthetic surface were provided, along with all-weather training facilities, they could be rented out for community use. It could be a wonderful community facility, for the benefit of young people in the town.

There should be a get together between the board of Cowdenbeath FC, the management of the stock car racing company and Fife Council to hammer out a win-win solution. This Championship victory has been a public relations boost for the town and for Fife, and now is the time for firm plans to be made. And if there is to be a much-needed new stadium, it's essential that supporters are consulted on its design.

******

July 26, 2006

King Abdullah of Saudi Arabia warns that the entire Middle East could be engulfed in war if Lebanon peace moves fail. He tells world leaders: "If the option of peace fails, then the only option remaining will be war, and God alone knows what the region would witness in a conflict that would spare no one."

The conflict gives a glimpse of the gates of hell opening in the Middle East. A senior American politician, Newt Gingrich, says that the Third World War may have started, and goes on with total crassness, "Bring it on!"

The struggle for resources is at the heart of these conflicts. We are dependent for oil on some of the most volatile areas in the world. Russia stops its flow of gas to Chechnya for a spell to teach them a lesson, and to teach the world a lesson. Will some "uneconomic" pits have to be re-opened in this country? Any comments, Baroness Thatcher?

In the Middle East, the conflict is also fuelled by injustice and stories – some of them poisonous. Peoples are imprisoned by the stories of their past. Lies About Our Fathers.

Every Cowdenbeath Championship win has been followed by a world war. Will George W. Bush invade the Black Isle, mishearing it as "The Black Oil"? There are some laughing matters that are not really all that funny.

July 28, 2006.

The SPL2 clubs announce that when the changes come into effect, no club without a stadium with at least 3000 seats will be admitted. This means that if Cowdenbeath were to win the Second Division Championship on merit, they would be excluded. These are exactly the kind of tactics the First Division clubs objected to when the SPL was set up. Have they no sense of irony? If they really want to do something creative for Scottish football, let me suggest a much more productive criterion – no club will be admitted to SPL2 unless they have been granted SFA performance League Status for their youth set-up. This means that only Cowdenbeath, Hamilton, Livingstone and Ross County will currently qualify and the others will have to get their act together quickly. Discuss, you sods.

August 1, 2006

Davie Irons, assistant manager of Gretna, predicts that Cowdenbeath will finish bottom of the Second Division.

August 5, 2006

Gordon Brown unfurls the league flag at Central Park, as Cowdenbeath play their first game of the season in the Second Division. Somehow. you expect to hear the sound of a helicopter.

Cowdenbeath 6 Alloa Athletic 1. A big hello to the Second Division from the Blue Brazil. Cowden play some exhilarating. attacking football, bringing the Chancellor to his feet.

Here's a thought. Will the helicopter come for the prime minister-in-waiting, or will his Holy Grail be snatched from his grasp in injury time? Championships are for the brave.

After the sensational opening game, rival fans suggest it was beginners' luck.

August 8, 2006

CIS Cup round 1: Cowdenbeath 4, East Stirling 1.

August 12, 2006

Ayr United 0, Cowdenbeath 4. This is one of the best Blue Brazil performances I have ever seen, as the young strikers put Ayr to the sword.

August 15, 2006

Challenge Cup round 1: Cowdenbeath 4, Stirling Albion 0.

August 19, 2006

Cowdenbeath 1, Brechin City 3. Ouch.

August 22, 2006

CIS Cup round 2: Cowdenbeath 0, Falkirk 5. The quality and fitness of full-time Falkirk, second top of the SPL, tell. Rival fans ask: has the bubble burst?

August 26, 2006

Raith Rovers 1, Cowdenbeath 3. A comprehensive victory over local rivals. The Blue Brazil play wonderful attacking football. Humiliated Raith sack their manager and appoint Craig Levein as their new boss.

August 29, 2006

Challenge Cup round 2: Morton 3, Cowdenbeath 2.

September 3, 2006

Cowdenbeath 4, Peterhead 2.

September 9, 2006

Cowdenbeath 1, Morton 2. No disgrace to lose to the full-time league leaders.

September 16, 2006

Forfar 1, Cowdenbeath 1. Cowden sit proudly in second place in the Second Division. Who would have believed it? The Mixu Revolution continues to roll.

David Allan, banker and historian extraordinaire, gives me the startling information that although it is correct to say that 2006 did bring our first title for 67 years, it was actually only 51 years ago that Cowden last won a national trophy. In 1955 Cowdenbeath beat Rangers to win the McKie Cup. (Why was there no Mason in Black to award Rangers a penalty deep into a mysteriously-long injury time?) Championees! Why are we so good? Bring on the helicopter!!

What on earth is the McKie Cup? I hear you ask. Well, it's a dominoes trophy for blind football supporters. In 1955 the Cowdenbeath team of David Hotchkiss, William Young, Jim Douglas and Peter Honeyman – heroes all - took the honours in the final against the mighty 'Gers at the annual outing of Scotland's blind football supporters.

I thought you'd like to know that.

206

A final thought. At this time of celebration – maybe never to be repeated in your life time and mine, gentle reader – spare a thought for the wise woman who boarded that train for Glasgow during the reign of Queen Victoria, knowing exactly what she wanted, and returning with a gleam in her eye and a precious thirteen-shilling leather football. Yes, her two sons formally founded the club, but it needed a practical and determined woman to bring along a ball.

Without a football, there is no football club.

I want to rewrite the founding myth – making it more true, if you understand – by giving my great grand aunt, this far-seeing mother of twelve, the place of honour at the head of the banqueting table. A Lie About my Mother, relatively speaking. I want to declare the ancient antiques dealer of Cowdenbeath to be one of a trinity of founders of the club we know and love so well. With a crystal glass overflowing with Blue Nun, I give you the loyal toast: the Queen of Blue Brazil!

In the pantheon she now inhabits – and probably organises – does Margaret Pollock have a smile on her face?

Bless.